SWOLE

SWOLE

THE
MAKING OF MEN
AND THE
MEANING OF
MUSCLE

MICHAEL ANDOR BRODEUR

Beacon Press,
Boston

BEACON PRESS
Boston, Massachusetts
www.beacon.org

Beacon Press books
are published under the auspices of
the Unitarian Universalist Association of Congregations.

27 26 25 24   8 7 6 5 4 3 2 1

This book is printed on acid-free paper that meets the uncoated paper
ANSI/NISO specifications for permanence as revised in 1992.

Text design and composition by Kim Arney

The names of some individuals in this book have
been changed to respect their privacy.

Frontispiece: Charles Meynier (Paris 1763–Paris 1832), *Milo of Croton,
Attempting to Test His Strength, Is Caught and Devoured by a Lion* (1795),
oil on canvas, 61 x 50 cm, the Montreal Museum of Fine Arts, purchase,
the Montreal Museum of Fine Arts' Volunteer Association Fund.
Photo: MMFA, Brian Merrett.

Library of Congress Cataloguing-in-Publication Data is available for this title.
Hardcover ISBN: 978-0-8070-5936-4
E-book ISBN: 978-0-8070-5937-1
Audiobook: 978-0-8070-3505-4

There is not the slightest evidence of sham about him. On the contrary, he is just what he pretends to be.

—NEW YORK WORLD, 1893

For Rosie & Doug
&
in memory of Rob

CONTENTS

MIKEY

THE OLD MAN PAINTING the hallways of our building just wheeled his paint cart into the elevator with me to go up a floor. He looked me up and down and flexed his free arm. *Yeah! All right!* he growled. *Hulkamania! Runnin' wild, brother! I like it!* Then the doors parted, and he wheeled his cart right back out, grinning a big, satisfied grin.

That might be the sweetest thing anyone's ever said to me.

Now granted, while not actively soliciting this kind of feedback, I was wearing a shreddy purple string tank that, at this point in its stay on earth, functions more effectively as a symbol of the idea of a shirt than as an actual shirt, its neckline nothing but plunge, its nipple policy leaning toward complete liberation. This time-tattered tank was paired with silken polyester short shorts—my 2.5 inchers, known as "silkies" or "ranger panties" in the military, or so I'm told. (I thank you for your service, and I adore your shorts.)

I also sport a little moustache, one which has been variously referred to as a "copstache," a "coach-stache," and a "pornstache," if that helps you sketch it out. It's serving old-timey strongman in a leopard print loincloth. It's serving frightened librarian in a Slim Jim commercial invaded by "Macho Man" Randy Savage. It's giving a little Mike Ditka, a little Teddy Roosevelt, and an increasing amount of Wilford Brimley. My dad once asked if it was OK to compare my mustache to Tom Selleck's, unsure if the actor's vastly differing politics would disqualify him as a muse. I assured him that the general idea of Tom Selleck's mustache was perfectly acceptable, even if it wasn't quite accurate as an analog. His iconic character, Magnum, P.I., sported a broader, thicker moustache, more settled into its wide (smolderingly sexy) horizon of an arc. Mine's much tighter and fussier, thus nimbler, like a kitchen broom. I entrust it with nuanced stage directions, treat it like an auxiliary eyebrow.

It seems relevant to add that printed on the front of my string tank was the image of another shortish bald man, wearing his *own* deteriorating string tank. He's visibly but nobly struggling against the burden of lifting an impossibly bending barbell. I was also quite sweaty, which I tend to be in general, but extra so today, having just completed a demanding Push Day at the gym.

This, in turn, means I was also rather pumped at the time—or "puffy," as my husband prefers to say—"the pump" being that coveted, ever-fleeting super-inflated state that immediately follows a rigorous lift and visibly tightens one's tank tops. In pump-state, my whole body pops: my traps become stony mounds, my pecs reveal a hidden atlas of veins and arteries, my arms attain the slow undulations of a thick hunk of rope, my pecs shelf out, and my butt gets all pert in my pants. In the right weather, I might steam from the shoulders, my traps Olympian peaks awoken by a cool dawn.

All of this taken together means I'm fine being immediately assessed and addressed by strangers as a meathead.

This is because I *am* a meathead.

After many years of denial, I came out (for a second time) about ten years ago, admitting to myself and confirming what family and friends alike had long suspected: I am trying to get Big, and doing it very much on purpose. No, I am not sure why. Yes, you can feel my arm.

I go to the gym five days a week, and on the other two days, I think about what I'll do there when I return. In fact, for many years I've run on parallel subconscious calendars: the traditional Sumerian week, superimposed by what I call the *swolar* calendar. The fundamental unit of this latter calendar is a shorter four-day sequence composed of Push Days, Pull Days, Leg Days, and Greg Days (a core workout named after the friend who sent it to me) with irregular intervals of one or two Rest Days thrown in for good measure. While my calendar is built around a regimen, it retains a flexibility you just can't get from the standard week—a given Tuesday might feel like a Friday, but you cannot make it so; meanwhile, I am free to Push whenever I wish.

When I go to the gym, I go for ninety minutes, minimum. I work hard. I move constantly. I leave everyone alone. I leave myself alone. I put in four to five sets on each exercise, continually increasing the weight and performing reps until I can no longer move, i.e., I go "to failure." My workout scheme is built around a holy trinity of compound exercises—exercises that involve entire systems of the body's mobility: the bench press, the dead lift, and the squat. A second tier of support/"accessory" exercises are just as important: things like push-ups and pull-ups, barbell rows and overhead presses, lunges and good mornings. Rounds of machines ("circuits") follow these: a lightning round of pulleys and cables and plates and thick pins slipped into stacks of weights. I love the sounds of the gym—the clang of metal, the thump of tumbling dumbbells, the growl of faraway grunts. I enjoy the textures of rubbery mats cracked by decades of sweat, the rusty knurling of the bars, the ancient padding on the benches. I like how the gym assigns me exclusively to the present moment, how it reduces me temporarily to a task, a set of gestures. I love my sweaty romance with failure, and the meditative capability of hard, pointless work.

But I also really love how my ass looks.

When I first started beefing up, my gay friends all presumed I was trying to appear more straight. Meanwhile, my straight friends were certain I was just becoming more gay. And while there was enough truth in each assumption to pull me in two directions, like the Pillars of Hercules, my true motivations lay somewhere in the middle. As best I can tell, every time I go to the gym, I am trying, in a very literal way, to become *more myself.* Put another way:

I want to be a Big Man.

And ho-ly shit, that felt just as gross to type as it did to think, if not more, and I'm pretty sure that one day I'll have to speak that line aloud—and that, my friends, is going to suck. Be there.

But it's the truth, and it's important just to say it, type it, acknowledge it.

I've wanted to be big since I was Mikey—a wispy, waify string bean of a boy with a high-flying falsetto and a bowl cut lifted from the baby brother of every sitcom. I was effervescent but shy, a tiny twister blowing gayly (whether I knew it or not) through the playground.

If I take an overhead view and examine the better part of my forty-eight years treading this planet—the general vectors of my innermost desires and outermost interests over the last four decades; my aesthetic preferences in museums and the patterns of my sexual tilts at bars; the investment and allotment of my own time and energy and focus, from rep to rep, set to set, workout to workout, meal to meal, week to week, pound to pound, year to year and onward by the decade; how I eat, what I wear, what I watch, who I know, what I click and double-tap, where I go, and how I go about being in my white male body—I see few forces that have so dependably shaped my physical, emotional, and philosophical trajectory more profoundly than the pursuit of Big.

Ask any man who is actively engaged in attempts to attain some objective state of Big—whether that process means going from thin to thicc or embarking upon the opposite course and carving off body fat—and you'll find that while individual motivations differ widely, swole tends to be a reliably retreating goal for those who seek it. The pursuit of Big is a cruel, existential form of cardio that lures men into an endless chase toward an impossible and constantly changing standard. There's something mythic, tragic about it: this dogged commitment to what we regard as noble Herculean labor is actually a mélange of Icarian folly, narcissistic vanity, and Sisyphean pointlessness.

And yet, off I go anyway. Every morning. Ass-early, when the sun is barely up and the sky is as gray and serious as a bottle of mansoap. I wake, I work, I wait for the next opportunity to do it again.

But why?

There are plenty of practical reasons I go to the gym.

As I trudge into my late forties, the goal of fortifying my body while I'm still physically able is certainly one of the big ones. Strength training has been tied to longer life, better sleep, improved circulation, reduced risk of disease, and other assorted healthy shit. Strength training has also been tied to lessening depression and anxiety, effects I've observed firsthand. (To wit, the anxiety attacks that sometimes visit me when I'm home alone or out reviewing a concert for work never find me at the gym. A loaded barbell seems to impart a quelling calm akin to a weighted blanket on a dog.)

The routine of the gym has also allowed me to impose structure upon the increasing blur of passing time, and the results encourage me to stick to the routine. The sense of regimen and ritual I've attached over decades to my individual workouts and larger cycles of training have come to feel like a form of devotion or worship—and I don't mean of the lummox in the mirror, but rather the push and pull of the everyday, the tug of time. Like the nuns had us do in Catholic school once a year, I move from station to station. I kneel. I dab my brow with a shroud of terry cloth.

Additionally, lifting weights has given me a greater sense of physical stability and personal security. For a gay guy, muscles function as both attractant and repellant, as armor and invitation. (For many of us, muscle embodies this duality—a feedback loop of defense and desire.)

But there's more to it than that.

And while I'm coming out as things, I might as well add to the pile of potentially unsavory character revelations: I also identify as a critic.

I've been writing about art, literature, music, food, films, TV, and whatever else ends up in front of me for various publications for about twenty years, roughly as long as I've been lifting heavy weights.

These parallel paths have inevitably tangled together. In fact, part of what keeps me coming back to the gym are the surprise connections that emerge between the books and the barbells. The weights in my hands have felt like proxies for great philosophical dilemmas in my mind. Grasping the bar, I have struggled against issues of form and discipline, of resistance and repetition, of purpose and failure. Night by sweaty night, I have discovered both a means of escape from the normal and a mode of productive engagement with the absurd. (It's not for nothing that the colloquial definition of insanity—doing the same thing over and over and expecting different results—doubles as the defining ethos of the gym.) It's easy to imagine the gym itself as a permanent exhibition of cruel interactive sculptures, each built in betrayal of its nature as a machine, designed to make its sole purpose more difficult. The gym is a theater of the absurd, a hall of mirrors where our forms vanish into diminishing iterations (sort of like the little dude on my string tank).

Lifting weights has trained me to understand my body not just as a consensus of cells, but as a critical mass—a medium where meaning is made. It's also helped me come to understand my own unsteady relationship with masculinity, not because I'm some big strongman in foxy Lycra pants who hogs the squat rack (though probably all of that too) but because it's breaking down my existing ideas of what manhood means and forcing me to rebuild them in my own image.

Generations of American men have historically been instructed, through suggestion, inference, risk, reward, and punishment, not to express themselves, especially when that means sharing our feelings.

It's why the class poet gets shoved into a locker. It's why the theater kid gets pushed down the stairs. It's why simply walking down the hall in junior high with my admittedly giveaway gait was enough to earn me the accolade *faggot*. Casually but clinically, men are trained to read each other's silences and parse each other's bodies; from an early age, we are raised to understand that once boyhood gives way to manhood, the only emotion permitted full expression is anger. (And if you're going to bother, you might as well make it rage.)

We generally portray this tendency in parenting as a necessary part of bringing up boys, a way to curtail blooming weakness from the get-go and plunge boys' reactions to pain, jealousy, anguish, or other corrosive emotions into a cold bath of stony silence. This hammering of white-hot human emotion into an opaque, impenetrable surface is the way we forge hard men from soft boys.

Given the myriad ways American men are taught to suppress real manhood in service of the preservation of Real Manhood, it's no stretch to suggest that we have turned our bodies—over two centuries of relentless repression and refinement—into our primary mode and means of self-expression.

What men don't put into words, they broadcast with their bodies, whether it be sizing each other up in a confrontation, projecting dominance in a social setting, revealing meekness or weakness through nothing but posture or volume, or projecting all manner of nonverbal social and sexual discourse into every room they enter. We acquire this silent language of the body almost unconsciously, but most men are keenly aware of the ways their bodies shape the spaces they occupy.

Perhaps this is why I'm so worried about them lately.

I love men. I really do. But more so than ever before, men appear to be short-circuiting. And I have to wonder if it has something to do with the body.

Our culture has moved, rather abruptly, from socializing in a physical world where a man's mere physical presence earned him a kind of ambient respect, to interacting in a high-stakes virtual one where he must now present himself almost entirely as precisely selected configurations of text and image. The entire mythology of masculinity—let's go ahead and term it *mythculinity* because it's useful and fun to say—is founded in a belief that a man's value is determined, realized, and expressed by his physical form, whether through size or strength or work or violence or sex or some combination thereof.

The diminishing role of the physical world has therefore had major consequences for men in search of dominance. To these men, the wild frontier of the Web has been democratized beyond reclaim, their speech restricted and their thoughts suppressed under the ill-defined but nonetheless repressive regime of "wokism."

"Can we be surprised that after years of being told they are the problem, that their manhood is the problem, more and more men are withdrawing into the enclave of idleness, and pornography, and video games?" Missouri Republican senator Josh Hawley rhetorically asked an audience at the 2021 National Conservatism Conference, ultimately blaming liberals and priming buyers for his 2023 book, *Manhood: The Masculine Virtues America Needs.*

The specter of "modernity" looms like the shadow of doom over "traditional" men who find themselves online, an ever-present reminder of a perceived dilution of masculinity. "Confrontation between men has been watered down to texting or posting on social media," reads a tweet from a now-defunct account named "americancockfidence" (and no, that is not a typo). "It's simple. You have an issue. . . . Do it face to face like a man not behind a device to do it for you."

Big scary modernity, the Internet, and its subtraction of the physical body have, according to the contemporary lore exciting the "manosphere" online, created a society of "betas," "soy-boys," "simps," and "soft men."

The world of "real men," meanwhile, made from earth and dirt and blood and oil, has disintegrated beyond recognition into a cloudy silt of data, digits, and anonymous avatars. One's identity, one's "brand," even one's personal pronouns are now self-selected, self-constructed, and self-defined quantities. Identity in the age of the Internet is limned primarily from disembodied language, image, and ideas, and their fluid exchange.

This dissolution of definition seems to have stranded those men for whom *identity* was just another word for their bodies. For many men, especially white ones, our society's movement from the physical realm to a virtual one has felt like a demotion. The "other" had always been theirs to define; now men are the ones getting subjected to definition. They've become white men. Or white cisgender men. Or white straight cisgender men. And boy, do they not like it.

The result is a perceived "war on masculinity," an attempt by the shadowy forces of "modernity" to tame "real men" through systemic emasculation. As culprits, men will point to the wrath of umpteenth-wave feminism, the expansion of human sexuality, and the collapse of gender binaries as tectonic shifts that threaten to topple ancient structures into ruins, though perhaps not in terms so gentle. The discourse around gender online—in tweets and TikToks, in Reddit forums and Discord chats, and in darker corners of the Internet where I cared not to leave footprints—has turned sour, vitriolic, and violent. A new wave of anti-gay, anti-woman, and anti-trans sentiment has come to characterize large swaths of a new masculinist movement online—an exploitation of negative space in service of shaping a primary figure of acceptable masculinity.

Online, men scramble into formation like drone bees surrounding their queen to protect the same tenets of masculinity and manhood that made their own boyhoods so miserable, ensuring the continuance of their suffering. As bell hooks points out in *The Will to Change*, her 2004 treatise on masculinity: "[T]he emotional lives of boys cannot be fully honored as long as notions of patriarchal masculinity prevail. We cannot teach boys that 'real men' either do not feel or do not express feelings, then expect boys to feel comfortable getting in touch with their feelings."

It's weird: men can perceive the full spectrum of, say, musical pitches just as well as anyone else (and, having been in several bands myself, we can often linger for entire shows in the spaces very much between those "notes"). Most men can precisely perceive and identify a vast spectrum of colors—even if they can't coordinate them for shit and remain obsessed with navy blue. They can successfully sniff out faint hints and subtleties in wine, weed, and cigars. They can hear the finest imperfections in the hum of their trucks' engines or in the hardwood cabinets of high-fidelity speakers. The impossibly detailed latticework of statistics and variables undergirding men's engagement with their favorite sports offers a time-tested and empirically proven model of their collective ability to process nuance, occupy vast gray areas, parse difference, and navigate uncertainty.

But bring up gender and suddenly the range of perception that men demonstrate in every other realm of human experience suddenly shrinks like a nutsack in a frigid pool to a bing-bong binary of *he* and *she*.

Part of the problem is that any investigation of gender would also require men to investigate—and invariably reconcile with—our own masculinity. A coming-to-terms with the raw-getting-rawer numbers surrounding men and their mental health: How men die of suicide up to four times as often as women. How men are more likely to develop substance abuse disorders and antisocial behaviors, but less likely to ever get them diagnosed. How men are also more likely to manifest depression and anxiety as physical disorders like indigestion, insomnia, and chronic pain. How men are twice as likely to experience homelessness as women. How women tend to outlive men by five to ten years. And how the rules of manhood as we know and enforce them now directly contribute to this decline in our mental health. That is, there's only a war on masculinity insofar as men are dying to defend it.

Among men, undiagnosed and untreated mental health problems are rampant, according to research conducted by organizations like the Mayo Clinic. Men's feelings are rerouted by "traditional masculinity" into silos of rage or antipathy—an underacknowledged fact that seems to invisibly caption our country's endless procession of mass shootings, carried out almost entirely by mentally unstable or culturally unmoored white men.

Men have ended up at a regrettable intersection of contradictions, where their longing for connection and community is stunted by a macho commitment to hyper-individualism. Where their posture of self-determination is often fed to them like formula from a cast of grifters, gurus, pseudo-intellectual thought leaders, and life coaches. Where their overbearing tough-guy defenses of traditional power dynamics translate as the colicky whining of babies whose dreams were disrupted by sunlight. Meanwhile, younger "chronically online" teenage boys at formative stages in their development are being weaned on a steady algorithmic diet of misogyny mislabeled as masculinity on platforms like Instagram and TikTok, spewed from a growing industry of artificially trending social media manfluencers and profiteers.

Adrift and allegedly emasculated by the mass rejection of "real masculinity," men are now balls-deep in an imaginary Internet-based civil war with themselves. At its crux are thousands of unironically self-designated "alphas," somehow unable to safeguard a mode of masculinity they insist is instinctual from a growing coalition of ineffectual "betas." Alphas don't curl up in a corner and cry, but if they did, they'd probably be doing it right now.

All of which brings us back to the body, and back to the gym.

Ten years ago, when I took my training up a notch, started powerlifting, and really began putting some weight on the bar and my body, the changes were swift and visible. My shirts all seemed to shrink in the wash at once. My seams kept splitting when I'd squat to tie my shoes. The closures of my collars all struggled against the slow disappearance of my neck.

But perhaps the biggest change I experienced from slapping on twenty pounds of beef was that I gradually became visible to other men: The guy at the 7-Eleven who upgraded me from "Boss" to "Big Boss." The little boy in the grocery line who asked his mother if I was a wrestler. (We said yes.) The Lyft driver inspired to break the silence by sharing his own best bench press with me. The old man in the elevator. *Runnin' wild!*

In man-land, to build the body, to put it to work, to form and shape it with purpose and deliberation, to turn it from one thing into another, to make it more visible to other men, to wear a body the way you would share a narrative is to acquire fluency in an unspoken tongue.

I know this because I picked it up through years of immersion. Making myself bigger inexplicably unlocked my access to those men who otherwise couldn't, wouldn't, or didn't want to see me—the big men, the strong men, the straight men, the "real men." For the first time in my gay life, those men could see me back, and I was speaking their language.

Big gets a bad rap. And maybe rightly so. We associate big men with roid rage and bar fights; troubled pasts or trouble brewing. And fine: I'm all but certain that part of the allure I've always found in giant dudes has to do with the flash of fear they stoke in me just by existing in close proximity.

The descriptive lexicon of Big only serves to showcase these violent and antisocial associations: one gets *ripped, shredded, jacked;* you *torch* your quads and *destroy* your pecs; you are a *freak,* a *beast,* a *monster,* a *mutant,* a *god.*

Muscle is also fairly equated with vanity and narcissism—overblown egotism made meat. Some consider big muscles to be big red flags—bulging signals of deeper burdens to work out. (And as someone who absolutely uses the gym as a method of physical—pause—therapy, I can't quite argue with this. I did once refer to my muscles as "issue tissue," which I thought was pretty impressive for a Sunday morning.)

In the movies, we meatheads are the token bullies, bodyguards, and numbered thugs. We're brutes, boors, barbarians, and Blutos. In the ads for Planet Fitness, we "lift zings up and put zem down." In a Mentos ad, we assemble on command to helpfully free a small car trapped in its parking spot. In a spot for Geico, the whole gag is that customers are "happier than a bodybuilder directing traffic," with the massive Kali Muscle flexing and posing in a busy New York City intersection. Little is expected of the big.

There's something anachronistic about the beefy body, like men who drive expensive classic cars that use too much gas. Why do we need so much meat? To some, our deep investment in something as ephemeral and garish as muscle can only signal an equally significant divestment from the mind (in ancient Greece, the two were once an inseparable pair!). Translation: people presume we're thick in a less flattering sense.

To a large extent, bigness—and the muscular male body as an idealized form—is also an extension of whiteness. Since the Renaissance, the "classical" form has been a representative of European values of which bodies were designated to embody beauty and which were to be left unseen, rendered invisible. And in contemporary culture, a big white body continues to be received and interpreted (in both real life and representative media) differently than, say, a big Black body, upon which are projected centuries' worth of racist tropes characterizing Black men as hypersexual, violent, athletically inclined. Bodies determined ideal (like that of turn-of-the-twentieth-century "father of bodybuilding" Eugen Sandow), bodies canonized (like that of Steve Reeves, the most worshipped Hercules of the silver screen), bodies designated "classically" perfect (despite the inhuman proportions required to earn the title of Mr. Olympia) are always done so at the expense of other bodies. It would be silly, not to mention impossible, to try and distance the symbol of the buff male bod from its long and wide lineage of unsavory cultural signifiers. As a mascot for classical beauty, the meathead must also embody white supremacy, hetero-patriarchy, and a vast panoply of nationalisms.

So what gives? Why is big such a big deal to men? Where did these ideals and images come from? Who are we doing all this work for? How do we want to be seen? In building our bodies, what else are we constructing?

Every body is different, and what follows is the story of my own.

From the twelve trials of Hercules—a to-do list of ostensibly impossible tasks through which the mythical demigod earned both his penance and his legend—I split my own story into twelve chapters. And inspired by the action of lifting itself—the stretch of an extension, the flex of a contraction—I've broken each chapter into a pair of symmetrical pursuits: one to rebuild my own path to built, and one to examine the culture that shapes us as men. In the personal memories and critical inquiries that follow, I revisit the men and the myths that shaped my own understanding of manhood in hopes of decoding the story of my body.

In telling this tale of my own journey from twig to big, I hope not to suggest that my relationship with my body is somehow representative of others. I can only pilot this one around, speak from the experiences I've had, and relate those others have shared with me. In an attempt to authorize any generalizations I may make forthwith, I interviewed dozens of men from a wide range of backgrounds for whom size plays an outsized role in their identity and sense of self-worth. I also consulted old-timey fitness manuals and newspapers from the dawn of physical culture, beefcake and "physique" magazines from bodybuilding's golden age, hours of films and days of TikTok and YouTube clips, bodybuilder biographies and scholarly studies, histories of art and advertising, and a fast-growing virtual culture of thong-busting morphs. The story of men and muscle is a long and complicated one—a centuries-long wrestling match between men and their bodies.

While my story is mine alone, I do think that sharing it with others—especially with other men—serves a bigger purpose.

We talk a lot about issues of body image as they pertain to women and femmes, and we should talk about those issues more. But when it comes to men and mascs—who are bound by self-imposed rules of masculinity not to seem vulnerable or seek help—we seldom hear about the burdens of our bodies: the way we rely on them to show strength and perform masculinity.

I think of my body as material that can be read, interpreted, and (with enough hard work) revised. I also think of my body as a form, a shape shaped as distinctly by the weather of culture as the processes of biology and time. And I can't help but think of my body as an inheritance of fantasy—of ideals and images handed down from man to man over centuries.

Selfishly, I also hope that by telling this story, I can clear space for the muscular male form to adopt some new associations. As laden with negative stereotypes as we meatheads are, I'm a firm believer in muscle as an expressive medium, and in Big as a force that can be used for good. My going to the gym tightened a lot of things up, but it also very much loosened my notions of what masculinity is, how strength can be worn, and what muscle can mean.

I also hope that men whose bodies have grown into expressions of their own isolation can find a familiar form in my story—a reflection of themselves flexing back.

I

ADAM

I N THE BEGINNING WERE THE LETTERS. The little plastic multicolored ones with the magnets fitted into their backs. I filled beach buckets
and grocery bags with them. I hoarded and guarded them like gems.

My office, at age three, was sited in front of the refrigerator, an in-
convenience that steered the selection of my Christmas gift in 1979: a
Fisher-Price school desk with a green plastic chair and a pristine white
desktop that flipped open to reveal storage enough for all of my alphabets—the makings of a universe.

Once the tree and its garlands of popcorn were dragged out to the
street, my deluxe new study situation was permanently relocated to the
living room, where I also managed a small private art space on the wall
behind the recliner in the corner, featuring primarily abstract works in
crayon. There, between the steady glow of the console television and the
blank void of my desk, I learned to manifest entire worlds from nothing-
ness—that is, I learned how to spell.

I'd pull letters out and press them together, turn MAKE into MIKE
into MINE into MIND into WIND into WILD and then wipe the whole
thing into oblivion. Words formed and disbanded like the legions of pi-
geons I'd disrupt at the playground. Whenever the television would blare
a memorable tagline or a particularly compelling jingle (like the "Byyyyy
Mennen!" at the tail end of every ad for Speed Stick), I'd set the type on
my desk and stamp the words out of slices of American cheese. So began
my long relationship with print.

All of this is to say that language was my first playset, letters my first action figures. The puffed chest of the P. The manly stance of the M. The big belly of the B. The leaning repose of the Z. I perceived letters as characters in both senses and felt a kind of tenderness toward them, the way they required one another to mean anything.

My early embrace of letters and words was, I think, a way of learning how meaning is made and unmade—through difference, combination, context, and proximity. The words on my desk felt as delicate as the barely frozen puddles in our backyard, their thin scrims of ice creaking, then cracking under the press of my Moon Boot.

The youngest of three brothers, I was slender and restless, showy but shy, gentle and strange in terms that wouldn't be flung at me for a few more years. In the textual noise of my scattered alphabets I detected something like an echo of myself, my own unfinished image articulated in a cloud of undone words, their nonsense an assurance that everything was made of difference. I'm pretty sure every boy's first game is some form of god.

In the fall of 1983, when I was eight, He-Man—or Prince Adam, his alter ego—invaded our living room five afternoons a week via one of the UHF channels that our antenna struggled to fully intercept. Even with the iffy reception, the body of He-Man was the clearly detailed focal point of his flagship syndicated series, *He-Man and the Masters of the Universe*. Each frame of the animation struggled to negotiate with the impossibility of He-Man's body.

I'd never seen bodies like He-Man's in real life, though I had seen them on TV before. Like when the *Creature Double Feature* would fill entire afternoons with mythologically inspired peplum (i.e., Italian sword-and-sandal) epics from the 1960s. I loved watching Hercules in those old overdubbed Italian flicks, embodied by unfathomably proto-swole beefcakes like Reg Park or Steve Reeves or Alan Steel, each strutting in his own specific interpretation of the legendary demigod, half-naked, heavily bronzed, thickly bearded, and perfectly coiffed, battling cheaply wardrobed "moon-men," or strangling massive animatronic snakes.

I'd also seen bodies like He-Man's on those rare occasions when *CBS Sports Spectacular* would air the annual World's Strongest Man competition, which featured a pantheon of real-life small-town giants in trucker caps, tinted sunglasses, and tight-fitting singlets performing eye- (and tendon-) popping feats of brute strength: pulling trucks, pressing logs over their heads, racing down a track while carrying a refrigerator, squatting a platform crowded with Playboy bunnies. I'd seen their bodies soaked with sweat and caked with chalk, racing to hoist progressively heavier Atlas Stones onto their pedestals. I'd seen them tense into trembling Titans— holding upright the Pillars of Hercules or bending bars of iron over their toweled heads. I was entranced by their majestic forms and ridiculous grudges against gravity, awed by the ample evidence of their bodies.

And I'd also seen bodies like He-Man's on the walls of the comic book store on Main Street, its walls plastered in posters of beefcake warlocks and barbarians, many of them drawn by fantasy art's godfather of fleshy detail, Frank Frazetta. They hung over bins of costume-stretching superheroes and hyper-jacked mutants. If their aggressive chiaroscuro and suggestive pyramid formations (often climaxing in a thrust sword) weren't exactly erotic, they at least expressed an unabashed adoration of muscle, an indulgence in the fantasized form of men that managed to sneak by as standard-issue objectification of women—that is, for every preternaturally jacked Viking, there was a scantily clad Valkyrie bursting out of her pelten bikini.

I'd seen bodybuilders on TV commercials, where they flexed their biceps and posed their bodies in service of analogy—the strength of a detergent, the reliability of a tire, the power of a battery—propping up their brands like telamons supporting the corners of a temple.

And while I was too young to behold him on the big screen myself, I was fully cognizant of the R-rated cult of *Conan the Barbarian*. Arnold Schwarzenegger hadn't yet Terminated a soul (and wouldn't for another year), but his musclebound form, fresh from a historic domination of the Mr. Olympia stage and amplified by his breakthrough appearance in the 1977 documentary *Pumping Iron*, was already ubiquitous by the time he took up the role of the renowned warrior in 1982.

At the mall I'd gaze upon Arnold flexing across the covers of the muscle magazines, which they kept half-hidden by little metal barriers due to their adult-adjacent content. I'd nag my parents to take me to the poster store (a thing that existed) just to steal glances at his body, rendered in spectacular vascular sword-hoisting glory by the Italian artist Renato Casaro (also responsible for some of the more iconic images of Sylvester Stallone as

Rambo that would soon arrive). I downloaded them to my memory and hung them all over the walls.

Holding him in my hand, I felt tiny.

Even in action figure form, He-Man was broad and stout, thicc before thick was a thing. He and his legion of allies and nemeses arrived as part of a larger influx of *Masters of the Universe* action figures led by my two older brothers, who had taken over an entire corner of our living room with a rolling battlefield of crumpled blankets fenced in by a canyon of stacked sofa cushions.

There, a cross-mythological force of *Star Wars* troops and stray G.I. Joes combined and clashed, the front lines advancing behind rows of wheezing Stomper trucks fueled by struggling AA batteries. Day after day, they'd storm and swarm each other's playsets in a hail of mouthed explosions and little death screams, all in the name of intergalactic justice, the killing of villains and time.

But He-Man and his ilk quite literally didn't fit in.

Not one of them could man the tanks, fly the X-wings, drive any of our fire trucks, or even stand upright in the Millennium Falcon. He-Man and his friends stood 5.5 inches to the G.I. Joe's 3.75, making miniatures of the Real American Heroes. He-Man and his universe were completely incompatible with the imaginary status quo of our toyscape. It was as though the only mythology He-Man could fit into was his own. This was by design.

In 1980, executives at Mattel, having perhaps unwisely passed on the pricey licensing rights to the then-untested *Star Wars* brand (which had gone in 1978 to Kenner Products), went on to enlist designer Roger Sweet to design a new line of action figures, vehicles, playsets, and accessories for boys.

(Side note: If you've ever handled a bottle of Downy fabric softener or poured out a smooth sip of Scope mouthwash, you're familiar with Sweet's handiwork as an industrial designer—his way with curves, his understanding of tactility as a means of connection.)

For the base body of his prototypes, Sweet used a Big Jim—the leader of a pack of foot-tall tough guys produced by Mattel through the 1970s to compete with G.I. Joes, Hasbro's similarly statured military men.

Big Jim and his cohort of clones were a lot more casual about following the heroic paths predicated by their heroic forms, opting instead for lives of leisure (camping, playing baseball) or occupations of relative peril (astronaut, cowboy). These proto-bros also emerged from their boxes barely clothed until such time as you outfitted them otherwise. Big Jim, Big Jack (who was Black), Big Jeff (who was blond), and Big Josh (who had a beard, a denim vest, and serious vers-top vibes) rolled into American homes wearing nothing but bland grins and red PE shorts—and something about it felt as aspirational as a Barbie Dreamhouse.

Their spring-loaded arms (much like He-Man's snapback waist) allowed Jim, Jack, Jeff, and Josh to simulate "smashin' karate action," as touted on the box, and throw a variety of miniature sports balls (a tiny baseball was included and likely immediately swallowed). You could also "flex" their biceps to activate "bulgin' muscle action"—enough to pop off an enclosed "muscle band." To ensure that their pump was eternal, the dolls also came packaged with dumbbells. Sold separately were dozens of outfits, uniforms, getups (hunter, boxer, spy, pirate), and conveyances (copters, fan-boats, dirt bikes, jets), allowing Jim and company to drop in anywhere to bestow their suddenly acquired expertise in a number of specialized realms upon whichever crisis demanded it.

Jim and his gym buds were buff—clearly limned in the image of the short-shorted beefcakes strewn across the covers of bodybuilder magazines, their imposing, sand-kicking bully vibes slightly tempered by Jim's barely discernible smile and gummy helmet of wind-tousled hair. But neither Jim nor his crew were imposing enough to, say, master a universe.

For his prototypical trio of He-Men, Sweet amped up the body of a Big Jim doll by gluing it into a fighting stance inspired by the hulking heroes in Frank Frazetta's illustrations and heaping on additional clay, thickening his already stacked proportions and expanding his form into a distinctly Herculean one.

Much like Big Jim and his look-alike ilk, Sweet's He-Men arrived in multiple forms, intended to demonstrate the boundless vision of the creator's budding mythology. Sweet created a dark-haired barbarian hailing from the distant past, a "mid-tech" contemporary soldier outfitted for enhanced warfare, and a futuristic intergalactic warrior to cover the *Star Wars* bases, each of them inviting a different kind of boy, each of them outlandishly jacked.

Mattel executives reviewed several contenders for their new action figure and, upon examining Sweet's transdimensional trio of hulking brutes, they pointed and said, with unexpected prescience, "Those have the power"—a distinct pre-echo of He-Man's skyward sword-thrusting catchphrase. (According to Sweet, those same executives would later order him to lighten He-Man's deeply tanned complexion and the doll was made "more clean-cut and changed to a blond.")

In interviews—as well as in response to a lawsuit filed and lost by Conan Properties International, with whom Mattel had canceled a prospective licensing deal before stamping out their new fair-haired barbarian—Sweet has denied that the pop-culture shadow of *Conan the Barbarian* played any role in shaping the silhouette of He-Man. He was thinking more conceptually about what boys would be after—and what would appeal to the men buying the toys for the boys. He drafted a list of over forty names for his manly hero in the making: Mighty Man, Megatron Man, Strong Man, Big Man, you get the idea. He ended up settling on the name that felt most like a blank to be filled in. One size fits all—i.e., big.

In interviews, Sweet seems to regard his prototypes as more representative of his original vision than the toy line that eventually emerged and proliferated into over seventy characters, saying that other designers "weakened" the concept with their input. This makes sense considering his original gang of "three huge tough guys" weren't just modeled on Big Jim and his buddies. Sweet had built them upon foundations of manhood that seemed wicked from his own experience. In a 2005 interview with *ToyFare* magazine, Sweet points to his own past as a beanpole among brutes as a key inspiration for He-Man.

"When you were a boy, you were a 'small man,'" he said. "Kids were not coddled. That had a great bearing on my originating He-Man. Where I grew up in Akron, Ohio, with the rubber factories, there were thousands of guys there who were factory laborers, and they were tough guys. And I saw a lot of tough stuff happen. And I'll tell you another thing. I've always been slender. And when I saw or got into tough situations happening, there were many times I wished I was a He-Man."

Same.

He-Man's origin story on Sweet's desk cuts a much clearer path than the character's in-world genesis, which was blurred to a point that seems intentional. At the time most superheroes had a relatively clear point A: they were launched here from another planet, or bitten by a radioactive spider, or bathed in gamma rays. With He-Man, such questions seemed superfluous; it was as though he had always been He-Man.

A tiny comic book series that accompanied the figures revealed that He-Man's official tale began as an ending: He-Man waving farewell to his tribe and their jungle home, which he had protected as their strongest warrior. According to the broad strokes of the provided lore, He-Man was the first of his people to venture beyond the jagged cliffs that marked the margins of "the outside world."

"He might have preferred to stay," read the strip, "but had a noble mission to accomplish"—vanquishing vaguely identified "evil forces" threatening the mysterious Castle Grayskull, "a fortress so ancient that no one knew its origin." He-Man immediately encounters a sorceress imperiled by some furry beast thing and rescues her, earning himself an arsenal of enchanted weaponry (that she didn't use against the furry beast thing herself for some reason) as well as a super sexy harness. Bam: He-Man is born. He finds a suitable valley, punches his new home into the side of a mountain, and begins perpetual battle against his blue-bodied skull-faced nemesis/frenemy, Skeletor—who, fun fact, came packaged with the other half of He-Man's Power Sword, the two of which could snap together into one. Interesting!

Meanwhile, *Masters of the Universe*—the companion Filmation cartoon series in which I and many other boys first caught sight of He-Man—offered a sweeping revision of the hero's mythology. "He-Man" was actually the secret identity of lavender-leotarded royal layabout Prince Adam, the inexplicably super-jacked son of bonus zaddy King Randor and Queen Marlena of the Kingdom of Eternia. Adam was the keeper of a dry, sardonic wit as well as a large, green, chronically terrified cat named Cringer. This telling did retain the Sorceress as the bestower of He-Man's magical powers, though here they were derived through the mysterious forces of Castle Grayskull and channeled quite dramatically through the Power Sword. He-Man broke it all down in his introductory voice-over, the end of which you should drench in reverb:

"Fabulous secret powers were revealed to me the day I held aloft my magic sword and said, 'By the power of Grayskull, I HAVE THE POWER!'"

With this, a flood of iridescent energy would course through Adam's body, Cringer would transform into the far more ferocious Battle Cat, and Adam would burst out of his work-from-home outfit into full regalia as He-Man, the Most Powerful Man in the Universe, a.k.a. Adam in drag.

Masters of the Universe was an opening salvo in a larger-scale siege on American living rooms during the Christmas of 1983. Not long after Ronald Reagan took office in 1981, he appointed one Mark Fowler as chairman of the Federal Communications Commission (FCC), the agency charged with the regulation of radio, television, and cable. Think of Fowler as the He-Man of deregulation.

Fowler did everything he could to make the FCC itself as feckless and redundant as possible, relaxing limits on how many radio and television stations could be owned by the same entity, removing restrictions that prevented advertisers from completely infiltrating children's programming, and otherwise inviting the market to determine what made it on the airwaves, regardless of who was on the receiving end.

This was not good news for children's television as I had come to know it. Shows like *Sesame Street, The Electric Company,* and *The Great Space Coaster* had been welcoming youngsters like me into a happy-go-lucky, seemingly more than slightly stoned fantasyland whose big furry puppets and grown-up human neighbors were primarily concerned with ensuring that I understood which words started with J, what a conjunction is, and how crayons are made.

Back in 1969, an FCC review of *Hot Wheels,* a children's television program based on Mattel's popular toy cars, had determined the show was little more than an extended commercial for the toys and moved to ban such product-centered programming. Fowler began his tenure by swiftly undoing these restrictions, thus opening the gates of daytime TV wide open for a decade of highly lucrative partnerships between cartoon creators and toy companies, who raced to reverse-engineer flimsy mythologies to fill hours of airtime and sell millions of pieces of plastic.

In 1982, Pac-Man was the first character to serve as ambassador from the mall, making the quantum leap from the arcades to the Saturday morning cartoon lineup (acquiring arms, legs, implied dimensionality, and a Flinstonian swagger in the process). Liberated from the hopeless mazes that had made him a household name but still pursued by a relentless pack of adversarial ghosts, the Pac-Man of the animated dimension had a life, a wife, a kid, and an influential presence over Pac-Land, a custom-crafted universe quite literally fashioned in his suddenly spherical image (even its bright yellow sun had a Pac-Man-esque wedge bitten out of it). As a commercial trial balloon, it succeeded in prompting competing networks to develop their own arcade adaptations, like CBS's *Saturday Supercade*. As a Saturday morning cartoon, it sucked.

One year later, *He-Man and the Masters of the Universe* made a similar leap. Having already stormed a good portion of American households as an action figure, He-Man now took to the TV screen to spread awareness to the remaining masses, including my brothers and me. Around the same time, Hasbro relaunched its longstanding G.I. Joe brand with the more compact 3.75-inch figures my brothers collected, and also released a companion cartoon, *G.I. Joe: A Real American Hero*—which remains a favorite of meme-crafters to this day.

A line of warring vehicles emerged over the TV horizon next, with *Voltron* (featuring robotic lions that assembled into a multicolored colossus), *Transformers* and its iconic "robots in disguise," and *Challenge of the GoBots* (a.k.a. Transformers if you ordered them from Wish.com) all vying for the hearts of boys and the paychecks of parents.

(Make no mistake, girls were, of course, squarely targeted in their own set of merchandising crosshairs, with another Filmation and Mattel collaboration, *She-Ra: Princess of Power*, launching in 1985 and leading its own charge of the pink half of the toy store, along with other TV-to-Christmas-tree offerings like *Poochie*, *My Little Pony*, *Rainbow Brite*, *Jem and the Holograms*, and the clearly jealous-of-Jem *Barbie and the Rockers*.)

By 1985 there were no fewer than forty cartoons on the airwaves with matching toys on the shelves, and toy store aisles had grown to look like miniaturized theme parks dedicated to after-school TV. But it was *He-Man* who was king of the mountain, reaching 2.9 million households on weekday afternoons and selling over 125 million figures (representing seventy some-odd characters) for $500 million in sales.

This rampant commercialization of what was once educational television's turf naturally caused plumes of steam to shoot from the ears of children's advocacy groups. "If there were a show for adults based on . . . Hoover vacuum cleaners, it would be boycotted," asserted the chairman of the American Academy of Pediatrics' Task Force on Children and Television. "A commercial by any other name is still a commercial," said Peggy Charren of Action for Children's Television (a group that spent the rest of the decade doggedly attempting to rebuild the regulatory dam against the flood of commerce).

When pressed, Fowler defended his FCC's deregulation crusade by pointing to the ever-widening variety of educational programming for kids available across the fast-growing cablescape, a sudden abundance that, he claimed, rendered the reins of regulation redundant and burdensome. Fowler also managed to make it about other people's parenting, throwing shade at parents for letting their TVs play babysitter to begin with: "Maybe sometimes it is that we want Johnny to play baseball," he told the *Washington Post* two days before Christmas 1983, when parents across the country were gift wrapping their *Masters of the Universe* purchases. "We ought not lose sight of religion, the family, school. There are lots of influences on children."

In 1985, a Christian day school in Manhattan hosted a "He-Man Workshop" for concerned parents to voice grievances over this new vanguard of barbarism. In a *New York Times* article covering the event, one father was quoted expressing deep concerns about the extreme violence and "one-dimensional nature of the characters" he saw in the cartoon. Peggy Marble, the school director, agreed, saying that He-Man and his friends "are devoid of human characteristics—they have no emotions and no humor," deficiencies that had little apparent impact on their appeal to children. "I would say in terms of boys age 3, 4 and 5, it's almost a national obsession for them," she said.

Lou Scheimer, the president of Filmation, argued that He-Man never hurts another living creature—which is technically true, as his Power Sword was usually drawn to deflect laser beams or demolish obstacles. Scheimer also claimed the show often addressed important issues ranging from gun control to child molestation, "and the good guys always win." Paul Cleveland, a senior vice president at Mattel, chimed in, arguing that the concept of good guys and bad guys didn't originate on the mean streets of Planet Eternia. "Little boys played that way 1,000 years ago," he said, throwing in some choice whataboutism: "Look at 'Road Runner.' Can anything be more violent than that?"

The parents' workshop additionally lamented the impending arrival of an animated adaptation of *Rambo* for children. A spokesperson for the production company assured a *Times* reporter that *Rambo* in cartoon form would be a "total departure" from the bullet-riddled, R-rated bloodbath of the feature film.

"There won't be any violence," she said. "He will have giant muscles and all of that. But he will be a guy who loves nature and won't look for trouble."

As with He-Man, Rambo's big built body in and of itself was read as a vessel of violence, as if the potential energy dormant in their muscles could only be activated for combat or destruction. One Yale psychology professor and television researcher echoed what the school director had observed among her students in the schoolyard: "What we have noticed is that the play with toys like He-Man tends to be rather aggressive."

He wasn't wrong. Most of the very first games I can remember playing with other boys at recess in the St. Bernard's Catholic Elementary schoolyard were little more than violent impulses searching out means of expression. We started with rocks, sitting in circles on the ground where a curb had crumbled into a ditch, banging them together, making big rocks into smaller rocks and sometimes generating little sparks, a magic that seemed like a flicker of creation. We moved on to trucks and spaceships, whose only imaginable courses were to collide with each other.

By second grade, most of the boys in my class were arriving to school lugging backpacks full of little barbarians. They'd dump their respective hordes out on the cafeteria tables at lunch and swap armors and axes, shields and swords, bludgeons and other tiny tactical choking hazards. They'd faction off their figures into arbitrarily warring tribes whose missions seldom aligned with the supplied mythologies. The details and reasons for the ongoing conflicts were imagined as the battles—which usually took the form of just slamming their bodies together—were waged. Little boys fighting as giant monsters. My men against your men. If two boys had copies of the same guy, one of them was designated the evil one. Battle was the fundamental organizing principle of our free time in boyland. Boy was a simple language to master. Together we grew fluent in each other: bodies in proximity spelled war.

But Adam on his own was a different story.

Unlike most barbarians, Adam had a soft side.

It's hard to say what about He-Man made his otherworldly figure so relatable to me. I wasn't particularly drawn to medieval warfare (or any warfare for that matter) or any of the other fantasy references aesthetically conjured up by his regalia.

In fact, when I played with He-Man, I tended to disarm him completely, stripping him of his weapons, his shield, his harness. My brothers' assorted Stormtroopers and Cobra Command forces were all identically outfitted or emblazoned with insignia representing their respective sides, but their power was derived from their anonymity and uniformity.

He-Man, meanwhile, was nothing but his body: a glossy colossus in fur briefs and matching boots. He was high camp the likes of which I wouldn't experience again for another decade, when as high schoolers we'd drive in to Cambridge to sing and shout through midnight screenings of *The Rocky Horror Picture Show* in Harvard Square, and where I'd spend half the film drooling over the titular lab-grown hunk, perfectly embodied by Peter Hinwood.

Like Rocky, the He-Man of my imagination was a misunderstood meathead, a gentle giant stuck in a world built for somebody else's proportions. It was this difference that became the center of gravity for my play. I'd have He-Man wander, lost and alone, through the hinterlands of a rumpled blanket before stumbling upon the outskirts of my Legoland, its placid plastic Main Street cutting through the wild shag of our carpet.

There, the perma-smiling townsfolk would gather around him and tilt back on their planted heels to take in the spectacle of his body, its bulging curves in stark contrast with the right angles of the Legos. In this setting, He-Man was more about awe than shock. While in town, he might rescue a cat from a green plastic tree; or hoist a car by hand to its spot in a questionably constructed parking garage; or he might just stand in the town square like a statue, flexing to the silent thrall of his audience. Whether I was playing the part of He-Man or his adoring audience is the only detail I can't recall.

—

My body-first fascination with He-Man now seems to be a trend among men my age—and not just the gay ones who have made quick Halloween homages out of the harnesses they already own.

The writer John DeVore recalls "clutching the brawny plastic figures as if they were magical totems" in his youth, but he regarded the animated character of He-Man as a model for the type of man he wanted to grow up to be: in possession of grace and humility and a jolly, no-fucks-given demeanor. "He-Man wasn't a barbarian," he writes in a piece titled "He-Man Is My Gender Icon." "He was a human being confident enough to run around half-naked, fighting evil with his pet cat."

A 2020 article in *Men's Health* speculates aloud that He-Man, with his lavender-legging'd alter ego Adam, is difficult to imagine as anything but "super gay," citing eavesdropped locker-room talk among Filmation animators about designing Prince Adam as a "soft prince" and He-Man as having "ten pounds of balls."

I've even seen connections drawn between the strange relationship (or duality) of He-Man and Skeletor, interpreting the antagonism between the fresh-faced Adonis and the skull-faced monster as unconscious analogues for the endangered gay self amidst the first fatal surges of the AIDS crisis. Were the two men truly enemies or two sides of the same mirror? Or two ends of the same lifetime? There was something tender about their antagonism, as though they needed each other to mean something. How else to explain that their little plastic Power Swords snapped together into one?

He-Man's muscles were strong enough to pry open the gates between the boardroom and the living room and rip them off their hinges, but were they truly of zero educational value? Right now, sitting here, I can't summon the details of a single one of his adventures from memory, despite my formative year or two of watching his world expand from the screen to every surface of our house. But I did learn some valuable things that I wouldn't be able to articulate for another forty or so years.

He-Man—or Adam, as he'd rather not be known—taught me that men find more power in the generic than the specific. The wide-open conceptual space of the He-Man—not as any specific character but as an ideal of masculinity—has been sold to young men since the 1950s, when fitness magnate and Schwarzenegger mentor Joe Weider started hawking home strength-training courses with booklets titled *How to Develop a He-Man Personality* and *Be Popular, Self-Confident and a He-Man*, which posited the body as the foundation for a growing man's sense of self.

"Grasp the truth that there are hidden powers within you which you have never yet uncovered," Weider wrote in the *He-Man Personality* booklet in 1959. No mention of the Power Sword or whether those powers were also fabulous.

As an artifact of the mid-1980s, the body of He-Man (the superhero) remains a hulking emblem of Reagan-era excess, a greed-is-good hunger for economic and geopolitical domination that was only beginning to whet its appetite.

To me, the violence that He-Man's critics so easily read into (or projected onto) his de facto threatening muscles could as easily be understood as a plasticine manifestation of Sweet's own boyhood pain, a realization of his own extinguished wish to be "a He-Man" that could handle the "tough situations" faced by the "tough guys" he had encountered through his hardscrabble upbringing.

He-Man was, at heart, a doll for "small men."

As such, he let us pretend: the blur of He-Man's half-fabled origins, the implied disposability of his past, even the open brackets of his name, all made his impossible form an easy imaginative space to inhabit. He struck me as the shape I was supposed to grow into, my body the universe I was meant to master.

I was equally drawn to his ample embodiment of transformation. He-Man and his afternoon ritual of self-actualization was drawing something out of me, his growling grimace urging me to hoist aloft my own sword, invoke my own figurative Sorceress, and begin my transformation from whatever I was to whatever I would be.

Of course, some aspects of He-Man's appeal wouldn't become clear until later, like in 1985, when the beefy Swedish bodyguard, bouncer, and Fulbright scholar (!) Dolph Lundgren would channel the momentum he'd gained playing the interchangeable Russian antagonist in *Rocky IV* to don He-Man's harness in the live-action iteration of *Masters of the Universe*. Or when, much later, I realized that He-Man's bestie and advisor,

Duncan—the mustachioed and similarly stacked Man-At-Arms—had somehow assumed the position of style icon in my subconscious. Still, my attraction to He-Man had more to do with his ineffability than any budding sense of his . . . effability.

I probably learned more from He-Man about how to properly accessorize than how to properly behave myself, but even still, his body had plenty to teach me about the ways my fellow boys and I would come to understand each other through the silent speech of our physical presence. In my hands and my imagination, He-Man was an articulation of everything I was not yet, and yet, his impossibility seemed attainable, graspable. For a boy already eager to grow, the fantasy of his body was a mere technicality of time.

But now, decades later, He-Man's body represents something much simpler, and far more complex. His superpower seems less like the product of another universe than a persistent symptom of an ongoing syndrome, less the gift of a sorceress than an inheritance of the big white musclebound body: the ability—the audacity—to deepen one's voice, summon the heavens, and declare, with all of the confidence in the world, that you have the power.

FORM

READERS SOMETIMES express surprise when I come out from behind my byline, as if my body doesn't properly fit the shape they've cut out for me.

A writer's body, after all, is supposed to reflect some measure of hunger, isolation, and deprivation. And a critic's body is supposed to take this even further. We're to appear wan and unsunned from long hours reclining in dark theaters, tubby from idle time plus snack bar diets, hunched from long sedentary stretches spent on our couches consuming media from multiple screens at once, our only energies expended through spindly bitter fingers batting at our laptops. In composition, writers are supposed to be soft and squishy, our bodies evident of an unwavering commitment to inadequately masculine labor.

Dusty stereotypes imagine writers as introverted hermits, starving artists, decrepit academics, or bookish nerds, starved of sunlight and cloistered away in cluttered studies. Some prefer their writers to be altogether formless—a vapor of persona hovering in the spaces between the type, a specter lurking behind the opaque curtain of the page, suspended in the realm of language and protected by a veil of fantasy. (The Internet has only made this worse, the byline of an author carrying about as much weight as the username of a troll.)

What a letdown it can be to follow the fine tether of a perfect line of prose to the clunky meat sack of a human body. Talk about disappointment incarnate.

Much of this has to do with long-ingrained notions about body and mind existing at opposite ends of a spectrum with no overlap. A focus on muscles is generally understood to indicate a corresponding neglect of the intellect. I first encountered the dumb jock archetype as Moose from *Archie*, Slater from *Saved by the Bell*, Kubiac from *Parker Lewis Can't Lose*. Often the dumb jock archetype comes bundled in a pair—the dumb lummox and the nefarious mini mastermind, passing their sidekick status back and forth. Every cartoon I watched growing up seemed to confirm this division between physical presence and intellectual prowess—a Yogi and Boo-Boo effect that delineated the two types as distinct but also utterly symbiotic. It offered a forecast of how I'd make my own way through high school as a pip-squeak: befriending and aligning with the Mooses and Oxes and Tanks of the world as a strategic means of protecting my proverbial queen—me. I remember when I was ten years old, latching on to a refrain from the Pet Shop Boys cassette I wore thin in my bedroom: "You've got the brawn, I've got the brains."

Indeed, an old acquaintance from grade school recently commented on an admittedly thirsty gym pic I posted to Facebook in what I can only describe as an acute outburst of "felt cute." The pic was me in a Speedo standing in a vaguely menacing slouch by the pool on the roof of our apartment complex. I was fresh from Push Day and was admittedly pumpy and shiny. My old schoolmate said something to the effect of "the new you looks like he'd slam the old you into a locker." Not gonna lie, I blushed. Some guys just know exactly what to say.

Despite how unrelated writing and lifting may seem on the surface, the two have long felt to me like alternate ways of performing the same exercise, making something out of nothing. The things that draw me to the gym each morning are, in large part, the same things that bring me to my desk to write each afternoon. I write and lift in equal measure each day precisely because of how complementary they feel, as though each endeavor contained a little of the other.

On the obvious side, both writing and lifting require discipline and dedication for any perceivable progress to be made. They demand the do-er show up and do. Weak spots left untrained will inevitably reveal themselves over time, and will do so all the more distinctly as the areas of greater focus tighten up. Both writing and lifting demand you see through the surface of the mirror or the blank page, forcing you to project your vision forward in time, to believe fully in things that don't yet exist. And yet, each also demands you engage directly with an unbudgeable present. Whether writing or lifting, I show up whether I want to or not. I make their respective practices as nonnegotiable as the sun's entrance and exit.

Writing and lifting also necessitate a measure of solitude. Of course, most writers have a confidant or two with whom they share drafts and pending disasters without fear of humiliation. An obvious meathead analogue exists in the "gym buddy," a contemporary form of bromance predicated on long-term commitment, mutual improvement, and the glory of shared "gains."

But for the most part, lifting and the long physical and psychological road of consciously building one's body is, by default, a solo mission. It's ultimately you against the pull of the earth as channeled through a bar, a rope, a pulley. Pick things up and put them down enough, and you start to develop a more acutely felt relationship to your motor system, a one-to-one connection between your body and, well, everything.

This may explain why klutzes who sucked very conspicuously at team sports as a teenager (ahem) grew up to opt for the weight room over the battlefield or the ball field, or why those predisposed to long stretches of me-time (ahem again) find themselves at the gym ass-early in the morning or at their desks late into the night. It may explain why so many of my biggest, beefcakiest friends share origin stories of being bullied into the weight room, escaping extreme loneliness and isolation through a connection they forged with their own bodies, offsetting the impossibility of fitting in with the possibility of busting out.

Most writers will also confess that the process of writing—reduced by many into a purely mental exercise—is in actuality a gruelingly physical trial. The process of moving one's thoughts through the body, down the arms and out through the fingertips, the act of sustaining these bursts of tension and release for hours on end, the labors of creation and output can feel, themselves, like acts of resistance training. (And that's assuming you can drag your body weight to the desk in the first place.)

Similarly, many lifters will attest to the extreme mental demands of lifting weights, which often rival the physical difficulties. Lifting weights—especially ones that are heavier than you—requires the recruitment of intense concentration, clarity, and connection. In personal-trainer lingo, this cultivated rapport between one's mind and one's musculature is known as *proprioception*: an awareness of one's body, of its motion through and occupation of space. Longtime lifters develop a downright dancerly control over the minute mechanics of their bodies, and yet each rep originates as pure abstraction, mere intention, volition transposed into action. If lifting is mindless, it is mindfully so.

Both writing and lifting require reporting to a specific mental and sometimes physical place. Both involve a close courtship with failure. Words, like weights, are just dumb representations—one of gravity, the other of meaning—awaiting activation, realization, elevation.

But in my thinking, one thing aligns writing and lifting more closely than anything else. Both are formal concerns. In lifting, as in art, form is everything.

Form is, ideally, the first thing you learn in the gym. In a tautological treadmill of sorts, good form is what allows for the continued pursuit of good form. With good form—the proper and safe execution of a given exercise—you can grow big and strong. Without good form, you invariably obliterate yourself: bring down a bench press in an unstable or awkward way, or lower a wobbly body into an iffy squat, or twist to catch a peek at a heavy dead lift in the mirror and you could screw yourself up a thousand different ways, leaving yourself unable to lift for weeks, your precious "gains" (progress) scattered in the wind and softening on the bone.

That little whisper of morality that haunts the phrase "good form"— and implies a neat binary "bad" as the sole alternative—is there for a reason. Good form is admired and praised in gym circles. It earns you back pats and approving comments in male-dominated ecosystems where such complimentary exchanges are exceedingly uncommon. To this day, I have close friends whom I only met because my barbell squat was visibly ass-to-grass enough to properly break the ice. Good form is read as good behavior: a signal of seriousness, a show of control, a sign of dedication. Good form is mastery of a secret language.

Bad form, meanwhile, is what allows you to get seriously hurt in public and possibly go viral on Instagram, YouTube, TikTok, or (depending on how bad the form) GoFundMe. Across these platforms, thousands of accounts dedicated to the compilation and preservation of especially bad form caught in the wild—a.k.a. "gym fails"—draw millions of gawkers and likers. Click and you can watch one doomed dude after the next, their mere inclusion in the reel a bellwether of impending disaster, their sloppy workouts always just moments away from dire physical consequences. The sight of dropped dumbbells, "stapled" benchers, snapping resistance bands, and flailing newbies contorting themselves to incorrectly wrench into random machines serves as both popular entertainment and as preemptive admonishment of violations against good form.

To slip into trainer mode for a moment, more often than not, various types of bad form are a direct result of the same bad decision: to take on more weight than one can handle. Beginners beguiled by the optics of heavy weight can often forego proper form for the sake of getting a good take on camera. It is the origin story of every fail video. Thus bad form is parsed with all the moral simplicity of a nursery rhyme, with a much larger chance of internal bleeding.

But subtract this value system and it becomes something more pure and more profound. Form becomes something like an essential element, a guiding principle, the physical equivalent of a spiritual tenet. Form, at its core, is a relationship between your body and your intentions. An enactment of an ideal way of moving, doing, being. A worship of motion.

Most form boils down to eliminating the separation between your body and the bar, connecting with the floor through your feet, embracing the weight, distributing it through the architecture of your body, holding gravity in your arms. You become momentarily more.

When I lie on the bench and pinch an imaginary pencil between my shoulder blades as instructed by the coach who dismantled my bad form and rebuilt it in his own image ten years ago; when I construct a little suspension bridge from the arch in my back, ensuring that my butt ever so gingerly grazes the bench (as is compulsory in competition); when I plant my heels and grip the bar hard enough that the hatch lines of its knurling stamp my palms; when I take in a big breath of air, store it in my belly, and dislodge the bar from the rack; when I draw the bar down to my chest as though I were pulling open the drawer of a flat file; when I store that tension in my lats as though I were drawing a bow threaded through my back; when I fire each muscle and launch the bar back up toward the fluorescents and lock out my arms; when I do it again, and again, executing each repetition precisely like this, just as I was shown and told until I could show and tell you; and when I do reps until I can no longer do them in precisely this way, I am not only following good form, I am carrying forth an inheritance, I am bearing a tradition, I am embodying an ideal, an attempt at perfection, an expression of desire.

When you zoom out from the individual motions of an exercise, when you widen the frame to fit the structure of one's workout, here, too, form makes an appearance at a different scale. In the rhythmic systems of reps and sets and workouts and cycles, I have found something like an anabolic analogue to the formal structures of writing.

In graduate school—where I studied poetry, because it was the early aughts and that's where the money was (lol, love that joke)—I signed myself up for a bunch of classes on formal poetry. (That is, poetry written according to long-established schematics, like the fourteen lines of an English sonnet, or the limited quiver of end words made available in a sestina, or the various rules and regulations of forms from other traditions: the ghazal, the pantoum, the renga.)

I did this not out of a desire to crank out a thesis's worth of villanelles, but as a way to consciously rein in my own personal craving for abstraction. I loved blank verse, free verse, poetry that said fuck you to other poetry, poems that slid into the gutters of their books, or walked a different path around the margins. I liked poetry that refused to behave like poetry. I saw myself in abstraction the way you can still recognize yourself in the surface of a disturbed pond.

Forcing my ideas into the predetermined shapes and schemes of sometimes ancient poetic forms was a way to force my own path through my thoughts, making the journey to the poem more of a hike through a thicket than a stride to the podium. I found myself embracing the obstacles. There was something about these arbitrary conditions—the enforced rhymes and end words, the rigid metric and syllabic demands—that felt like a dress code that could only do so much to contain me. Sneaking into poetry wearing these dusty old disguises felt like a caper, an infiltration.

But it also felt like I was joining a lineage of shared struggle, however small the stakes. I liked thinking of forcing myself into the same formal predicaments of William Shakespeare, Edna St. Vincent Millay, or Ted

Berrigan—each of whom put the sonnet to vastly different but vivid use. Squeezing into these hand-me-downs felt like donning the uniform of a tradition—and delighting in busting the seams.

Years later, with hundreds of hours of gym time between me and those creative writing workshops (which I always think of—positively—more as destructive writing), I realize my rigorous engagement with poetic form had actually been itself a form of exercise: poetry as resistance training. In poetry, and in art of all sorts, form serves as both a barrier to entry and a point of departure. The way an artist enters, occupies, and fulfills a form is a showcase of their ability to surface ideas and images through the limits of language.

Form enforces a level of sameness and predictability, yet it is form that allows us to perceive difference and divergence: Form can be the three chords of a punk song, the rhyme scheme of a limerick, the nautilus of a sonata, the size of a page of copy paper. Form is the shape of the instrument, the atlas of a symphony; it is both vessel and vehicle, limit and liberator. When an artist claims to be "free-form," freedom steps in as the form.

As such, the rhyme and meter of one's writing, the particulars of how time and breath and movement are managed from one line to the next, and the overarching importance of invisible structure to individual style all contribute to our understanding of voice—of who it is filling the form, a shadow of identity.

Even this book is a composite of forms, its structure the product of a process of modified and adapted shapes. At one point, I wanted it to echo the four movements of a symphony (complete with a melancholy andante adolescence). At another, this was all going to be letters to myself at different sizes. At another, a subtle model of the twelve trials of Hercules, traced like a frieze beneath the text.

I settled on something like a workout. Twelve sets of two.

It feels crazy to write "after the pandemic" because you're probably reading this a year from now and it's probably reared back up in a new variant, but: After the pandemic, I joined the gay gym.

By this I don't mean that the gym had exquisite style or longed to have sex with other gyms. (Although I did know a Jim and James who dated briefly, and I always wanted to refer to them as the Jim Buddies, but I really did not know them well enough to release that absolute fart of a joke in their presence, so you all get to enjoy it.) By "gay gym" I simply mean those naturally occurring (or precisely located) gyms in the heart of their cities' gayborhoods.

These gyms essentially assume the role of a queer commons—one of a vanishing stratum of "third places" where members of a physical or conceptual community can share real space together, which, not gonna lie, felt charged with extra significance when the gyms all reopened. In gyms, queer communities find not just reflections of ourselves (though, that) but proof of each other's reality. Another great feature of gay gyms is that you never have to wait for the squat rack. (Zap!)

In any case, at my new gay gym the men's locker room is very easy to find. The entire wall adjacent to its entrance is overtaken by a large-scale photograph: a creamy white, precision-chiseled torso, its surface dusted with evenly trimmed blond hair and defined by cleaving shadows and photogenic washes of light. The photo cuts off at the top of his traps and the lower ridge of his pelvis—the pre-convergence of what my husband would call his "cum-gutters." I think it's a real body, but I can't be sure. Screwed into the wall and his left shoulder is a big silver capital *M* (for "Men's"), which also seems to pose. I remember my first day at the gay gym getting stopped in my tracks by this image, closing my eyes to see if I could feel the pull of its current: *I am supposed to want this. I am supposed to want to be this. I am supposed to want to want to be this.*

This, says the wall, is where the *M* go, which is me. The body spells it out. Sometimes I imagine my own picture, laser-printed at high-resolution and lit by the crisscrossing beams of a pair of industrial LEDs: The crashing white wave of my belly's overhang, the crumples of fat at my armpits, the garden of unaddressed skin tags, the accidental-seeming distribution of body hair, the scars from my hernia surgery, or the ones from my bike crash when my forearm snapped into an intersection of bone. My dry skin and moles. My ingrown hair and calloused patches. My body eroding like a shore. This is where the men go, which is me.

The world of men is a world of forms.

Masculinity is a formal concern stricter and more unforgiving than music or poetry (and actually frowns on both). To be soft, or fat, or femme, to occupy a male body while rejecting the regulations of form, is considered by some to be squatting, trespassing, a defiant violation of the rules of occupying this body. Men are loathe to suffer their manhood alone. Ours is an alliance of captivity.

Masculinity is also a cult of ideals. The forms of strength and power that the men of the Western world abide by today were forged thousands of years ago in the golden age of Greek sculpture (around 450–400 BCE), when ancient artists were moving toward a convergence of extreme realism and exquisite fantasy.

"Perfection comes about little by little through many numbers," the fifth-century BCE sculptor Polykleitos of Argos famously declared. While his original bronzes made it to modern times, his legacy rests most strongly on a lineage of Roman marble copies and a paper trail of historical accounts from first- and second-century CE writers like Plutarch and Galen. Polykleitos was singularly interested in creating the ideal physical embodiment of the human form. To achieve this, he looked not just to the young soldiers and athletes that surrounded him but to Pythagorean ratios (the octaves, thirds, and fifths of the harmonic scale) and Hippocratic principles (like *isonomia*—i.e., equilibrium). Through Polykleitos's hands, the idealized male body became an instrument of visual music, an expression of harmony, a unification of body, mind, and spirit that the Greeks referred to as *arete*.

We know that Polykleitos sometimes depicted specific gods in his sculpture. In *Naturalis Historia* of 77 CE, the Roman author Pliny the Elder documents that Polykleitos had created "a Mercury that was once at [the Greek town of] Lysimachea" and "a Hercules now in Rome." At the Metropolitan Museum of Art you can behold Roman marble copies of an elegantly poised and posed Hermes attributed to the sculptor dating from the first or second century CE.

But Polykleitos was clearly most inspired by the mortal men around him. As historian Andrew Stewart notes, "Polykleitos' statues of gods or *agalmata* were apparently as neglected by the copyists as were Pheidias' statues of mortals . . . though this did not prevent occasional attempts to furnish his figures with divine attributes." His bronze sculptures of young male athletes, meanwhile, created a new standard of male beauty—the body itself as a work of art.

The principles that shaped his vision of perfection are outlined in his treatise, known as the Canon. Though the original text is lost to us, through scattered extant references to and quotations from the Canon, we can derive a sense of how Polykleitos calculated the perfect man. The Greek philosopher Plutarch of the first century CE recounted the importance the artist placed on proportion: "the numbers must all come to a congruence through some system of commensurability and harmony, for ugliness is immediately ready to come into being if only one chance element is omitted or inserted out of place."

The Greek physician Galen of the second century CE later noted that the perfection of Polykleitos's forms emerges "via an exact commensurability of all the body's parts to one another: of finger to finger and of these to the hand and wrist, of these to the forearm, of the forearm to the upper arm; of the equivalent parts of the leg; and of everything to everything else."

To demonstrate these principles, Polykleitos created an exemplar statue also called the Canon, though it is more commonly known today as the *Doryphoros* (or "Spear Bearer"). Cast around 440 BCE, the Doryphoros is known to us only through marble copies created centuries later by the Romans and represents Polykleitan proportions down to the finger.

In his study and speculation of the treatise Canon's contents, the historian Andrew Stewart surmised that while Polykleitos was likely not a card-carrying Pythagorean, "in considering the various formulae that Polykleitos could have used, it is fair to conjecture that he made his choice from what was available in the field of mathematics at the time, that is, around 450 B.C." This put him well within the influence of Pythagorean models—and the whole number ratios akin to those from which the harmonic scale is derived—and well before the fine-tuned and "arithmetically irrational" golden ratio that would come to undergird the slightly extended torsos of Renaissance proportionality.

The Doryphoros stands asymmetrically, or contrapposto, with a slight cock of the hip. His pose is an effortless expression of *isonomia*, a balance of opposites (or the 1:1 ratio Pythagorean duality)—stillness and motion, tension and release, hard and soft, flesh and stone. But his form also articulates a precisely calculated proportionality—from knuckle to finger, finger to hand, hand to forearm, and so on. His body is perfectly balanced, its parts precisely commensurate—a quality the Greeks called *symmetria*.

He's also nude. In ancient Greek sculpture, male nudity was a show of cultural refinement, the elegant aesthetics and physical prowess of an advanced civilization. But cast in bronze or stone, the body here also becomes an impenetrable suit of armor—a show of force rendered forever still. It also becomes a blank surface for projection—he represents no man and every man, featureless and awaiting identity, offered as a body to be worshipped, donned by only those worthy to die in it.

Polykleitos's statues were snapshots in bronze of everyday men, but they also represented a vision of the perfect Grecian citizen: strong, confident, beautiful. Through Pliny we know he sculpted a young man scraping his skin with a strigil (a tool used in ancient Grecian gymnasiums to clean off dirt and sweat before bathing); a pair of boys "playing at knucklebones" (an ancient game that falls somewhere between jacks and dice); a man tying on a fillet (a cloth or leather headband worn by ancient athletes)—each figure a perfectly proportioned negotiation between the real and the ideal.

The realism of Polykleitos's mortal men inspired a fresh perspective on the unreal body. It was Polykleitos's student Lysippos who, in the fourth century BCE, cast his own divinely inspired hit single: a beefy bronze figure of Hercules that would loom large over the next two millennia of Western art.

This particular Hercules—who at the time of his creation was known by his original Grecian moniker, Herakles—is often referred to as the "Weary Hercules." It captures the mighty son of Zeus late in his mortal life, having freshly completed his twelve redemptive and heroic trials, undertaken to appease his asshole cousin Eurytheus. (And having bulked up into an absolute unit.)

Like the Doryphoros, Herc stands with a slight tilt. He leans in repose, at long last able to rest. Unlike the Doryphoros, he is a mass of meat—every muscle taken to a superhuman state of swole. The work-worn Hercules leans on his club, over which is draped the skin of the Nemean lion (his first labor). Behind his back he clutches the Apples of the Hesperides (the stolen fruits of his penultimate trial). His body tells the story of his body. This is a Hercules no longer charging forward; his work is done. And though he stands still, everything about him is evidence of movement, strength, resistance, power.

Seven centuries later, in 216 CE, this preternaturally jacked Herc would be enlarged and reproduced in marble by the Greco-Roman sculptor Glykon, featured in the portico to the courtyard in the astonishingly beefcake-strewn public Baths of Caracalla in Rome. (The idea of decorative celestial studs rendered in oversized marble might seem strange until you recall Mr. Headless Torso at my gym.) Among the divine Greek figures adapted by the Romans into their own culture, Hercules took up a large space in their hearts, not to mention the baths. This original copy (which is not an oxymoron here) of Lysippos's Hercules stood a little over ten feet tall and presided over the baths' main swimming pool. For those Romans who visited the baths to exercise, he was there to pump you up.

In the mid-sixteenth century, Glykon's Hercules was excavated in pieces from the site of the baths—a head here, a leg much later—and moved to the Renaissance palazzo of Cardinal Alessandro Farnese, whose particular taste for classical antiquity aligned with a heightened cultural attention toward Olympian deities, and where Hercules was surrounded on high by equally meaty fresco renditions of the big man's excellent adventures.

If you're wondering what happened in the millennium of meantime, the answer is many things—the fall of the Roman Empire and the rise of Christendom, to name two big ones. In the monastic-ruled world of medieval Christian Europe, representations of the male body, let alone sumptuous nude ones, had not been part of the paradigm. "The human body ceased to be a candidate for glorification," writer Kenneth R. Dutton notes, "and became rather a vessel doomed to condemnation unless supernaturally saved by God through the instruments of grace."

Dutton describes the sixteenth-century artistic rediscovery of the body and the transformation of attitudes surrounding it as "one of the distinguishing marks of the Renaissance."

"The physical body, which in the medieval period had been drawn purely naturalistically because it was not seen as a figure or type of a higher reality, now took on again the symbolic status which it had abandoned at the breakup of the Roman Empire," writes Dutton. "The nude could once again take shape as a creative idea."

Lysippos's original bronze Hercules is long gone—it was likely melted into coins after the sack of Constantinople in 1204 CE—but the reconstructed Farnese Hercules (a.k.a. *Ercole in riposo*, or "Hercules at rest") still stands, permanently posted at his own super spacious first-floor walk-up in the Museo Archeologico Nazionale in Naples. But he's one of a million copies.

You can find them in museums and universities around the world. You can page through centuries of etchings, engravings, and prints paying homage to his divine bulk. You can spot him topping fountains and guarding gardens. You can buy miniatures of the colossus to sit on your desks or mantle. He can be custom-printed on T-shirts and aprons to make you look jacked. Artists have recast him in plaster, gold, polystyrene, and car parts. On Etsy you can order a 3D-printed Farny (my name, not theirs) cast a ravishing rip-off of Yves Klein blue.

Or you can just go to any gym and see his progeny in person.

For as big as Hercules must have seemed to those mere mortals he once presided over, there's something increasingly common about his demigod bod. This ancient Herc looks like any number of contemporary action heroes, pro wrestlers, UFC (Ultimate Fighting Championship) heavyweights, or beefcake influencers. He could occupy any square in the grid of big bodies Instagram suggests to me: men selling supplements, pushing programs, telling men how to be bigger men. He looks like the juiced-up giants I see at my gym, each of us taking turns kneeling at the altar of the ab machine. Hercules was once a god; now he's a goal. A form to fill.

One of the reasons I aspire to a certain form is so that I can break it.

Like the forms I used in poetry class, I like to feel in defiance of my physical shape. I enjoy being a secret softie in a hard body. A nerd in bully's clothing. I've always been drawn to the gentle giant, the chummy beast, the terrifying teddy bear. I like the idea of form as a gentle betrayal, a decoy, a shell.

But what is form when it comes to my own body? Is it something I pour myself into or something that emerges from within? In the mirror, I see a composite of forms—a pastiche of archetypes and antecedents: elder Athenian senator; old-timey strongman; mustachioed stranger from a Tom of Finland vignette; Venice Beach meathead; ironic cop. Sometimes I feel like an action figure in search of a playset.

What form do I hope to take? Who is this man I am trying to be? Do I know him?

II

PETER

I'M PRETTY SURE a truck turned me gay.

His broad crimson cabin. The gleaming six-pack of his silvery grille. His glassy windshield pecs with wipers where the nipples would go. His iron biceps and calves of steel—both of which were actually plastic. Out of all of my toys, and out of all of their beefy animated avatars appearing on the television screen in our living room each afternoon, Optimus Prime was my ride or die.

Real quick Transformers universe primer: Optimus Prime is the leader of the Autobots (the good guys), sworn enemies of the Decepticons (the bastards). Millions of years ago, the Autobots attempted to ghost their war-torn home planet of Cybertron, taking off in a spaceship to search for resources elsewhere. Obsessed, the Decepticons trailed the Autobots into space, eventually hijacking their ship and starting shit. During the resultant melee, the ship veered off course and crashed into prehistoric Earth, where it remained lodged in a dormant volcano until 1984. That's when an eruption triggered a full system reset of the ship's onboard computer, dispatching drones to scan the local mechanical landscape and create effective camouflage forms for the soon-to-be-reanimated robots. The Decepticons were the first to rise from their rusty slumber, taking a plainly threatening range of earthly forms—Skywarp, Starscream, and Thundercracker all turned into F-15 fighter jets. Ravage turned into an angry Jaguar. Rumble was a pile driver. Megatron, the leader of the pack, could turn into three different types of gun. Freshly re-fabricated and ready to do evil, the Decepticons fled the scene to build their own lair.

Meanwhile, the revived Autobots were remade into an array of foxy Earth cars—like a Datsun Fairlady 280ZX (Bluestreak), a Mitsubishi J59 (Hound), a Ligier JS11 Formula One racer (Mirage), a Lamborghini Countach LP500S (Spin-Out).

For his part, Optimus Prime was modeled after a Freightliner FL86 cab-over triple-axel semitrailer truck. And as a truck, he was honestly just so-so. He had a cool blue racing stripe down the side of his trailer, but it was clear to me that his wheels were mere decoration—they weren't actually made for playing *truck*. I knew a thing or two about toy vehicles. My older brothers saw to it that our toy boxes were full of functional trucks, cars, and construction equipment: chunky Tonka cranes that could crank an imaginary wreck from the trenches of crumpled blankets; Tyco slot cars that would fling around electrified tracks spitting little sparks and leaving the scent of burnt circuits; battery-powered Stompers that could climb couch cushions; a massive fleet of driverless Matchboxes and Hot Wheels, little avatars of ambition and drive.

Optimus in truck form never quite transcended his disguise, but we tried. My brothers and I had him running deliveries of imaginary supplies all around our Lego village—or we'd dispatch the "Roller" drone that lived inside of his trailer. Or we'd have him navigate dangerous passes atop the couch as though he were hauling cargo through a plush, garishly floral version of the Rocky Mountains. But it always seemed forced. Optimus was clearly built to be something else.

I'd like to think this outsider status was at the bottom of my innocent affinity for Optimus Prime, this shared feeling that our visible form was a ruse. That we could only reveal our true natures by transforming into something else. That one could blend in with the traffic jam of the world around them or transform, fly away, to hell with the Decepticons.

With the clarity of hindsight, I think I was just horny for his voice. On TV, Optimus Prime spoke in this captivating, deep, and deeply calm bass-baritone rasp that seemed to drag on the ground like a torn mud flap. "Autobots," he'd intone with boot-on-gravel authority, "*transform*."

And we were all like "Yes. Sir." Or, you know, the Autobots were.

There was a grit, a texture, a realness to his voice—far removed from the forced depth of He-Man's whenever he would slip out of Prince Adamhood into something more comfortable. He-Man was voiced by John Erwin, about whom you can't learn much by searching online. Peter Oppenheimer, the far squawkier voice of He-Man's nemesis Skeletor, once said at a toy expo that Erwin was an extremely shy man who regularly balked at appearing in public as a representative of his character: "I don't even *look* like He-Man," Oppenheimer recalls him saying.

Optimus Prime was voiced by a man named Peter Cullen. It was at one of the lowest points of his life that Cullen found himself suddenly called to lead the Autobots.

At the time, Peter was sharing an apartment with his brother, Larry. The two were extremely close. Larry was the older brother by thirteen months, bigger by five inches and several pounds. He was a boxer who had left their hometown of Montreal for the States (where he also had roots), graduated from college, and joined the US Marines, intending to play football for the corps. Immediately after officer training, he was sent to Vietnam, where he did service tours along the northern border, earning the Bronze Star and two Purple Hearts. By the time the brothers were sharing an apartment in 1984, Larry was forty-three years old and a decorated captain, keeping a close eye on Peter, a self-described "grunt" struggling to find work and purpose.

You can watch a YouTube video from the 2018 TFCon—and here I should mention that since the Transformers' first appearance on TV in 1987, the franchise has expanded into a vast multidimensional universe with a matching empire of products, games, reissued toys, and fan communities, about all of which I know virtually nothing—where Cullen stands before an audience and shares a conversation he'd had with Larry before heading to the audition for the part:

He said, "Peter, where are you going today?"

I said, "Why, do you need the car?"

He said, "No, no, I just want to know where you're going."

"I'm gonna be auditioning. As a truck." [Crowd laughs.] *He did the same thing!*

I said, "But Larry, he's evidently a hero truck. He's a hero."

And his face got somber and he said, "Peter, if you're gonna be a hero, be a real hero. Don't be a Hollywood hero type with all the BS and all the yelling and screaming and trying to be tough."

He closes his answer with something that—goddammit—makes me fucking tear up as I'm transcribing it because his voice is still that voice:

"Be strong enough to be gentle."

"OK, Lar. Yeah." [And the audience stays stone still.]

So his voice is ringing in my ears as I'm driving to the audition. And I read the copy and Larry is just coming out: His voice. The way he talked to me. And it wasn't "MY NAME IS OPTIMUS PRIME!" It was "My name is Optimus Prime."

After the audition, not knowing that he would get the part, Peter sat in his car in the parking lot and wished Larry had been there to hear him. In telling the story seven years after Larry's passing, you can hear Peter's voice struggle under the weight of his memory. "I think he would have been proud of me because I really think I nailed the character," he said. "It was just Larry."

When I was twelve, skidding into junior high, the only thing I wanted was to become something else.

At home I was always the smallest, until my kid brother arrived in 1985—and then his small overtook mine, which only made me less visible. When *Honey, I Shrunk the Kids* came out in 1989, it held a strange resonance for me.

I was awkward and ungainly, squealy and flamboyant, with bony legs and a bowl cut tousled by tornadoes of cowlicks. At school, I was equally fascinated with and fearful of the older boys, who seemed to double in size each year as I remained the same, and with whom I seemed to have less and less in common as the years passed and our bodies changed.

Or theirs did, at least. My puberty was somehow both light- and lead-footed, the other boys lapping me on the proverbial racetrack, their high voices cracking like eggshells, their armpits suddenly smuggling small tufts of dark hair. The boys in my class started to smell and smell each other. I felt detected and undetectable at once. The whole pride of boys was sorting itself out.

As if to mock me, transformation was suddenly everywhere. The success of the Transformers inspired copycats all over the toy store: GoBots were the closest analog (rip-off)—the Pepsi to the Transformers' Coke. Rock Lords (a spin-off of the GoBots) were robots that could turn into (double-checks notes) rocks. McDonald's came out with its own line of

Happy Meal toys called Changeables—robots that could turn into plastic fries and burgers.

But even beyond this, every respectable hero from my childhood was the product of transformation: Bill Bixby's David Banner devolving into Lou Ferrigno's Incredible Hulk, Christopher Reeve's Superman phone-boothing out of his dorky reporter persona into the Man of Steel, or most impactfully to me, Michael Keaton as Batman.

Tim Burton's 1989 live-action reboot was the reboot that arguably launched Generation Reboot. Without the benefit of contemporary CGI fluffing, costume designer Bob Ringwood said he faced a challenge in creating a Batsuit that would convincingly transform the dad-bod star of 1983's *Mr. Mom* into a "big six-foot-four hunk with a dimpled chin."

Ringwood declared Lycra and leotards out of the aesthetic question, opting instead for a black rubber costume designed from a full cast of Keaton's body, piled and padded with heaping muscles made of latex. In some spots, the suit was several inches thick.

I could have really used a heavy-duty exoskeleton at the time. When I reached seventh grade my parents, tight on cash and low on faith in the local parish, decided to pull me and my brothers out of Catholic school and enroll us in the public school system. For my brothers, this meant a return to the high school my mother had attended when she first came over from England. For me, this meant the middle school up the street with the stabby reputation. Before I left for the summer, my friends all wished me a somber farewell, some of them articulating the fear that I was going to get shivved in the yard like the kid they'd heard had gotten shivved in the yard. I wasn't sure what to expect beyond the fact that I'd finally have a locker like the kids on TV.

B. F. Brown had a completely different energy from the hushed dominion of nuns that was St. Bernard's. Lockers slammed, intercoms blared sterile attention tones followed by inscrutable announcements. A wild wind of relative sartorial independence swept through the halls: the two school-permitted hues of blue to which I was accustomed were here replaced with expressions of actual individual style—or 1988's version of it.

There were jocks and punks and stoners and roughnecks and goth kids and nerds and metalheads and theater fags. And while they would mix in the halls, the lunch tables would distill the mob of students into their distinct elements.

The opening bell of the school year felt like the launch of a countdown to formulate what I was, who I wanted to transform into. But by the end of my first week, I knew.

I wanted to be Coach Chauvet.

An absolute tank, Coach Chauvet had a first name none of us were permitted to say. When he wasn't helping coach the high school football team, he was teaching morning period Phys Ed, glaring at us like a pissed-off hawk from over his clipboard or through the iron grate screwed over the window of his office just off of the basketball court. He had a neck like a tree, a perfect flattop that looked like he'd chainsawed it in one swipe, and a hard disapproving brow that shadowed his eyes. Imagine Sam Eagle from the Muppets but insanely jacked.

Coach Chauvet's arms were huge: they looked like thick coils of cable, stretching the sleeves of a T-shirt precisely selected to struggle against them, to signal a constant state of busting out. His forearms were thick as hams, his hands like massive mallets. He had the legs of a lineman, filling out his sweatpants with a deep shelf of butt.

We had gym class twice a week, an experience I had fully expected to dread, as rosters were assembled based on arbitrary alignments of class schedules and regardless of students' grade levels. Thus the sixth, seventh, and eighth graders—separated by only three years of Earth time but multiple dimensions of puberty—would size each other up in every imaginable sense.

The boys around me, even those younger than me, had gotten off to bounding starts on their development. In class, their voices leapt between registers as they read aloud; in the schoolyard, the honking din of their voices could have been mistaken for free jazz from a distance. And up close, their bodies were growing like the plants in the time-lapse filmstrips from science class. Their upper lips and chins started sprouting hair, their cheeks and backs broke into swaths of acne, their bodies were growing out as well as up. Coach Chauvet would make us hurl dodgeballs, climb ropes, and run laps, and when I'd inevitably find myself at the back of the pack, it wasn't even a metaphor. In every sense I was running behind.

In the John Hughes movies I'd watch in my earnest but unsuccessful attempts to decode the social order of my chaotic new milieu—*The Breakfast Club, Pretty in Pink, Weird Science*—this would be the part where the coach would humiliate me in front of the class, highlight my pathetic wormhood, and use my weakness as a worst-case example for the rest of the class.

But Coach only looked like a brute. When the day's exercises were over and he'd dismiss the class downstairs to the ancient-seeming belly of the locker rooms—where the ritual of the mandatory gang shower added an epilogue of humiliation to each class—he'd check on me.

Nothing big. Just a "Hey. Brodeur. You OK, buddy?"

I probably looked like I was about to cry. And I probably was. Not because I hated climbing the rope (though I did). Not because I could feel myself naturally gravitating toward target status for the older boys in my class (though I could). But because I felt alone, abandoned, invisible to the naked eye.

I wondered if he knew my older brothers, using my last name like that. Or maybe that was a military thing. Or maybe it's just because that's what he barked out when taking attendance. I remember how strange it was to be addressed that way—as one in a lineage, a Brodeur, a form, a space to fill. I also remember the thrill I felt from him simply seeing me beyond his taking the roll; the rush of his body registering the existence of mine. The answer was yes, I was OK.

I was fascinated by the lair of Coach's office, which I'd take a mental snapshot of whenever I'd walk past. It was spare but selectively cluttered. The Tupperware of whatever he was eating between classes sat open on a defunct wooden teacher's desk dragged in from a classroom. A small bookshelf to the side sported a row of his own football and weight lifting trophies—little gilded plastic musclemen hoisting loaded barbells overhead, or frozen forever in a classical bicep flex. Next to these he kept a bottle of Hai Karate cologne—a partial source of what I found to be his intoxicatingly acrid musk. I remember he often kept a short stack of bodybuilding magazines on the edge of his desk that I was too shy to join my classmates in paging through: *Flex, Muscle & Fitness, Iron Man.* They felt like forbidden texts written in a language I'd never understand. An instruction manual for a body I would never have.

There was a Midas auto repair that we'd pass on the drive home from school, and behind that, there was, apparently, a gym. I'd see the sandwich board for the Flex Factory out on the sidewalk when we'd drive by—a thick flexing arm like Coach Chauvet's pointing down a gravel road that curled toward a row of what I thought were empty garages. I never saw anyone go in or out of the driveway, and I was far too terrified to pedal my bike back there on one of my *Goonies*-inspired solo adventures. I'd never seen any other men in real life who looked like Coach. I hadn't known his body was humanly possible. Was this where it came from?

Though my memories of this time of my life are worn about as thin as Coach's T-shirts, I can say with some certainty that I wasn't sure what I wanted—I just wanted. I wanted to somehow pilot Coach's body like the kid who gets hexed into adulthood in that movie *Big*. I wanted to be him. To know what it was like to be him. To be seen as me but mostly as *that*.

At the same time, my fascinations with Coach filled me with fear and dread. Coach became an icon of a desire that had to be ignored or repurposed. His brawn and bulk didn't intimidate me—it made me terrified of myself. I disqualified myself from the idea that I could occupy a body that anyone would see the way I saw Coach's.

I longed to forget I even had a body. I started thinking of myself as my thoughts.

ON MANLY
HEALTH

WHEN THE PANDEMIC WAS RAGING, the quarantine in full swing, I did what everyone else did: I disappeared a little. I sank into the couch and shrank into myself. I softened. I felt my cells lose their grip on each other. I fell out of form.

Attempting to remember details from 2020 is like trying to scoop up soup with a slotted spoon. I remember the movers hauling stuff out of our old place in Houston in mid-February as we prepared to relocate to DC, where I was about to start as the new classical music critic at the *Washington Post*. I remember the flight into DC with my husband and spotting in first class Representative John Lewis, who I'd not have noticed were it not for the (then) strange sight of his N95. I remember my first staff meeting at the *Post*, and I remember that meeting's uncertain adjournment, which sent us home to work remotely for a period that certainly, we imagined, would only last a week or two.

From there, it all just spills back into the same tepid sludge of images—the sunlight's daily crawl across the kitchen wall, the sickly verdant landscape of *Animal Crossing* lighting up our living room by night, every TV channel a chart of rising case numbers, a spiking graph of deaths.

In the interest of feeling less like a heap of human laundry and in the absence of an open gym, I started searching for ways to build one at home. At this point my fellow lifters had already drained the nation's limited supply of retail gym equipment in the Great Online Iron Rush of 2020, so my options were few. After several failed attempts to win gnarly old weight plates from shuttered gyms on eBay auctions, I found a guy on

Facebook Marketplace making oversized dumbbells. He'd pour quick-set cement into matching plastic sandcastle pails, join the set wads with a crude aluminum handle, and dip the finished dumbbell in black latex paint. They were cartoonishly huge but barely weighed twenty pounds each. Desperate, I bought two for sixty bucks. They arrived in the trunk of an Uber two hours later. They sucked.

Instead of depending on my DIY dumbbells, I slid the couch back to clear floorspace to do push-ups and crunches and searched the new neighborhood for sturdy-looking scaffolding on which to attempt pull-ups. I repurposed items around the house, deadlifting boxes of vinyl LPs on repeat. I'd stuff backpacks full of my heaviest books about Verdi and Wagner and squat them. I'd climb the ten flights of stairs in our new building, walk down the hall to the south stairs, and go back down—a captive *tour de stade*. I'd venture outside with the one resistance band I'd hung on to in the move. I'd sling it around park bench legs or tree branches or the soles of my feet. I'd pull against its pull until my arms were torched with lactic acid (the feel-the-burny by-product of anaerobic metabolism). I'd walk long yards in deep lunges until my thighs ached and my eyes teared. I'd find a field where I could be alone. I'd gorge myself on air and drain myself with effort. It felt defiant to do something, anything—the more pointless, the more repetitive, the better.

For millions of gym bros like me, the closure of gyms nationwide amounted to the loss of a primary habitat, a source of identity.

And for many of the men I watched unravel online—throwing tantrums on social media over the perceived oppression of public health measures, mask mandates, and home quarantines—the loss of the gym compromised a key source of their manhood. Many men found themselves going stir-crazy, fashioning their own improvised backyard gyms out of disused sawhorses, five-gallon buckets of paint, sandbags, and barrels.

This type of resourcefulness, I imagine, is how it must have been for the meatheads of yore—those sepia-tinted nineteenth-century strongmen, wrestlers, and assorted swole-timers we envision when we think of the vaudeville stage or an old-timey circus: twirly moustache, leopard loincloth, massive barbell. You know the ones.

Those sturdy, swarthy Halloween-ready archetypes are inspired by a real-life pantheon of fin de siècle fitness phenoms—formative musclemen of the late nineteenth century like Eugen Sandow (a.k.a. "The Father of Bodybuilding"), George Hackenschmidt ("The Russian Lion"), Louis Cyr ("The Canadian Samson"), and Arthur Saxon ("The Iron Master").

And each of these iconic beefcakes was himself the product of a sweeping "physical culture" movement that originated in nineteenth-century Europe and swept across the Atlantic to the States. A wave of widespread cultural shifts and political upheaval through the 1800s set the stage for a wholly revised vision of manhood, masculinity, and "manly" health that still shapes our perception of the American male body.

The history of American gym culture can be indirectly traced back to the influence of one notably diminutive and highly figurative strongman. If it hadn't been for famed French emperor Napoleon Bonaparte's decisive trouncing of Prussian forces at the 1806 Battle of Jena-Auerstädt, young Johann Friedrich Ludwig Christoph Jahn (who settled on "Friedrich") might never have declared his own personal war on weakness.

Born in 1778 in the Prussian state of Brandenburg (in current-day eastern Germany), Jahn studied history, theology, and philology as a young man before moving to the capital city of Berlin to teach secondary school physical education. This was a period of remarkable innovation for the young athlete and educator, who devised several of the apparatus that remain central to modern gymnastics, including the rings, the balance beam, the pommel horse, the parallel bars, and the horizontal bar.

A proud Prussian in a time prior to a unified Germany, when clusters of Germanic principalities (once part of the fallen Holy Roman Empire) were fending off the advances of France, Jahn was deeply stung by Napoleon's swift victory and subsequent occupation of Berlin. His response to the defeat was visceral in more ways than one, inspiring him to establish his own center dedicated to the training and strengthening of young Prussian men of fighting age.

For his gymnasium—which, to honor Germanic etymology, he termed *Turnplatz*, derived from the German *turnen*, "to practice gymnastics"—Jahn likely drew inspiration from two influential figures in the growing field of physical education: Johann Guts Muths, a teacher and gymnastics pioneer whose 1793 treatise *Gymnastik für die Jugend* served as a primary phys ed manual, and Franz Nachtegall, a gymnasiarch (gym owner) in Copenhagen who directed Denmark's Military Gymnastic Institute under King Frederick VI.

Nachtegall shared Muths's view of a physical fitness shaped by Enlightenment ideals—a properly exercised body was itself an extension of moral, social, and intellectual fitness. These are tenets directly transposed from the gymnasia of ancient Greece, which drew as much admiration from Muths as "soft and effeminate people" attracted his ire.

Jahn opened his first Turnplatz in 1811 at Hasenheide, an area outside of Berlin. It was nothing special: a simple but useful array of ropes, bars, beams, blocks, dumbbells, clubs, and other rudimentary gymnastic equipment. A vast open turf was reserved for running drills, playing field games, and practicing gymnastics—and its members became known as Turners (German for "gymnasts").

The spartan setup of the Turnplatz makes sense considering its ancient inspiration. Jahn modeled it after the gymnasia of ancient Greece. These public centers of athletic, academic, and military training were far removed from our modern fitness palaces of iron, chrome, and mirrored glass. But like the overcrowded gyms of twenty-first century America, the gymnasia of ancient Greece were cultural hubs—home to storied Panhellenic athletic contests like the Pythian games (which started in Delphi around the sixth century BCE) and the Olympics (which started around the eighth century BCE in the sanctuary of Olympia).

Only freeborn men and boys and authorized resident visitors were eligible to attend ancient gymnasia—it was a small fraction of ancient Greece's largely enslaved population—and those who benefited from access were privy to elite military training, studies with influential philosophers and sophists, and the benevolence of the gods.

The primary pursuit at ancient gymnasia was to maximize one's individual potential as a citizen—one's *arete*, described by scholar Stephen Miller as an amalgam of "virtue, skill, prowess, pride, excellence, valor and nobility."

Similarly, the thrust of the Turnplatz, and the network of *Turnverein* (or Turners unions) that sprung up to connect about 150 clubs operating by 1815, was primarily about Germans building a strong Germany. Historian

Eric Chaline points out that Muths and his disciples flipped the script of the nature and function of physical education: "Physical fitness, or fitness for purpose, was not an individual attainment freely offered to the state by the citizen, but a social obligation demanded by the state of its citizens."

"As long as man has a body, it is his duty to take care of, to cultivate it, as well as his mind, and consequently gymnastick exercises should form an essential part of education," Jahn writes in his 1816 fitness manual, *Deutsche Turnkunst*. "Where man exists, there gymnastick exercises have, or at least ought to have, a place; they are the property of mankind, not confined to any one nation, or part of a nation."

As universal as Jahn's phrasing (translated by fellow Turner Charles Beck for the 1828 English edition, *A Treatise on Gymnasticks*) may be, athletes at any given Turnplatz weren't just there to develop their bodies but their sense of *Deutschheit*, or Germanness. The Turnverein weren't the only places where fitness served a sense of nationalism. Sweden established a Royal Gymnastics Institute, and the similarly physical Sokol movement spread across the Slavic region and Slovene countries in the mid-1800s. Their impact has carried into the twenty-first century; even today's Olympic gymnastics culture carries with it a vestigial but vital nationalistic charge.

In 1813, Jahn helped to form the Lützow Free Corps, a volunteer force supporting the Prussian army's fight against Napoleon, and led a battalion to halt the expansion of the First French Empire. Following Napoleon's ultimate defeat at Waterloo in 1815, Jahn returned to Berlin for a short-lived reprise teaching gymnastics. In 1819 Austria's foreign minister, Klemens von Metternich, instituted the Carlsbad Decrees—a set of brutally repressive laws intended to quell pro-unification activity and sentiment across the German Confederation by censoring the press, removing liberal educators, disbanding *Burschenschaften* (nationalist fraternities), and banning gymnastics, especially those practiced by Turners, perceived by authorities as a clear threat. Jahn was promptly arrested for revolutionary activity and imprisoned for nearly one year. After a five-year period of confinement to Kolberg, his freedom was granted on the condition he avoid cities with schools and universities and abstain from any further instruction in *turnen*.

Though the politics of the Turnverein were liberal enough to attract the ire of the state, Jahn's own patriotism edged into ethno-nationalist *völkisch* territory. In 1810, for instance, he wrote, "Poles, French, priests, aristocrats and Jews are Germany's misfortune."

Jahn's calls for the preservation and empowerment of a German homeland made for easy appropriation a century later, offering the National Socialist Party a ready-made conceptual template for propaganda promoting Germanic superiority, all steeped in repurposed imagery of classical antiquity (even as the Nazis themselves banned independent Turnverein). The writer Daniel Kunitz describes Jahn as "an exemplar of that Romantic idealist generation which combined an admiration for ancient Greek culture and the struggle for freedom from absolute monarchy that, for some like Jahn, devolved into an inward looking, racist parochialism."

After Jahn's arrest and release, his Turnverein would continue operating quietly around Germany, with the official ban on them lifting in 1842 and the *Damenturnverein* opening gymnasium doors to women in 1845. But the failed revolutions of 1848 against the German Confederation sent many devoted Turners into exile—part of a larger contingent of "Forty-Eighters" that landed on American shores with very specific ideas about how men and their bodies fit into the making of a nation.

It was two of these Turners who helped launch the physical culture movement in the States: Charles Beck, who in addition to translating Jahn's writings founded the Round Hill School for gymnastics in Northampton, Massachusetts, and Charles Follen, a professor turned abolitionist who, in 1826, opened the first college gymnasium at Harvard. By 1855, there were nearly one hundred Turner societies in the States, with about 4,500 members. By 1860, more than 50,000 men belonged to over three hundred clubs.

The American Turner movement benefited from a wave of fresh enthusiasm for gymnastics and physical fitness in America. There are a number of reasons for this. For one, a different kind of revolution, well under way, was actively changing the relationship between men and their bodies. The technological, social, and economic change brought about by the Industrial Revolution—that period of accelerated cultural advancement commonly mapped onto the years between 1760 and 1860—turned the country into an international superpower. But in many ways, it also reduced free American men to cogs in the machine of the far greater enterprise of modern capitalism.

The Industrial Revolution completely upended Americans' relationship with work. The boom in manufacturing created thousands of new businesses and services—many, like cotton brokers, textile factories, and meat processing plants, driven by the labors of enslaved people in the South.

These new jobs employed thousands of Americans but introduced laborers to a harsh new reality of tiny roles within massive factories, and repetitive work that encouraged a mechanistic drive toward efficiency and productivity. Advances in technology like the cotton gin (1794), the steamboat (1807), the sewing machine (1830), and the telegraph (1844-ish) each launched their own revolutions in manufacturing, commerce, and communication. Post–Civil War, a branching bloodstream of railways, steamship canals, and roads offered something like stitches to suture together a country that had been torn asunder.

The Industrial Revolution also changed Americans' relationship with their own health. The dire conditions faced by factory laborers, as well as the open sewers and unsanitary conditions endured by residents of urban slums in overcrowded cities, forced advances in medical science that remain vital to our survival today—from vaccines (1797) to blood transfusions (1818) to anesthesia (1842).

In 1858, the *Atlantic Monthly* bemoaned the state of American men— "how few carry athletic habits into manhood," positing that "a race of shopkeepers, brokers and lawyers could live without bodies."

As more and more men migrated away from farms and menial/manual labor and into sedentary office jobs in the booming fields of business and finance, as incoming waves of immigrants filled jobs in the manufacturing centers, and as cities grew crowded with white-collar workers putting in long hours and getting little use of their bodies, American men began to experience their first identity crisis: What were men for?

(To this perceived emasculation, stir in the threat posed by the steadily increasing presence of a women's rights movement. It was in 1851 that the formerly enslaved author and abolitionist Sojourner Truth gave her "Ain't I a Woman?" speech at the Women's Rights Convention in Akron, Ohio. Susan B. Anthony would commence the burgeoning push for women's suffrage in 1869. The rise of the desire among men to cultivate their physical power tracks quite neatly with the timeline of women cultivating their own political power.)

All of these factors played a part in the rise of physical culture. But a more direct influence on men's bodies in nineteenth-century America seemed to come from on high. A large swath of American physical culture was guided by a philosophy that directly conflated physical prowess and spiritual purity: Muscular Christianity.

In the framework of this informal movement, which took root in England in the mid-nineteenth century through the writings of Church of England priest Charles Kingsley and spread worldwide, the body is understood as a divine gift from God. Thus, man should make the most of it through hard work and rigorous discipline and training. The body (the male one, at least) should be properly developed as both tribute to God and in preparation for the hard work of spreading His word (which, I suppose, must be quite heavy). Primary proponent and author Thomas Hughes believed "a man's body is given him to be trained and brought into subjection, and then used for the protection of the weak, the advancement of all righteous causes, and the subduing of the earth which God has given to the children of men."

Part of the seeming urgency behind the Muscular Christianity movement was the suspicion—largely among men of the cloth—that the church was growing soft. Lamenting the sickly shape of his fellow American clergy, Thomas Wentworth Higginson penned in an 1858 *Atlantic Monthly* article titled "Saints, and Their Bodies": "There is in the community an impression that physical vigor and spiritual sanctity are incompatible. . . . One of the most potent causes of the ill-concealed alienation between the clergy and the people, in our community, is the supposed deficiency, on the part of the former, of a vigorous, manly life."

To be clear, here "manly" doesn't so much mean "hairy and smells like engine oil or whiskey." It means "of man," related to that collection of virtues and qualities purported to compose the core of a man's true nature: strength, honor, courage, control (if you know what I mean). A strong, healthy body played a crucial role in the cultivation of them all.

As historian David Chapman puts it, "many mid-Victorian religious men had been alarmed at the encouragement of 'feminine' virtues in the church. Such qualities as humility, acceptance, and meekness were rotting the church from the core—or so they believed." Chapman points to Hughes's "Tom Brown" books—formative British "school novels" that folded schoolboy life lessons into tales of athletic prowess—as essential tinder to stoking what grew into a "cult of 'manliness.'"

Muscular Christianity "provided a Christian avowal of physical exercise and bodily health, of a sort of masculine self-sufficiency and strength," writes Kunitz, "but also of a bigoted violent machismo" that ultimately "provided an excuse for ignoring traditional religious proscriptions against idolizing the inherently sinful body." (Even today, whenever I spot an airbrushed depiction of a steroidal Christ on a flag or in a meme, I realize the movement has only grown—and grown unsettlingly literal.)

The Turners, the Sokols, the Muscular Christians, and the growing number of amateur physical culturists in the nineteenth century all sprang from different traditions but shared a binding tenet that emerged as a pressing concern for American men: manly health.

In 1834, the Victorian British writer and outdoors enthusiast Donald Walker published the first edition of *Manly Exercises*, a series which grew in popularity among American readers and expanded in subsequent editions to detail proper form and execution in "rowing, sailing, riding, driving, racing, shooting and other manly sports," like running, described as "precisely intermediate to walking and leaping."

"Active exercises," he wrote, "confer beauty of form; and they even contribute to impart an elegant air and graceful manners." Regular exercise could "inspire confidence in difficult situations, and suggest resources in danger." And he seemed, in his mid-nineteenth-century way, to extol an early version of "the zone," i.e., losing yourself completely in the physical demands of a workout, remarking that exercise wasn't suited to reflection or "labours which demand the assemblage and concentration of all the powers of the mind."

"It is, on the contrary, in the absence of external impressions that we become more capable of seizing many relations, and of following a long train of purely abstract reasoning."

My favorite example, by manly leaps and bounds, of manly fitness literature of the period is undoubtably "Manly Health and Training," a series of short columns on male vitality and fitness composed for the *New York Atlas* in 1858 by one Mose Velsor—a sore thumb of a pseudonym for none other than Walt Whitman.

Whitman's prototypical screen name (first discovered in 2016 by University of Houston graduate student Zachary Turpin) appears to be a mash-up of sorts. In a loving nod to his mother, Louisa, Whitman constructed his alter ego upon the sturdy foundation of her family name, Velsor.

As for that mysterious first name, it was most likely selected in honor of a beloved roughneck of New York City lore named Mose Humphrey, a street-brawling, beer-swilling brute who doubled as a baby-saving, danger-facing, fire-fighting proto-superhero. Mose had been a volunteer fireman with the Bowery Engine 40 in the early 1840s, a period in which an influx of disaffected working-class men streamed into New York City and blew off steam in gang fights and melees in the streets. They dressed to impress and intimidate—their tall silk top hats and brightly hued coats accessorized with pins designating their respective engine companies, their boots hinting at an inclination to kick ass.

Among these tough guys, Mose was considered King Shit, so to speak. According to legend, "His cigar was two feet long, and with one exhale he could send sailboats in the harbor out beyond Staten Island before the captain could drop the sail. He could swim the length of Manhattan in two strokes and leap from the Bowery to Brooklyn."

Punch-drunk antics, violent hijinks, and general largesse of stature and charisma earned Mose mythic status in his own lifetime. But more than for his violent streak or his temperamental temper, he was valued for his valor, vigor, bravery, and hapless but reliable heroism. One moment he could be digging a tunnel to drain the Hudson and drown a fire, the next he'd be whooping one of the Plug Uglies (a rival gang) with a wagon tongue. You never knew what would go down when Mose was around, but you could be sure he was, in a Herculean way, absolutely convinced he was helping.

After the real-deal flesh-and-blood Mose Humphrey up and decamped to Honolulu (shortly after getting his ass handed to him by Henry Chanfrau, a fellow "fire laddy" from rival Engine Company No. 15), the name he left behind took on a folkloric glow.

In 1848, the thicket of tall tales detailing his superhuman feats of strength was developed into a series of stage shows—originating with a "gentleman's sketch" by Benjamin A. Baker titled *A Glance at New York in*

1848—as well as a stack of penny novels. To portray Mose on stage, Baker cast the surly, burly actor Frank Chanfrau (Henry's kid brother). Frank, another fire laddy with a flair for the stage, was a perfect fit for the role—and came to regret ever bearing the weight of the name.

Chanfrau played Mose on and off in various dashed-off productions until 1871. Through Frank, Mose became a mix of fact, fiction, and outright fantasy, a collaborative projection of how men in and out of the Bowery supposed they should behave: outrageous, outspoken, outsized.

The role of Mose launched Frank Chanfrau into stage stardom, but it also capped his potential, penning him into a persona he'd spend the latter half of his life struggling to get out from under. "Mose was a detriment to him as an artist," reads his 1884 obituary in the *New York Clipper*, which goes on to describe Chanfrau as an actor capable of playing characters "from Rip Van Winkle to Richelieu. . . . He himself often complained that for a long series of years, he was unable to get an engagement at a first-class theatre in the city because his name was associated with Mose." It was as though he was trapped in the body of a fantasy.

Whatever Mose-borne stink Frank Chanfrau was trying to wash off, Whitman was actively trying to pick up in adopting the moniker for his fitness columns, where he vivaciously opines on the wonders of "manly health."

"Is there not a kind of charm," he writes, "a fascinating magic to the words?"

And I have to agree, there kind of is.

Whitman's articles present not so much an exercise program for men as an attitude adjustment for their bodies. His tenets target a set of budding American vices—lethargy, idleness, oversleeping, indigestion ("the great American evil").

"WE DO NOT INCULCATE A MERE PASTIME," announces one of his many all-caps headings. And indeed, Whitman covers every imaginable aspect of acquiring manly power. He devotes an entire column to waking up early: "in nature, there is no example of the bad practice of an animal, in full development of health and strength, in fine weather, lingering in its place of rest, nerveless and half dead, for hours and hours and after the sun has risen."

Whitman impugns the lazy habits forming among a growing population of office drones: "To you, clerk, literary man, sedentary person, man of fortune, idler, the same advice. Up!"

He warns against the "syphilitic taint" of sexual overindulgence and assures readers that physical training helps moderate the runaway libido of the weak man: "the almost unnatural indulgence in licentiousness, of the desire for it, which previously, perhaps, characterized the man, sinks away, and a different, more wholesome and more salutary habit of feeling and practice succeeds."

Whitman discusses foot care, proper dress for cold weather, and the merits of dancing, swimming, and bathing. He praises the "Virtue of Out-Doors, and a Stirring Life," warns of the vices of "Too Much Brain Action and Fretting," and stresses the importance of "Not Too Violent Exercise."

Like the ancient Greeks and his contemporaries the Turners, Whitman was interested in developing something like *arete*—that quality of integrated moral and physical virtue. A pair of lines from his 1855 poem "I Sing the Body Electric" declares man "is all qualities, he is action and power / The flush of the known universe is in him." But for Whitman, this push toward manly health was inspired less by a drive for domination and more by a longing for friendship (or maybe the conquest of lust). For if there's a real takeaway to "Manly Health and Training," it's that Whitman's primary focus was something that most men, no matter what the era, are loathe to talk about.

"Manly Beauty—The True Ambition" reads the heading of a column at the midpoint of the series. "Be not afraid or ashamed definitely to make your physical beauty, of form, face and movement, a main point of interest you have here in life, at all of its periods, and whatever position of wealth or education you may be.

In other men, Whitman didn't just see individual beauty—though he makes clear that he certainly saw that. He also regarded their bodies as the building blocks of democracy.

"Could There Be an Entire Nation of Vigorous and Beautiful Men?" he asks in one heading. "We are encouraged to hope that these articles, among many means now at work, may help toward producing that most desirable result."

Is the "we" him? He and Mose? All of us? It was only a few years before, in section 51 of "Song of Myself," that Whitman had offered a clue that grew into his calling card: "(I am large, I contain multitudes.)"

Sometimes I wonder what Walt was trying to hide by masking himself in the musk of Mose. Maybe he just wanted to disappear a little. Or perhaps the name was a path to a part of himself he'd fenced off?

Certainly "Mose" was grabby, the kind of name that could seize the attention of any young man absent-mindedly scanning the *Atlas* for signs of themselves in the heroic forms of other men. But it also carried with it a kind of renegade vigor, a rhetorical punch in the gut that the gentle poet may have otherwise struggled to deliver.

You can even see hints of Mose in Whitman's poems, as in "I Sing the Body Electric," which opens with a celebration of working men, including "the march of firemen in their own costumes, the play of masculine muscle through clean-setting trowsers and waist-straps." Elsewhere Whitman was beguiled by the sheer presence a farmer "of wonderful vigor, calmness, beauty of person": "You would wish long and long to be with him, you would wish to sit by him in the boat that you and he might touch each other."

With the poem's late revelation that we are in fact observing a "slave mart"—"a man's body at auction" and "a woman's body at auction"—the divinity of the body is swiftly and cruelly commodified, and Whitman recoils:

Within there runs blood,
The same old blood! the same red-running blood!
There swells and jets a heart, there all passions, desires, reachings, aspirations,
(Do you think they are not there because they are not express'd in parlors and
*   lecture-rooms?)*

It's possible Whitman thought he'd command more respect posing in the paper as a tough guy. He had already developed a habit of anonymously writing glowing reviews of his own books of poetry (and only occasionally getting caught). But as the scholar Jimmie Killingsworth observes, Whitman would act as his own critic "not, as is usual, in the voice of the autobiographer or memoirist, but in the guise of a created persona presuming to represent, and redirect, the tastes and cultural trends of his times."

Maybe the name itself—the slow, mumbly roll of *Mose*—could lower his voice an octave in print, lend his byline some bulk and knuckle, allow a persona to push through the page. Maybe wistful Walt felt the only way to be heard was to become less of a poet and more of a man?

The ancient Greeks viewed a man's physical health as a realization of human potential and a show of civic pride, the Turners regarded strong bodies as essential to the preservation of national identity, the Muscular Christians linked bodily vigor directly to moral and spiritual virtue. But Walt Whitman's vision of manly health combines all of these into an embrace of male beauty that can barely contain itself to the column.

I identify with the teeter-totter of hard and soft that was Walt's alter ego—his invocation of a roughneck fantasy secretly sweetened by a shout-out to his mom. Sometimes I am a Mose, a tough-guy persona I put out front; other times I'm a Frank, an actor trapped in the role that helps him survive.

But what I love most about Walt as Mose is the space he makes for men to discover the joy locked within their own bodies, buried somewhere beneath the burdens of modern life—and easily excavated through exercise. Whitman believed men should proudly pursue and embrace their manly beauty as "a main point of interest you have here in life"—not for the sake of vanity, but for the good of humanity: "It is a germ, implanted by nature, that you should make grow. And out of it will come a prolific growth of good results, besides itself. It is a main part of that reception of friendship, admiration and good will which all desire, and which can always make life sweet."

III

LOU

THE INCREDIBLE HULK wasn't big in our house.

My brothers kept comic books all over the place—short stacks of *X-Men*, *Superman*, the occasional *Teenage Mutant Ninja Turtles*. And while I admit to ambiguously doting over the detailed renderings of various heroes' increasingly hyperswole bodies—the strained terrain of Wolverine's thighs, the taut webbing of Aquaman's wet suit, the incredible hunk that was *The Incredible Hulk*—I couldn't have cared less what they were all fighting about. I just liked the costumes. And the way sounds took form in blasts of all caps: POW, WHAM, THUD.

As for the Hulk, his entire existence seemed like little more than a big green object lesson in the workings of the bigger boys who intimidated me at school. The central message of CBS's live-action show—which first aired in 1978 and left eighty episodes, five TV movies, and countless shredded dress shirts in its wake—seemed painfully plain: Don't get them mad or else.

When I rewatch the show now, the message seems even more refined: anger curdled into rage essentially changes a man into a beast to which he can claim to have no connection and over which he can exert no control. Hulk alter ego David Banner, played with iconic nice-guyness by Bill Bixby, is innocent but for the gamma rays that he exposed himself to in a laboratory, which exposed his inner rage—or what the intro calls his "raging spirit." His monstrous alter ego, the Hulk, played by Lou Ferrigno, is one of his multitudes, essential to the engine of David's nature.

I always found it strange that there was no Happy Hulk, or Sullen Hulk, or Jealous Hulk (I suppose green was already taken). Just the angry one. Which is strange because the Hulk is meant to be an expression of repressed emotions, and my decades of living under the rules of masculinity have instructed me that anger is the one emotion we're fully authorized to display. The "raging spirit" that most men keep locked inside to fester and churn is actually their fear, their uncertainty, their sadness, and sometimes even their joy.

It could be that the Hulk was just a metaphor for the difficulty that men have in expressing just about anything, that the act of having to feel turns us inside out, forces us to contort into monsters who know only to smash. And the weekly ritual of the show reinforced the dependability of that anger—for what possible episode could unfold without it?

In *The Will to Change*, bell hooks describes the Incredible Hulk as "instrumental in teaching the notion that for a male, the exertion of physical force (brutal and monstrous) was a viable response to all situations of crisis." The writers' room for the show was known to begin by determining the circumstances of a given "Hulk-out" (the breaking point that triggers David Banner's violent transformation) and developing the story outward from there. The Hulk's existence was a series of narrative explosions. As a kid, the Hulk struck me as less incredible than overly credible, less a superhero and more of an omen of men to come.

It's not possible to talk about the Hulk and his body without talking about the body that was actually the Hulk.

Most of the dangerous stunts in *The Incredible Hulk*—and there were many—were undertaken by stuntman Manny Perry, one of the first Black stuntman to work on a major network television show. Calvin Brown had first opened the door to Black stuntmen in 1965 as Bill Cosby's double in the series *I Spy*, but jobs doubling for Black stars were few and far between, often going to white stuntmen who would undergo "paint-downs"—the stunt equivalent of blackface.

Perry, who still works in the business and now runs his own stunt company, has a long résumé that includes films like *Rush Hour*, *True Lies*, and *The Last Boy Scout*, but he's probably most recognizable as Big Jim Slade in *The Kentucky Fried Movie*.

"When I first came to Venice, I was trying to find Gold's Gym," Perry told *Flex* magazine in 2006 of his search for the legendary California gym, a temple of the storied stretch of coastline known as Muscle Beach. "When I finally found it, the door was in the back and the windows were hard to see through. So I went around the back, and all the while I heard the iron clanging. When I walked in, I saw Arnold [Schwarzenegger], I saw Franco [Columbu], I saw Frank Zane, I saw Dave Draper, I saw Robby Robinson. The top bodybuilders in the world were all there at the same time training in shorts and tank tops, and I was so intimidated I ran out."

This fear didn't last long. Perry eventually bulked his way into a big win at the 1976 Amateur Athletic Union (AAU) Mr. USA competition, a title that, more importantly, earned him a place in the Venice Beach muscle community he'd once felt too small to join.

Perry, at 6 feet, 5 inches, and 270 pounds when he scored the gig as Ferrigno's stunt double, was one of a handful of men on earth who could match Ferrigno's mass and far surpass his mobility.

"The problem," Perry told *Flex*, "was I'm Black and Lou's white, but they took a look at me with the green makeup on and decided green is green—and they weren't going to get a better match than me."

Now, whenever I watch an episode of *The Incredible Hulk* and the green monster crashes through windows and walls, gets hit by cars, and drops from great heights, all I can see is Perry putting in the work, Ferrigno maybe sipping on a protein shake in his trailer.

Hooks observes that (even sans Perry) the Hulk models a toxic racial stereotype transposed into fantasy: "A scientist by training (the ultimate personification of rational man), when he experiences anger, he turns into a creature of color and commits violent acts. After committing violence, he changes back to his normal white-male rational self. He has no memory of his actions and therefore cannot assume responsibility for them."

Despite Perry's achievements on *The Incredible Hulk*, it's still ugly to imagine the Hulk's body as yet another venue for disparity to play out—a white body takes the credit, a Black body takes the beating.

"When you play the Hulk, you're wearing a pair of cutoff jeans," Perry said. "There's no shirt or pants that could hide pads, like there usually is when you do a stunt. My padding was my muscles."

Or as *Hulk* writer Allan Cole put it in a blog post recalling his work on the show, "When everything was cool and safe as pie again, Lou would take off his robe for his closeup, flex his mighty muscles, take the cue and roar into the camera."

There's only one episode of *The Incredible Hulk* that I remember with any degree of plot-specific clarity. It's called "King of the Beach," and it aired in 1981, very shortly before Ferrigno would finish his name-making tenure as the Hulk and fly to Italy to embark on what was to be an auspicious film career.

The episode title was an obvious wink to early twentieth-century body-builder and fitness entrepreneur Charles Atlas's iconic "Hero of the Beach" ad campaign, which has appeared since the 1930s at the back of any comic book or magazine an American kid could get his mitts on.

In these efficient one-page comic advertisements, a scrawny "97-pound weakling" or "bag of bones" or "skinny scarecrow" would experience some form of degradation in front of his gal at the hands of some strapping bully at the beach. Cut to "later" and our single-but-strapping beanpole has blossomed into a full-fledged he-man—his shoulders broad, his jaw squared, his trunks no longer flaring like a skirt. His body is drawn in confident thick lines. The "Hero of the Beach" punches his tormentor's lights out, reclaims his woman (who announces gleefully, "You *are* a real man after all!"), and whoever was reading would be inspired to send away for Atlas's era-defining (in several senses) Dynamic Tension program.

In "King of the Beach," the only thing being sold is Lou. After four years of playing the Hulk without delivering a single line apart from non-verbal roaring and growling—most of which was either lifted from animal recordings or supplied by Ted Cassidy (Lurch from *The Addams Family*)—this episode gave Ferrigno his first speaking role of the series, as a new character named Carl Marino.

This step up was no mean feat nor small risk for Ferrigno, who grew up bullied for a speech impediment he'd developed being almost totally deaf, due to a childhood ear infection. In interviews, he credits his bullies for giving him a proverbial shove into the gym, where he started bodybuilding at the age of thirteen.

"I was just obsessed with power, the feeling of being powerful," he told Oprah Winfrey in 2014. "That was a path for me to survive—building the body, being strong so I could receive admiration and respect from different people."

Ferrigno's alternate alter ego in this episode—Carl Marino, an aspiring bodybuilder—was an echo of his 1977 on-screen debut in George Butler and Robert Fiore's bodybuilding documentary *Pumping Iron*.

The movie positioned as its center of gravity the young sensation Arnold Schwarzenegger, at twenty-eight already a ten-year veteran of the sport and, by the end of the film, a six-time Mr. Universe and Mr. Olympia winner. But the charismatic and outright manipulative Austrian champion is also surrounded by a pantheon of titanic also-rans—like the former New York Jet Mike Katz, who was brutally bullied as a Jewish kid with thick glasses in New Haven, Connecticut. Even as a behemoth, Katz is tormented by the towheaded Ken Waller, a meaty ex-Marine. The compact Sardinian ex-boxer Franco Columbu appears as Schwarzenegger's training partner in the gym and diminutive rival at the final posedown. And the French bodybuilder, actor, and author Serge Nubret, also known as "The Black Panther," makes a memorable second-place appearance.

But it's Lou Ferrigno who gives the most unintentionally heartbreaking performance as himself: the hardworking kid from Brooklyn who trains hours a day under the firm encouragement and ever-evident awe of his father. Meanwhile, Arnold represents a more adversarial form of father figure—the king of the hill. In Michael Small's title song for the credits of *Pumping Iron*, one line seems to italicize itself: "Everybody wants to be a hero / Everybody wants to be bigger than dad."

The prospect of dethroning Schwarzenegger from a five-year streak as Mr. Universe is a Herculean feat that Ferrigno pursues with Sisyphean determination. As Arnold models with models all over him, Lou is grinding away in some basement with his Pops and a small entourage. Ferrigno takes every moment of his training very seriously and lets that seriousness show, unchecked. Arnold sniffs out this vulnerability and spends the film toying with him like a lion messing with a mouse.

In the *Hulk* episode, the itinerant David Banner—who spends the series presumed dead, taking odd jobs and traveling from one locale to the next—is laying low as a dishwasher in the café of Ferrigno's Marino, who works as a hearing-impaired cook. After Marino opines aloud of his dreams to save enough cash to open his own restaurant, a foxy scammer named Mandy (Leslie Ackerman) spots the young muscleman's obvious physical potential and touts the lucrative prize money he could win by entering bodybuilding competitions like Mr. America or Mr. Olympia (the latter of which the real-life Ferrigno had finished second and third in 1974 and 1975). His only obstacle is the reigning champion, the King of the Beach, who, according to Mandy, has gotten "soft and lazy."

The preening, flexing "King" is played by Waller, who had proven in *Pumping Iron* he could play the part of pretty-boy villain, swiping Mike Katz's lucky sweatshirt and effectively psyching the man out of a podium finish. Another colossal (if uncredited) guest star was the bodybuilder Ted Prior, who went on to star in slashers like 1983's *Sledge Hammer* and 1987's *Killer Workout* (a horrible title, maybe, but a step up from its prequel, *Aerobicide*).

I remember the episode feeling like a fever dream, as if it couldn't or shouldn't have happened. It felt strange to see Ferrigno as himself, but not quite—as though the Hulk had smashed through the fourth wall and the screen might be next. What could have been the point of puncturing the illusion, tearing down the scrim between fantasy and reality?

Now I watch "King of the Beach" and I realize it was a screen test, an audition for Ferrigno's real dream and a prelude to the form he would soon become: Hercules.

As filming wrapped for the final episodes of *The Incredible Hulk*, Ferrigno's big body was in high demand overseas, thanks to a peplum (sword-and-sandal) revival in Italy, ironically fueled by Schwarzenegger's pillaging of the box office in 1982 as Conan the Barbarian.

Luigi Cozzi's *Hercules* was filmed back-to-back with Bruno Mattei's *I sette magnifici gladiatori* ("The Seven Magnificent Gladiators") in the summer of 1982. Photos of Ferrigno training for the role at the time find him at the top of his form. At 6 feet, 5 inches, he was close to 280 pounds of solid muscle. "The impact of the film will come from the character of Hercules and from my physique, and that's why I intend to be in the best shape of my life," he told an interviewer in a September 1982 issue of Joe Weider's *Muscle & Fitness* magazine. On the cover of that issue Lou appears tanned and supple, hoisting a sword, locking his torso in a tense twist as though about to strike. Lightning bolts crisscross a deep blue sky behind him, and above him hovers a logo of glossy chrome. "From the Hulk to Hercules" reads the inside spread.

"When I was a kid," he tells interviewer Bill Dobbins, "I used to watch the Hercules movies over and over and over. My father would come into my room at two in the morning and I would be watching Steve Reeves on the television and he would scream at me, 'All you do is watch Hercules! Why don't you get an education, Louie? You're just wasting your time with that stuff.'"

He described the phone call offering him the part to "a lightning bolt from the sky." He signed a contract within five days. Unlike the lux $20 million budget of Schwarzenegger's scarcely barbarian *Conan*, *Hercules* was made for a comparably paltry $6 million. ("A million dollars a week!" Ferrigno told Dobbins. "That certainly isn't cheap.")

Besides, Ferrigno's interest was more than financial, after spending years as Arnold's runner-up only to find success in the secondary spotlight of an antihero's angry green alter ego. Hercules represented a role that Lou had longed to pour himself into since watching Steve Reeves first play the part in 1958, when little Louie was just seven years old.

"Playing Hercules means more to me than playing the Hulk," Ferrigno said. "Honestly, it means more to me than winning the Mr. Olympia contest. Hercules is my all-time fantasy hero. He is the most famous strongman-hero in history. For a bodybuilder, Hercules is the ultimate."

And in Cozzi's vision, Ferrigno's would be the ultimate Hercules. (May the gods bless his heart.) Cozzi, who not only directed but also wrote the film, adapted elements of the traditional tale of Hercules—the protective Zeus, the vengeful Hera, the redemptive trials—into a sci-fi milieu. The gods, for example, live on the moon. What could go wrong? (Besides the gods living on the moon, that is.)

Perhaps getting a touch high off his own supply of confidence, Ferrigno took a prerelease swipe at Arnold, who had trained extensively in martial arts to convincingly swing Conan's sword. "In the world of Hercules, although the Greeks were trained warriors, complicated and stylized combat skills weren't as important as strength and individual courage," he said. "Besides, as great a bodybuilder as Arnold is, I'm really a better-coordinated athlete."

Five months later Schwarzenegger—who had cut his acting teeth in 1970 playing Hercules in the demigod-awful goofball comedy *Hercules in New York*—responded in his own *Muscle & Fitness* interview with a passive parry. By then, *Conan* had pulled in between $70 million and $80 million at the box office—close to four times its production budget—and secured Schwarzenegger as a fixture of the big screen. He made sure to make his lack of concern the main concern.

"I expect a bunch of Hercules epics in the next few months," he said, "but they'll all fall on their faces if they haven't more going for them than just muscles. Sure, muscles are in these days, but where movies are concerned, you also need good stories. You need excitement. [Director] John Milius and I had an agreement that *Conan* would not be sold like a Hercules type picture. Nobody wants that anymore."

The future Terminator calculated correctly.

Cozzi's *Hercules* earned just under $3.5 million its opening weekend, the demigod proverbially slain at the box office by the unlikely trio of Michael Keaton in *Mr. Mom*, a horny young Tom Cruise cavorting in his tighty-whities to Bob Seger in *Risky Business*, and beloved dirtbag Rodney Danger-field abandoning his vices for a fortune in *Easy Money* with the tagline "I was happy being a big fat slob, but for $10 million . . . I'll give up everything!"

As a child I had been able to stare blankly into Ferrigno's *Hercules* any time it found its way to our television, blithely ignoring its budget-crunch special effects and clumsy overdubs. My more recent attempts to make it through an entire screening have felt like the unfinished thirteenth Herculean trial.

If the movie has a single intersection with perfection, it's Ferrigno's body. He looks unreal, a vision of symmetrical development and obscene mass. The film's opening scenes depict the creation of Hercules, at the behest of a Zeus costumed in a store-bought Santa beard and Pope robe, and Lou's body materializing in space: first a skeleton, then a flash, and then Lou, perfectly lit, perfectly oiled, perfectly framed by the stars and galaxies, his body slowly rotating back and forth like an oscillating fan.

Later, before young Hercules fully grasps the true nature of his powers (and celestial patronage), we see him pulling trees from the earth and hoisting them overhead—Ferrigno's unfathomably muscular body a mountain of glistening boulders. Another scene, depicting Hercules crossing an aggressively campy rainbow bridge to the gates of hell, lives on as the wallpaper on my phone.

But the heroic quickly turns tragic in *Hercules*. Throughout the movie, Ferrigno does battle with ostensibly massive, poorly superimposed models of purportedly killer robots representing the beasts that Hercules famously vanquishes in his twelve trials. The effect is . . . special, somewhere between the most poorly funded *Godzilla* knockoff and the battles that young me staged in the bathtub between Transformers and the dinosaurs that doubled as sponges.

The film's depiction of the famous tale of the child Hercules strangling a pair of snakes sent by Hera to slay him in his crib might be the only time I've hurt myself laughing at the attempted murder of a toddler. An absolutely batshit wrestling match with the bear who mauled Hercules's mortal dad to death results in Hercules hurling what looks like a thrift-store teddy bear into deep space (where, true to the lore, it becomes the constellation Ursa Major) and releasing a primal scream.

Or, at least, pretending to. Ferrigno's dialogue was entirely dubbed, with voice actor Marc Smith providing the husky heroic baritone that here and there veers out of sync with Lou's lips. The effect is a strange form of ventriloquism, Ferrigno's formidable presence muted into a kind of meat puppetry, his body possessed, pure vessel.

Ultimately, *Hercules* failed, grossing only $11 million total, $5 million more than it cost to make, and $1 million more than Rodney Dangerfield's baseline for giving up everything, but not enough to exhume the film from the heap of savage reviews under which it remains buried. This being Hercules, it seems most reviewers assumed the big guy could take a beating.

"'Hercules' Labors in Vain" read the *Boston Globe*'s headline for a review that slammed the script and production as "inert" and the "revisionist mythology. . . stunningly inept." "Compared to sitting through this film," wrote critic Jay Carr, "the legendary 12 labors of Hercules are a snap."

In the *Tallahassee Democrat*, Steve Watkins swung hard at the "hackneyed tale" and its "K-Tel cut-rate special effects." "Ferrigno is supposed to shoulder a burden greater than any Atlas ever bore: he must move the story if it's to go anywhere, and it's a story that refuses to budge," wrote Watkins. "Ferrigno is a body-builder extraordinaire; he's a Hulk, he's even a Hercules, but he is no actor."

And in an August 1983 *New York Times* review, Lawrence Van Gelder was less than impressed. "Here Mr. Ferrigno, the bodybuilding champion best-known previously as the green-skinned creature who appeared when Bill Bixby's volatile metabolism caused him to burst his shirt and metamorphose into the Incredible Hulk on television, is once again called upon mainly to flex his inflated muscles and lend himself to the sometimes less than special effects," Van Gelder growled in print. "'Hercules,' as its cast makes one constantly aware, is not a production that staked its future on thespian art."

Ferrigno and Cozzi would reteam to produce a sequel, 1985's *The Adventures of Hercules*—memorable, to me, for one particular line that comes in handy from time to time: "I must find a way to overcome the fire monster's radiant hate!" And director Enzo Castellari, along with an uncredited Cozzi, would snag Ferrigno once more to play the hero in 1989's *Sinbad of the Seven Seas*. But Ferrigno's career as a blockbuster hero was essentially kaput.

Apart from a few film roles (including a cameo in the 2003 *Hulk* reboot starring Eric Bana, which grossed $62 million its first weekend), Ferrigno has mainly stuck to television, showing up everywhere from *Sharknado 3: Oh Hell No!* to *The Celebrity Apprentice*. He owns his own line of exercise equipment, and since 2006, he's been sworn in as a special sheriff's deputy in three different jurisdictions.

Despite the film's excessive cheese and unbearable dialogue, Ferrigno seems happy as Hercules—throwing trees (or bears), pulling plows, and breaking chains. When I watch, I try to imagine him in the moment of filming, finally filling the shoes (or sandals) of Steve Reeves. Finally getting a shot at Arnold's level of adoration. Finally getting the view from atop Olympus.

In becoming Hercules, in accepting the body of a demigod handed down from one generation to the next, Ferrigno—a man you could see from a mile away—somehow managed to disappear. It was as though he had sacrificed himself on the altar of Hercules. Anything for the chance to embody him.

WILD
AT HEART

$\mathbf{I}$ T'S SATURDAY NIGHT and I'm watching a live video of a man eating a pound and a half of raw ground beef out of a fat-streaked glass jar. As he eats, he sucks his fingers clean and apologizes to the 158 of us watching for being unable to eat more raw ground beef than he already has. He's getting full.

Comments and little hearts sent from his audience spray up from the bottom of the screen like an eruption of hyper-masculine magma. Some dude asks the man if he eats vegetables and he says no, he's trying to stay away from "toxic foods." Another viewer asks if he has a girlfriend, and after pausing to consider phrasing, he confesses to "having a female" once a week, as though it were a bodily function. A hater asks if he's under the impression that he's a samurai on account of his hairstyle (a shrubby man bun of white-dude dreads baled by rubber bands) and he says, quite earnestly, that no, he's no samurai, but he *is* a warrior.

In addition to waging a daily war on modernity, he's also a bouncer. Someone asks how he makes money and he says different ways—he was bouncing at a local club and then had to move to another. He says no one will ever dominate him, that he's an alpha, not some vegan soy-boy. A persistent person in the comments is asking him if he'd ever consider fighting UFC champ Conor McGregor. He says he would, and that he would most certainly knock him out, but that he wouldn't want to because it wouldn't be a fair fight.

He cores a papaya for dessert and cautions that papaya seeds are a natural spermicide, that the elite want you to be a vegan bitch-boy so they can depopulate you, so stay away from papaya seeds. Raw chicken, he says, can't get you sick either. He knows because he's been drinking chicken blood for three years. He compares the consistency of his bowel movements to wet clay.

He takes the camera into his kitchen and rests it against the back of the stove for the finale of his feeding ritual. Once he steadies the camera, he begins roasting coffee beans in a saucepan until they start to pop and smolder. Coffee, he says, is his passion. He says that instead of using deodorant, which is full of toxins, he likes to let the smoke from the beans season his body. He waves the smoking pot around his body like a thurible. He excuses himself from the frame for a moment so that he can season his balls without earning a community guidelines violation. He comes back on and tips the pot to show off his coffee, now fully roasted—it's black and oily and looks delicious.

When the live stream ends, I tap on his profile and get swept over to a grid of his recent videos—him feasting on lamb kidneys and veal blood, him dancing, flexing, and munching on a raw steak all at once. In one video he boasts that he gets to live with his idol every day. (Spoiler: it's him.)

What a weirdo, I think. I should start roasting my own coffee, I think.

For some reason, I joined TikTok. Just to see.

I shouldn't have done it. I know this. For one thing I'm forty-eight and—yeah. For another, upon quick inspection, TikTok strikes me as less of a platform than a bottomless bog of digital quicksand—the app version of that scene from *The Never-Ending Story* where Artax the horse gets slowly devoured by the Swamp of Sadness, only in this metaphor I'm genuinely unsure whether I'm Artax sinking or Atreyu helplessly tugging the reins from the muddy shore or the actual Swamp of Sadness itself.

TikTok's algorithms get to know you fast, and more so than any of its competitors in the social media space, they seem to gain a finer "understanding" of what content will slow your scroll.

After just a few hours of mutual sniffing, TikTok picked up on my meathead scent and started inserting little scraps of fitness and manosphere content into my feed—flexing bodybuilders posing to the sounds of death metal, squabbling CrossFitters hashing out internecine (proverbial) beefs, powerlifters broadcasting their workouts to a few hundred virtual gym buddies, ambush interviews with meatheads at hardcore gyms, and a bustling substrata of manfluencers who self-identify as "primals"—men who operate under the hardwired (and roughly approximated) tenets of our Paleolithic forefathers, a prime example of which would be our beef-slurping gentleman.

The self-appointed king of the primals is a manfluencer who goes under the name Liver King—a moniker honoring his consumption of at least one pound of raw liver per day, a replacement for his pre-dominant moniker, Brian Johnson. (In an interview with *GQ*, he claimed he "ripped open a cage and ate Brian Johnson.")

Though average in stature at 5 feet, 7 inches, Liver King is a mountain. His suntanned skin seems to strain to cover his muscles, leather-tight and beetle-hard. His pecs are perfectly sculpted and proportioned to sit between his equally impressive boulder shoulders. His biceps and triceps seem to scream even when at rest. His lats and back recall the trunk of a tree, the slab of his abs a thick corrugated grid of muscle. His legs are kind of whatever.

The polished marble sheen of his ever-shirtless torso stands in stark contrast to the softness of his long bushy beard and long mane of unwashed hair, ever tamed by a back-turned ballcap. He's a celebration of textures and forms (and presumably aromas). His body looks like a Photoshop of itself.

According to the *GQ* interview, Johnson lost his father at a young age. In keeping with the traditional muscleman arc, as a boy he was weak and meek, routinely getting punched and spat upon by bullies in his San Antonio school. When he was in middle school, his mother's boyfriend obtained a weight set and the budding King started lifting. After a few months, a kid at school compared him (favorably) to "Marky" Mark Wahlberg, who at the time was flashing his fashionably pumped pecs and washboard abs for Calvin Klein. Suddenly, Brian was visible, desirable, influential.

Decades later, the Liver King allure subsists almost entirely on a diet of raw mystery. The "realer" the persona behind Liver King gets, the less interesting he becomes. The *GQ* piece details that after high school he dropped out of medical school and went straight into pharmaceuticals—a path that led to the founding of his own lucrative line of "ancestral" nutritional supplements. But Johnson seems acutely aware that given too much power, a life story can easily eclipse an impossible myth.

Liver King's sprawling galleries of promotional videos on TikTok (3.4 million followers) and Instagram (1.7 million) catch him, by turns, deploying a flamethrower to char pizza dough, shooting machine guns from a low-flying helicopter, and rolling a tank out to the desert to detonate a fully made twin bed, much like our ancient ancestors once did. "Modern day, fluffy beds that look good like this one are laden with polyesters, plastics and petrochemicals that wreck [sic] havoc on your hormone health," Liver King says in a preface to the carnage. "That's why this has to be destroyed."

(Sometimes I like to imagine Liver King and his film crew making the bed in the desert before the commercial was shot, carefully tucking the corners of the blankets and fluffing the pillows just so.)

These dissonant intrusions of modern convenience are ostensibly leveled out by heavy-handed primitive restrictions on daily life—soap is said to rarely touch Liver King's body, and entire interviews are dedicated to probing (mercifully exclusively through conversation) whether he wipes his ass.

Liver King also uses his grueling "Barbarian" workouts as a way to suggest superhuman effort. This weekly ritual—walking a mile while dragging a weighted sled, wearing ankle weights and a weighted backpack, and lugging a pair of kettlebells—often commences online with Liver King heartily hollering a motivational speech that simultaneously invokes the ancestral spirits of real manhood and ignores the McMansion spotted in the background of the footage shot on his sprawling ranch property.

For a while, young men and elder podcasters swirled around Liver King's brand with glassy-eyed adoration, double-tapping his pics and defending his bulging body, against all available signs, as "natty" (steroid-free). Defenders raged against haters in the comments sections of his posts, insisting that his muscles were purely the spoils of disciplined "ancestral living." Johnson's reliable habit of deflecting to prefabricated talking points on the frequent occasions the topic of his suspected steroid use came up in interviews scanned as a wink from behind the Faraday curtain (the one he uses to block Wi-Fi signals from entering his bedroom).

"We live in a world where people who are muscular, fit, and ripped have to justify their fitness," he once told *BuzzFeed News*, adding, dubiously, that "in the same world, people who are obese, metabolically deranged, or skinny and osteopathically deranged, they don't have to justify their level of fitness."

This posture of aggressive self-justification seems foundational to the modern primal movement, yet remains glaringly absent from the list of nine "ancestral tenets" posted to Johnson's website, by which aspiring primals are instructed to abide: Sleep, Eat, Move, Shield, Connect, Cold, Sun, Fight, Bond. There's no way I'm going through all of these individually, but suffice it to say they amount to extolling healthy living with an explicit emphasis put on the intake of raw meat, regular exposure to sunlight, the evils of shoes and mattresses and other modern comforts, and the testosterone-boosting goodness of snacking on bull balls.

When, in December 2022, a fitness blogger published leaked emails from Johnson to his nutritionist detailing his use of a stack of various steroids that amounted to $12,000 a month, it did little to rattle his nearly two million followers, disrupt his $100 million supplement business, or strip away the flimsy mythology draped over his shoulders like a fake pelt. Johnson quickly pivoted the ostensible humiliation of exposure into a viral Herculean redemption, with each apology and penitent workout documented on Instagram and TikTok, his prototypical barbarian persona reflected upon and recast as "an experiment," his grift rebranded as a campaign for "awareness."

This, we were meant to believe, was the real Brian all along. Or the real Liver King. Whichever.

This antipathy toward the modern is hardly modern. As Mose Velsor in 1858, Walt Whitman was lamenting the physical ravages of our modernizing and increasingly deskbound nation. In a column titled "Modern Society—Employments," he explored—in his verbose and punctuationally asthmatic way—his ambivalence about city life, conceding that convenience would ultimately win the day:

> Because civilization, with all its banes, and the ill health of masses, as before alluded to, has still more antidotes, if the choice were to be made between a life passed in the solitary freedom of barbarous and inartificial nature, and the highly complicated, and, in many respects, morbid life of one of our modern cities, we think the preference might deliberately and safely be given to the latter, as more likely to confer not only a greater

longevity, but a greater amount of average animal happiness; and singular as it may at first appear, the chances of the latter are in favour of a higher and more robust degree of health than the former. The former, with its freedom from the artificial evils, is bereft also of the means of favoring life, and improving it, which belonged to the latter.

In a column titled "Present Condition of the Health of the Masses," Whitman/Velsor approached the increasing softness of his countrymen with the firmness of a disappointed coach: "We are not disposed to grumble or overstate the evil condition of the public physique; we wish to call attention to the fact how easily most of these deficiencies might be remedied," he wrote. "Our theory is that America has mentality enough, but needs a far nobler physique."

In his first book on physical training, strongman Eugen Sandow—the aforementioned "Father of Bodybuilding"—viewed the encroachments of the modern age like tentacles dragging men down into despair: "Scholarships, competitive examinations, speculations, promotions, excitements, stimulations, long hours of work, late hours of rest, jaded frames, weary brains, jarring nerves—all intensified and intensifying—seek in modern times for the antidote to be found alone in physical action."

In his 1908 manual *The Way to Live in Health and Physical Fitness,* wrestler and fitness guru George Hackenschmidt challenged the increasing anachronism of the muscular body in a modernizing world that demanded human strength less and less, arguing—much like Liver King would, over a century later—that it was a modern man's responsibility to rebuild that which modernity had washed away. But Hackenschmidt's answer also echoed that given by English mountaineer George Mallory after being asked why he had embarked on a series of expeditions in the early 1920s to climb Mount Everest: "Because it's there."

"It may be suggested that there is no reason why a man should go to the trouble and exertion of struggling with heavy weights, since there is no crying necessity for that particular man to acquire any phenomenal degree of strength," Hackenschmidt wrote. "To that I would reply by asking why a man should desire to be weak? He was endowed by his Creator with muscles and sinews which would enable him to cope successfully with such physical feats as he might be faced with during his earthly career. Modern social conditions have deprived him of that open air life and hard physical exertion which would have kept these muscles and sinews in good condition and sound working order."

Fast-forward nearly a century, and history offered another especially ripe opportunity for a full-blown masculinity crisis. The rise of a new high-tech economy in the late 1990s, as the World Wide Web started its spread and the dot-com bubble began to bulge, threatened to further alienate American men from their own sense of identity and purpose. Physical culture was experiencing the first licks of erosion from a rising digital culture, and men digging in their heels were beginning to feel the undertow of a rapidly changing tide.

The 1990s were aflutter with man-centric self-help books like poet Robert Bly's *Iron John: A Book About Men* (1990), which spent over sixty weeks on the *New York Times* Best Sellers list, and *Fire in the Belly: On Being a Man* (1991) by professor of philosophy and religion Sam Keen. Each book reinforced the idea that manhood springs from a primal source that modernity had smothered.

At the core of Bly's myth was another myth, a grim Grimm tale about a Wild Man covered with thick fur who lives at the bottom of the village lake. In the tale, the Wild Man is taken from the lake and caged in a castle. The son of the king gets hold of the key (hidden beneath his mother's pillow), frees the Wild Man from captivity, and rides off into the woods on his shoulders, where he learns about Life, scores a princess, probably makes bank, etc.

Bly presents this tale, then unpacks it and breaks it down into metaphorical parts like a raw chicken. He points to broken father/son relationships, to the death of the "interior warrior," and to the psychic wounds sustained by men as all being at the root of their pain—and, subsequently, everyone else's. "The grief in men has been increasing steadily since the start of the Industrial Revolution," he writes, "and the grief has now reached a depth that cannot be ignored."

Bly envisions American men as still collectively mourning the loss of a stable model of manhood and charts a seismic change from the isolated "Fifties male" ("Unless he has an enemy, he isn't sure that he is alive") to the young men of the sixties, disillusioned by the war in Vietnam and increasingly in tune with their "feminine side."

While Bly was supportive of the sweeping changes in sexual politics that had been ushered in by feminism—which, by 1990, had expanded into its intersectional third wave—he was also clearly unmoored by its rising tide.

"There's something wonderful about this development—I mean the practice of men welcoming their own 'feminine' consciousness and nurturing it—this is important—and yet I have the sense that there is something wrong," Bly writes. "The male in the past twenty years has become more thoughtful, more gentle. But by this process he has not become more free. He's a nice boy who pleases not only his mother but also the young woman he is living with."

He describes these men as "soft males," and while they are "lovely, valuable people" who are "not interested in harming the earth or starting wars," he sees a primal longing in their docile contentment.

"Many of these men are not happy. You quickly notice the lack of energy in them," Bly laments with Whitmanesque pity. "Here we have a finely tuned young man, ecologically superior to his father, sympathetic to the whole harmony of the universe, yet he himself has little vitality to offer."

Bly laments the loss of male authority—of what he calls "Zeus energy"—which, he says, has been "accepted for the sake of community." He points to "devious, bumbling" sitcom dads as avatars for a culture taking revenge on "remote fathers." He laments that "Zeus energy has been steadily disintegrating decade after decade in the United States," though he himself wields it readily in the form of rather personal-sounding verbal lightning bolts.

"In traditional cultures, the older men and the older women often are the first to speak in public gatherings; younger men may say nothing but still aim to maintain contact with the older men," Bly writes. "Now we have 27-year-olds engaged in hostile takeovers who will buy out a publishing house and dismantle in six months what an older man has created over a period of 30 years."

Bly's book goes on to directly overlay the myth of the Wild Man over the mess of the modern man. Some of it is insightful and incisive, a cold bucket of water tipped over the heads of the millions of "soft men" hungering for a scolding by a bearded father figure in a beaded hat. Most of it is a generous helping of word salad passing itself off as red meat.

Keen's book, meanwhile, through its own structural pantomime of male ritual, addresses the "new kind of man who is being forged in the crucible of the chaos of our time." In *Fire in the Belly*, Keen attempts to defend men from modernity by dismantling the "modern myths of war, work and sex" that he believes mold (and traumatize) contemporary men, and by breaking their "unconscious bondage" to women—or as Keen puts it, "WOMAN."

"I would guess that a majority of men never break free, never define manhood by weighing and testing their own experience," writes Keen. "And the single largest reason is that we never acknowledge the primal power woman wields over us. The average man spends a lifetime denying, defending against, trying to control, and reacting to the power of woman."

In Keen's view, the observable violence men commit upon women (by his own 1991 measures, three out of four American women would be victims of a violent crime in their lifetime) is a result of the violence culturally waged against men. "Men are violent because of the systematic violence done to their bodies and spirits," he writes, and in "being hurt they become hurters."

The sources of this hurt are the "modern rites of passage"—war, work, and sex—that attend American manhood. Keen points to men feeling "blamed, demeaned and attacked," a distinct pre-echo of the rhetorical grievances that characterize today's perceived "war on men."

"Rise a hundred miles above this planet and look at history from an Olympian perspective and you must conclude that when human beings organize their political lives around a war system, men bear as much pain as women."

A decade later, bell hooks would make similar observations in *The Will to Change*, without the need to replace one set of myths with another. Where hooks recognizes the harm that patriarchy does to generations of men and urges men to confront that harm in terms capable of apprehending the actual problem (sample sentence: "Patriarchy is the single most life-threatening social disease assaulting the male body and spirit in our nation"), Keen offers a hypothetical map for "the heroic journey" to a new vision of manhood—a "pilgrimage into the self."

Ultimately, Keen's approaches to reforming manhood feel like lateral moves, as he advises men to shift "from cocksureness to potent doubt," "from numbness to manly grief," "from false optimism to honest despair." Keen doesn't dismantle patriarchy so much as seek a more purified form of it.

Keen has valuable ideas of what men are missing, but he joins them in missing the point. Looking back to look forward, he bargains with men to listen to possible solutions to our problems by absolving us of responsibility for creating and enforcing them in the first place.

———

Bly's *Iron John* is largely credited (or criticized) for launching what's now known as the mythopoetic men's movement—often shortened to "men's movement." Something about the combination of those two words produces visions of ponytailed middle managers tearing open their dress shirts, donning body paint, and playing tablas. And justly so.

Bly himself led hundreds of gatherings for men he considered (or convinced) were disaffected and "soft." A 1991 *Washington Post* article, written by Phil McCombs, documented one Bly event where 1,500 men paid seventy-five dollars a piece to attend. "A Day for Men," held at George Washington University's Lisner Auditorium, featured long talks and deep rituals. Attendees would gather to "beat drums, share intimate self-revelations and listen to a poet and a mythological storyteller," i.e., Bly.

One attendee, the editor of a publication called *Wingspan: Journal of the Male Spirit*, told McCombs he believed the 1990s would shape up to be "the decade of men, just as the '60s and '70s were the decades of women."

"There's clearly been a feminization of American culture as a result of the women's movement," he said. "Our wives and children often don't see our innate humanity, our beauty, our essence as men."

One physics professor in attendance noted feeling out of place among the tribe, not least because "there was no mention that a considerable number of us are gay."

In an aside that feels wedged into the preface to *Iron John*, Bly asserts that "the mythology as I see it does not make a big distinction between homosexual and heterosexual men." But it's hard to imagine queer men not feeling a gap between themselves and Bly's macho mythology.

"At one point," the physics professor continued, "Bly was saying that women criticize men for being too aggressive, but that 30,000 years ago if men hadn't been aggressive against lions, there wouldn't be any women today. And the entire room of 500 men roared like lions at that point. It scared the hell out of me. I sat there with my jaw open."

Another attendee, a self-described feminist lured in by the mystery of the event, rolled his eyes aloud: "I mean, the guy's a poet—what's so tough about him?"

The same article details another assembly, one of the Men's Council of Greater Washington, described by the *Post* as "one of six such local groups salving men's deep inner pain through communal rituals of dancing and roaring, hugging and weeping."

The group was founded by "mild-mannered" federal lawyer Ed Honnold to accommodate the "large numbers of men wandering lost, in some personal wasteland of jobs with little meaning, personal lives with little passion, and massive confusion about the reasons why."

At the council's meeting, McCombs describes the following scene in the rented auditorium of the Washington Ethical Society: "The sweating windows shake with rhythmic thunder that reverberates up and down the street as they raise Honnold—gyrating and clapping—high overhead and parade him about the room. Then group leaders circulate with large feathers and clay pots, wafting the smoke of burning sage into waiting faces in what is termed a Native American ritual, designed to put you in touch with generations of male ancestors."

A whiff of condescension is as distinct as the smell of sage in the *Post* account, but McCombs also experiences an unexpected tenderness toward the chanting, roaring, weeping men he's come to lampoon. A "charming innocence," he calls it:

> harking back to clubhouses and high school locker rooms, and suddenly you remember the slap of wrestlers on the mats, the shouts of drill sergeants in the smoky pre-dawn chill down at Fort Jackson, or the way your bare feet toughened to the road gravel over the long summers when you were a kid running on it with your friends.

So why the cosplay? Why the need to present as a caveman or barbarian or Wild Man?

For one thing, the fear of emasculation fueling the conscious push toward premodern manhood turns out to be supported by a scientific reality. Studies since 2007 have confirmed a key storyline of masculinist doomsayers and primal advocates like Liver King: levels of testosterone in men around the world have been steadily declining by about 1 percent each year (since they started being measured in the 1980s).

The vast number of possible factors contributing to this decline have made it a topic of obsessive speculation for men online.

"Problem is the food supply," reads a randomly plucked tweet from the manosphere. "This is emasculating men, increasing hormonal related cancers in both sexes. . . . Part of the ultimate plan."

"Vaccines, GMOs, media, processed franken 'food' and hormone-laden factory farmed meat, can't be overlooked here," announces another.

"Obsession with craft beers that are high in hops, which are high in phytoestrogen," reads another.

Other possible culprits include pesticides, parabens, phthalates, bisphenol A, and—the most maligned of beans—soy.

Men met the revelation of this hormonal decline head on. From 2001 to 2011, prescriptions for testosterone replacement therapy tripled (clocking in at over two million men by 2013). A pair of studies prompted warnings in 2014 by the FDA about testosterone increasing the risk of myocardial infarction and stroke, causing a significant drop in men seeking and doctors prescribing the drug but also a steep rise in sales of mail-order/over-the-counter "test booster" supplements and various vials of expensive snake oil. Parallel to the pills, a rise of "wellness" sites geared toward men started designating "manly" grocery list staples like pumpkin seeds, goji berries, grass-fed beef, and pomegranate as natural (and often pricey) ways to jack up one's hormonal profile. If men addressed the rise of global temperatures with the same fervor as the dip in their collective testosterone levels, we wouldn't be sweating climate change.

But the push for a return to primal values is also just the latest front of machismo assembled against the project of modernity itself. Modernity has been characterized by the expansion of rights and access to groups historically relegated to the fringes: women's suffrage, the civil rights movement, gay liberation, increased immigration, and legal protection for trans and nonbinary people are just broad-stroke examples of changing power paradigms in America over the last century, many of which have been interpreted by white straight men as swaths of ceded cultural turf. A reassertion of "primal" values is, by default, a way of egging on regressive politics.

The erosion of traditional gender roles, as seen through a conservative lens, represents an identity crisis for the country. Extremely unlikely heroes of new machismo like erstwhile Fox News squeak-toy Tucker Carlson and lanky insurrectionist cheerleader Republican congressman Josh Hawley have joined a wave of high-profile masculinist catastrophizers, the former releasing an ostensibly serious 2022 documentary titled *The End of Men,* the latter offering a year later *Manhood: The Masculine Virtues America Needs*—a book America needs from Hawley about as much as it needs a book on engine repair from me. Carlson's documentary, for what it's worth, centers on advances in "bro-science," an imaginary field which works to stave off attempts by "soy globalists" to emasculate American men by decreasing our testosterone levels en masse. In order to fight back, Carlson's cast of self-designated experts recommend avoiding low-fat diets, eating organ meat and raw eggs, taking cold showers, and, perhaps the most surprising presumed simulation of prehistoric manly health, "ball tanning."

This twenty-first-century fetishization of prehistory also has political currency. Online, where the push for primitive manhood makes the least sense and thus has the most legs, this brand of hyper-mythculinity is knotted up in notions of hyper-individualism, every-man-for-himself survivalism, an almost fanatical concern with maintenance of "pureblood" health (yes, that's code for anti-vaccine and a dog whistle for eugenics), and a cruelly karmic vision of public health that forms a suspiciously snug dovetail with right-wing policies toward affordable health care.

"Modernity eats away at masculinity without a conscious choice to be better," reads a tweet from a manosphere star made briefly newsworthy by his viral refusal to shut down his suburban Pennsylvania gym during the Covid-19 lockdowns. "We are the softest men in our lineage by default. The men who came before were harder, tougher, more focused, they were less distracted and diluted. It's our duty to live hard. Reclaim your throne Kings."

"There's a PRIMAL intensity that a strong man has within him that he has to learn to harness and control to become stronger day in and day out," tweets an anonymous defunct account run by user "americancockfidence." "It's apart [sic] of him. It's who he is as a strong man. So when it comes time to be a savage . . . It's no act."

This, and thousands of similar howls from the manosphere, are echoes of Bly, if less poetic. (Bly: "Showing a sword doesn't necessarily mean fighting. It can also suggest a joyful decisiveness.") But they also ape the viral advice doled out more recently by nattily dressed psychologist and self-help author Jordan Peterson, whose warbling instructions to young disaffected men about the proper execution of their broken manhood (and his love of large microphones and long paragraphs) has ensconced him as the patron intellectual of men who are sick of the world no longer revolving around them. In teary-eyed interviews and frowny-mouthed public statements, Peterson rails against the perceived dislodging of men—whom he claims built the foundations of the world—from a default position of unquestioned dominance. Even with Peterson's wild imagination, it remains too much for him to fathom.

Peterson's biggest hit single in the overwrought aphorism department, however, is his line about the beast contained inside every man. "Everyone says, 'Well, you should be harmless, virtuous, you shouldn't do anyone any harm, you should sheath your competitive instinct. You don't want to be too assertive,'" Peterson tweeted in December 2021. "No. Wrong. You should be a monster, an absolute monster, and then you should learn how to control it." In other words, he grew up watching the Hulk too.

It's worth noting that this "monster under control" rhetoric is also what undergirds "nice guy" masculinity—where a man's touted abstinence from violence is intended to be an assurance of his "high value" rather than just him meeting the bare minimum of human interaction.

For many men, a devout faith in a true "primal" self—a wild beast within that they've simply lost touch with—is foundational to their identity, or the distance they've strayed from it. The body is both the Wild Man's prison and his escape vehicle.

One thing you'll notice after reading a century's worth of men lamenting the "crisis" of dwindling masculinity is that, in many ways, masculinity itself is the crisis: this fitful obsession with living up to an inheritance of standards that feels distorted beyond reason or recognition, the absurd conclusion of a game of telephone strung over millennia of men.

Men long to replace myths with other newer shinier myths, but they also need to convince themselves that these myths begin within, i.e., they are "biological." A pattern you'll notice is that the things allegedly destroying men are coming from the outside, while the things that Make Men Great Again have all coincidentally been there the whole time, cheated of their moment by this stupid era.

"Modern culture stands for mediocrity!" reads a meme on a Viking-themed fitness Web page. "Modern culture seeks out comfort instead of exploration. Modern culture does not support the idea of self-improvement. Modern culture is a plague. Abandon modern culture!"

Who knows? Maybe these primals have a point. Maybe the path forward for men requires us to start fresh, go back to our roots—our caves, as it were—and tap more fully into the fire in our bellies. Maybe this insistence on resistance, this hunger for difficulty, this aversion to convenience really is part of what it means to be a man.

Or perhaps this notion that, as men, we've been tamed into domesticity by feminism and Big Soy is a fable we tell ourselves to justify our unaddressed anger, our inexplicable rage, our monstrous violence—as though a man couldn't be a beast without a beast within.

IV

FRIEDRICH

WE STORMED the Capitol.

We howled through the halls, our sneakers squeaking on the marble floors, our screams echoing through the atrium. It was the spring of 1990, and we had just learned a new game, Ballbuster, in which you slap another boy's nuts through their jeans with the back of your hand, and it was catching on fast. I'm pretty sure Ballbuster was responsible for our guided tour getting canceled. We never made it into the chambers. They stopped us in the lobby and turned us around. We were out of control, clutching our crotches, squealing with laughter, boys being boys becoming men.

The eighth-grade trip to Washington, DC, was a rite of passage for students at B. F. Brown Middle School, and the perennial source of lurid lore that would persist for years. Each spring our school pooled funds with Memorial—the rival junior high on the other side of my hometown, Fitchburg, Massachusetts—and our combined numbers would fill a coach bus and both levels of a Beltway motor lodge. The purpose of the trip was ostensibly a civic and educational pilgrimage. We'd be shuttled and chaperoned around the nation's capital to various patriotic attractions: the Lincoln, Jefferson, and Vietnam Memorials; the National Mall and its various Smithsonians; Congress and the Library of Congress. But by all accounts—passed down through a rich whispered oral history of class trips prior—the real education happened back at the motel.

For most of my classmates, three full days devoid of parental supervision (apart from two unlucky chaperones) amounted to anarchy, the motel the equivalent of international waters. All rules were off, and only instinct remained. Among the boys there appeared to emerge a spontaneous competition to smuggle the most illicit object from home: a glass flask of peppermint schnapps, a full pack of sweet-smelling Marlboro Reds stolen from a mother's carton, a butterfly knife swiped from an older brother's backpack, a crumpled issue of *Juggs* recovered from a dumpster. Like birds flying bits of colorful foil back to the nest, we foraged fragments of manhood as we understood it and assembled them into a shelter.

The eighth graders of B. F. Brown and Memorial had experienced flashes of contact in the past. We had crossed paths through the occasional cross-country meet, cross-pollinated at skating parties thrown at Roll On America or through the random happenstance of the arcades at Searstown Mall and Whalom Park. A static electricity crackled between us.

But the trip represented the first sustained caucus of our two factions before the commencement of high school in the fall, when we'd be fully combined into the freshman class. This informal spring summit provided a crucial opportunity to establish preliminary hegemonic outlines and power structures. The cool kids self-identified and sorted themselves from the losers; the rich parsed out the poor; the jocks ditched the nerds; the white kids made sure they were surrounded by other white kids; the bullies bullied the bullied; and the straight boys started picking up on the scent of faggots in bloom. I was soon to be screwed.

My place in the mob of my fellow boys felt precarious, as though its riptide could suck me underneath at any moment. I knew that on every imaginable front I was either odd boy out or last boy in: still new to the school since joining in seventh grade, rib thin, terrified of anything that wasn't schoolwork, too shy to approach even myself, and feeling, in full for the first time, the weight of my difference.

For one thing there seemed to be a competition between the boys to present as winning the footrace of puberty. The Memorial boys stood taller, puffed their chests out, and pushed their cracking voices down like trash in a can. Their cheeks blazed with fresh acne; some sported faint whispers of whiskers on their chins and upper lips. One or two tucked small pinches of pilfered Skoal in the trench beneath their gums, furtively spitting trails of sour brown goo into fat Gatorade bottles.

These new boys chewed their gum more aggressively, like baseball pitchers on TV. They laughed like hyenas, glared like panthers, moved around together in tribes that split into packs. They were nosy—wanted to know who the girls were, who was with who. They all seemed trained in a script I hadn't read, fueled by a fire I couldn't feel. During the trip I learned to laugh along with lewd jokes they'd pilfered from their older brothers about tits and pussies and sluts and other things I had no reference for, because otherwise my silence would stand out. I sharpened the edges of my laugh, sneered at what the other boys sneered at, learned how to transform into them. I donned the hand-me-down camouflage of masculinity.

Together we detonated the silence of every space we entered. Outside of the National Museum of Natural History, one group of boys encountered a woman selling knockoff handbags and immediately appropriated her pitch into a mocking battle cry: "GUCCI GUCCI GUCCI! POLO POLO POLO!" A few of us had already seen the new *Lord of the Flies* movie in theaters, and it showed. As boys you learn the pack absolves each wolf.

We swarmed and surged through the museum galleries. We aped the cavemen models behind the glass, grunting and swinging our book bags like clubs as the dead-eyed hunters and gatherers dealt us vacant glares from their prehistoric tableaux. We surrendered ourselves into an aimless offensive. We submitted to the rush of pointless dominance. We were a menace, i.e., the future.

And like the cherry blossoms blowing open all around us, we were also in full-frenzied hormonal bloom. At night, once the chaperones fell asleep, the motel turned into a large-scale game of spin the bottle. Boys and girls darted between each other's rooms, and my roommates furtively returned hours later reeking of cigarettes and Scope.

I pulled a Ferris Bueller sick act and stayed in my room, unsettled by the feeling I had somehow missed the starting gun of adolescence and uncertain how any of the other boys had acquired their seemingly instinctual desires. I was convinced that to try and play along would be to fail and risk exposure—though I wasn't even yet sure what I was hiding.

I didn't yet have a name for it other than *faggot*, so I left it unnamed. It was a word the other boys loved to fire at each other across the bus like an elastic band, and I'd have to hide how the sound stung my ears. The slightest wince would give me away as prey.

I'd had practice keeping a poker face through the Ryan White jokes that were en vogue among my classmates. After the eighteen-year-old Indiana student acquired AIDS through a blood transfusion in 1984, his expulsion from the public school system thrust him into the spotlight and backed him into a particularly cruel corner of discourse on AIDS and public health. It also sparked a moral panic about AIDS and its infiltration from the disparaged fringes of various subcultures into "real America." White became the innocent teenage face of an incurable disease spread by culturally maligned deviants, the physical ravages of which the media largely shrank from showing. The community most decimated by AIDS was kept behind hospital curtains and statistics, news reports of clashes and protests, and the obfuscations of the Reagan-era culture war against queer Americans.

But the innocence reserved for White by the straight world didn't stop its young boys from invoking his name—fresh from the news of his funeral—as a punchline, a tag, an alias for *gay*, a byword for *faggot*, and a carrier for the condemnation that such an identity would guarantee. To be called Ryan White wasn't just to be called gay, it was to be charged with the consequences of being gay, a death sentence sung as a schoolyard taunt.

The spring of 1990 also marked a full year since the death of photographer Robert Mapplethorpe from AIDS, a bit of news I remember a hidden part of myself grieving over without quite understanding why.

I hadn't been able (and wouldn't have been allowed) to see Mapplethorpe's photos in all their supple flesh, but I remember seeing blurred and barred-out flashes of his art on the news. In 1989 a major stink had emerged surrounding a posthumous touring exhibition of his photographs, including some of the artist's most homoerotic and sadomasochistic images. In an attempt to dodge the ire of certain congressmen, DC's Corcoran Gallery of Art abruptly withdrew from hosting *Robert Mapplethorpe: The Perfect Moment*, citing "a major controversy forming over the National Endowment for the Arts' support" of the show and sparking a national firestorm about the place of government funding and the arts—especially when those arts happened to be emphatically or aggressively queer.

It was Mapplethorpe who had offered me my first stolen glimpses of men wrapped in black leather and chains, strapped to each other and gagged by leashes. His art (of which I'd sneaked peeks at the mall's Waldenbooks) showed me splayed nudes and glossy queer hardbodies, their muscles pumped and flexed, their skin shaped by shadow and light.

But despite the attacks levied against Mapplethorpe from powerful critics—including US senator from North Carolina Jesse Helms—his work wasn't merely about generating provocation in a post-Warhol world where shock was just a spiky form of camp. I didn't get it at the time, but Mapplethorpe was deeply interested in preserving form while staging a coup on content.

"I'm looking for perfection in form," he once said. "It's not different from one subject to the next."

One of Mapplethorpe's fondest subjects was Lisa Lyon, the first winner of the World Women's Bodybuilding Championship, whose powerful body he'd reduce to its parts: an ideal arm roped in muscle, a single breast, a striated thigh, an upturned chin. He dressed her as a dominatrix, a beauty queen, a beach bombshell; he draped her in scrims of fabric and had her flex in the pose of a classical statue.

His 1986 collection *The Black Book* attracted particular ire from his critics. A collection of ninety-six erotic photos of Black male subjects rendered as headless gods, it endowed the torsos of models like Ken Moody (a personal trainer and longtime muse to Mapplethorpe) and Derrick Cross (a Herculean modern dancer) with elegant depth and classical heft. One of his subjects for the project, Phillip Prioleau, told Mapplethorpe he'd "always wanted to be photographed on a pedestal," and the photographer obliged, displacing the white body from its usual place in the process.

Today these photos remain controversial as a document of Mapplethorpe's—and, more generally, white culture's—fetishization of Black bodies. But despite the permanence the artist attempted to evoke by channeling the classical, the bodies in Mapplethorpe's photos also possessed a fragility on which even preteen me could pick up.

Mapplethorpe died the day before my thirteenth birthday, and I processed his death precisely the way Helms and Reagan and the rest of their ilk wanted me to: quickly, and as a consequence of his "lifestyle," rather than as a product of cruel, intentional government neglect of a public health crisis.

"Partly we are seduced by the way he presents his subjects, as idealized as any classical sculpture, if a touch more ethereal," Andy Grundberg of the *New York Times* wrote of Mapplethorpe in 1988, a little less than a year before he died. He goes on to quote art critic Ingrid Sischy's trenchant observation on the artist and his place as a cultural outcast: "any image of sex, especially of male homosexual sex, filters into the culture through the screen of death."

In the context of AIDS, and my growing fear of it, the statuesque bodies of Mapplethorpe's subjects seemed as vulnerable as the paper on which they were printed. But his images also captured an embodiment of strength I'd never before encountered—and certainly had never associated with gay men, whose wasting bodies had only ever been shown to me as warning, and whose names I'd only known as insults.

The beauty of Mapplethorpe's men—or their disembodied bodies—was defiant, dangerous, stronger than death.

———

In DC, I found myself drawn to the strong silent type—mostly marble but sometimes bronze. As our chaperones moved us all through the Mall and the labyrinthine galleries of the museums, I kept stalling in front of the statues—massive, classical forms that, up till then, I'd only ever seen flattened on the pages of my textbooks.

At the National Museum of American History, I vaguely recall beholding Horatio Greenough's twelve-ton neoclassical Franken-sculpture of George Washington from 1841, in which the first president's pose is modeled in marble after the ancient Greek sculptor Phidias's "Olympian Zeus"—seated, shirtless, and unexpectedly shredded—but his head is copied from a bust of Washington by French sculptor Jean Antoine Houdon. On the sides of his throne are carvings of the Greek god Apollo and the infant Hercules. The sculpture was widely ridiculed upon its unveiling, inspiring gasps and chuckles among viewers who presumed the artist was a touch too high on classical gas. (Greenough, whose reputation never quite rebounded, blamed Olympian George's poor reception on bad lighting.)

And, perhaps due to my own wise repression, I even more vaguely recall the deeply creepy bronze monument near the Ellipse honoring the Boy Scouts of America. Created by American sculptor Donald De Lue and installed in 1964, it features a young scout in full regalia flanked (or stalked) by a woman and a man, the former scarcely draped in robes, the latter jacked and stark naked but for some strategically draped fig leaf of fabric. The two adult figures looked like lesser Grimm villains, but according to the description, they are icons of "American Manhood and Womanhood and the ideals they will pass onto the youth."

I do recall, with crystal clarity, craning my neck on our passing bus to catch a longer look at *Man Controlling Trade*, Michael Lantz's 1942 art deco sculpture for the Federal Trade Commission, which depicts a man wrestling down a horse. In 1938, the twenty-nine-year-old Lantz had won a $45,600 prize in a design competition bankrolled by the Treasury Department's Section of Fine Arts for this titanic diptych of beefcakes, in which the untamed allegorical steed of Big Business bucks against the regulatory reins of the Federal Government, here embodied by an absolute unit of a man that turned me, at least in part, to stone. Rearing up and biting at its handler, the horse strains against the hold of the unshirted hero, their identically rippling musculature a subtle reveal of their shared animal nature: but for our grip on the reins, the man silently says, we, too, are beasts.

I also recall falling instantly and deeply in love with the golden warriors guarding the entrance to Arlington Memorial Bridge, namely Leo Friedlander's *The Arts of War*. A colossal pair of bronze statues, individually titled *Valor* and *Sacrifice*, stands as a companion to another pair of equestrian figures by James Earle Fraser (*The Arts of Peace*) stationed at the entrance to the adjacent Rock Creek Parkway.

Commissioned in 1929 but not erected until 1951, Friedlander's massive figures portray a burly bearded man built to evoke Mars, the god of war, who sits astride a stallion as a woman walks alongside him. Their curvaceous bodies are ambassadors of Art Moderne, a late deco movement that endows their sculpted bodies with the sleek lines of a classical car's chassis. In the passing glances I'd steal from the bus windows at the beginning and end of each day in DC, I marveled at the soft hardness and dormant power of their bodies, the pinkish gleam of the sunset against the rolling bronze mounds of their backs. To this day I struggle to adequately describe the heavenly ass of Mars.

To be clear—horny, confused fourteen-year-old me did not want to have sex with these statues, did not fantasize about pulling a *Mannequin* and zapping them to life to launch a transdimensional love story. As far as I can tell, and as clearly as I can remember, I simply wanted to *be* them. I wanted to know myself in that shape, I wanted to feel what it felt to be alive in an impossible form—to be stony and strong, powerful and present. I wanted to be seen. In this, I was much like Eugen.

"As a child, I was myself extremely delicate," wrote Eugen Sandow of his childhood in Königsberg, Prussia (today Kaliningrad, Russia), where, in 1867, long before he'd come the "Father of Bodybuilding," he was born Friedrich Wilhelm Müller. "More than once, indeed, my life was despaired of."

In Sandow's 1897 training manual *Strength and How to Obtain It*, he looks back with detached pity on the sickly, frail boy who "scarcely knew what strength was" until he was ten years old, when "it happened that I saw it in bronze and stone."

"My father took me with him to Italy," Sandow writes, "and in the art galleries of Rome and Florence I was struck with admiration for the finely developed forms of the sculptured figures of the athletes of old. I remember asking my father if people were as well developed in these modern times. He pointed out they were not, and explained that these were the figures of men who lived when might was right, when men's own arms were their weapons, and often their lives depended on their physical strength. Moreover, they knew nothing of the modern luxuries of civilization, and, besides their training and exercise, their muscles, in the ordinary course of daily life, were always being brought prominently into play."

"His imagination repeopled the Corso and the Colosseum with the stalwart deities of Roman mythology," writes G. Mercer Adam of Sandow's visit to Rome in his 1894 biography of the rising star, "and he seemed to see, as in a vision, the great pageant of a past day, with mighty concourses of people applauding their laurel-crowned favorites in the wrestler's arena. But, practically, he liked most to frequent the art-galleries, and there to hang about and admire the finely sculpted figures of heathen deities and of the chiseled beauty of some Herculean athlete or wrestler in the throes of a life or death struggle."

One imagines that on his Roman holiday, the young Sandow may have laid eyes on the *Gruppo del Laocoonte* ("the Laocoön Group"), a colossal marble sculpture dating around 200–80 BCE depicting the doomed (but preternaturally stacked) Trojan priest and his sons, the bunch of them under siege by serpents. Or perhaps Sandow was struck by the father figure of them all, the Farnese Hercules.

Contemporary Sandow biographer David L. Chapman describes the lore surrounding the strongman's early childhood as an "enigma" for its blend of fact and fiction—much of the latter supplied by Sandow's own penchant for self-mythology. But regardless of how or when the young Eugen first encountered the bodies of Mount Olympus, and whichever earthbound gods he saw, they left a deep impression.

"Eugen, contrasting his own slight figure with the mighty thews and graceful forms of the statued heroes about him, conceived the idea to train his body to the utmost pitch of perfection," writes Adam, "and so approach, if he did not attain to, the ancient ideal of physical power and beauty."

(Side note: Can we bring back "thews" as a word for muscles? Thews!)

It was Sandow's early exposure to muscles of marble that inspired him to devote his life to the embodiment of a myth. His earliest athletic pursuits, however futile, began upon returning to Königsberg, where his first attempts to develop a routine at the local *Turnhalle* yielded unremarkable results.

"Though I used to try my strength and attend the gymnasium," he writes, "nothing came of my desire for some years. So until I was eighteen, I remained delicate."

Even so, his single-mindedness about his body started to show. Sandow made a Sisyphean sequence of failed attempts to run away from home to the "circus tent and the wrestler's arena," in direct opposition to the wishes of his controlling greengrocer father, who considered such entertainments "forbidden indulgences." His parents sent him off to the University of Göttingen and from there he proceeded to studies in Brussels, where he cloaked his interests in physical training under the guise of medical training—his most intensive study reserved for anatomy and the "muscle-ramification of the human frame."

Growing weary of young Friedrich's flights of fancy, Sandow's father cut off financial support in 1885, forcing the stubbornly aspiring athlete to subsidize his own path to physical perfection. Sandow left Prussia that year, avoiding his required conscription into the military and adopting a new stage name, Eugen Sandow—a Germanized take on his mother's Russian maiden name, Sandov. He trained as a gymnast and acrobat, attempted to work for a traveling circus, won scattered prize purses performing mean feats of strength. It wasn't long before the young fugitive found himself flailing, penniless, and far from a home to which he couldn't return.

At his lowest point in Brussels, he came under the thick arm of a music hall entertainer turned wrestler and physical culturist, Ludwig

Durlacher—stage name, Professor Attila—who would go on to be Sandow's most formative mentor and future rival.

It was Attila who, upon meeting Friedrich in 1887, would set the young strongman on his lifelong course of progressive resistance, encouraging the athlete's muscular growth by continually adding more weight. It's a principle with mythological roots—the ancient Greek wrestler Milo of Croton was storied to have acquired his legendary strength by carrying a calf on his shoulders every day until it was a full-grown ox. Attila also schooled young Friedrich in the feats of strength that were increasingly drawing audiences to theaters and fairgrounds: the Roman column, the Tomb of Hercules, the Human Bridge.

Sandow supplemented his measly income by hiring himself out as a model to sculptors, including Charles Van der Stappen, who cast the strongman in the role of the vanquishee in his *St. Michael Vanquishing Satan*, and the Flemish sculptor Jef Lambeaux, who put him in his *La Dénicheur d'Aigles*. In Paris, the persistent and borderline desperate strongman found work modeling the mythical Lapith warrior in Gustave Krauke's *Combat du Centaure*. The American artist Aubrey Hunt, during an 1889 visit to Italy, where Sandow was wrestling, painted him as a Roman gladiator draped in leopard skins.

After touring Europe, gradually winning fame defeating strongmen with names like Cyclops and Sampson, and coming to America to launch into stage stardom with the help of famed impresario Florenz Ziegfeld, Sandow would eventually become the subject of his own statue. When, in 1901, Sandow staged "The Great Competition" at London's Royal Albert Hall—understood to be the world's first major bodybuilding competition—the winners were awarded gold, silver, and bronze casts of Sandow's flexing form as trophies. Unique to "The Great Competition," and most formative to the century of bodybuilding competitions that would follow, was its focus, singularly trained on the physique: strength dethroned by spectacle. (And in 1977, the miniaturized metal Sandow—clutching a barbell and sporting a fig leaf—emerged anew as the top prize in Joe Weider's prestigious Mr. Olympia contest. Weider sometimes sold spare copies of the thing for $1,000 through ads in his magazine, *Muscle & Fitness*.)

Sandow's classical inspirations fed directly into his public perception. A piece in the 1899 *London Daily Telegraph* on Sandow claims, "It is no exaggeration to say that the statue of the Farnese Hercules is not more powerfully modelled; the muscles stand out under a clear white skin and high relief, and suggest the gnarled roots of old trees."

And an 1890 interview with Sandow from the *New York Herald* described him as "full-breasted and broad-shouldered beyond all ordinary men, and with thighs and lower limbs of wonderful balance and power" that "might rival in statuesque beauty the Farnese Hercules."

Sandow himself was not above singing his own praises, let alone writing his own myth, but he was also keenly aware of himself as a mortal form aspiring to something greater.

"My notion about the ancients," Sandow writes in his training manual, "is that they were not a bit better men than there are now living, but that occasionally they found a man incomparably better than his fellows. The classical statues are all idealized—the complete dream of the artist who found in individuals some perfect parts, and shaped a form in which no ingenuity could pick a flaw. Of course, a Hercules or Venus may not have been, is not, impossible: in beauty or strength nothing is impossible, but we don't see such men and women everywhere."

Most of it is a blur, but I remember a man in a yellow parka, flexing in the foreground.

By this time, the mob has already pushed its way into the Capitol, has used flagpoles to beat police officers and break windows, has infiltrated the chambers. They've tased and punched and crushed their way through windows and doors, they've smeared their own shit on office walls and ransacked files, they've posted grinning selfies to social media.

His parka's too puffy for me to parse his body. Whatever guns he may or may not be packing, figurative or otherwise, remain strategically implied by its bulk. But the meaning of his pose—the reflexive choreography of his flex—couldn't be clearer: *I'm a big man.* Deep in the crowd, a man waves a flag overhead—it's emblazoned with the outgoing president's head airbrushed onto Rambo's body, his vascular biceps ablaze as he blasts an AR-15.

The man in the yellow parka is surrounded by hundreds of other men, all blending into a roiling blur of red caps, clashing camos, black hoodies, and tactical khakis. They writhe in place and roar in unison. They churn and froth and fuse into what could easily be mistaken for a purpose. From a distance their frenzy looks cellular—a wriggling, splitting, growing organism. Up close it's just rage and spittle and slogans. Together, these men have transformed from thousands of angry individuals into the unstable blob of a mob. One big man.

My husband and I share a blanket on a couch one mile west of the Capitol and watch the rioters flood into frame. As we watch, an eerie quiet hangs in the sky—the helicopters that had roared overhead throughout the summer's Black Lives Matter protests are now nowhere to be heard.

On TV, the camera makes an aghast-seeming sweep over the mess overtaking the Capitol steps. I think about *Valor* and *Sacrifice* silently guarding the gates to the city, watching powerless from the far end of the Mall as the Capitol is trashed by a costume party of confused, alienated, gullible, dangerous men. Men making their way by force, desperately seeking purpose, their pose of hyper-individualism betrayed by the comfort they seek in each other's company. I wonder how many of my old classmates are in town this weekend, their trucks waiting for them back at the Days Inn off the Beltway.

"It was like the real-life *300*," Capitol Police officer Michael Fanone told reporters after surviving the beating he'd taken from the mob, "minus the six-pack abs—which none of us have."

FLEX

L EARNING TO BE A MAN means learning to turn to stone.
And I don't just mean the way we get all silent and still as granite whenever an emotion other than anger rumbles within us like a tremor. I don't just mean the way we compress our grief and pain until they branch through our bodies like veins through marble (a capture of metamorphosis, of emotions turning to flesh and blood). I don't quite mean the opacity of men or our ever-heavy dispositions, our emotional imperviousness, or our visible cracks.

I mean the way that we as men seize upon any opportunity to make ourselves harder. The way we puff ourselves up before entering a room and push ourselves out if that room is full of men; the way we turn our bodies into armored vehicles or heavily decaled shells of ourselves. The way we posture for power and pose to impose ourselves. The way we stand and walk and sit and manspread, the way we flare our lats and weight our gaits to scan as forms of mercifully tempered force. These aren't just moves we learn; they're modes we move between.

Soft as I may be at heart, I'm no different. At the gym, before a wall of mirrors, when I am alone or close enough to it, I find myself a shaft of light and I interrupt its fall. I catch it like a prism, shape it around me. I tense and tighten, I harden and hold my breath. I turn to stone. I flex. I look. I take a mental snapshot. I hope no one is looking. I hope they can see me. It lasts only a moment before I disappear again. My time is short, my form is fleeting. If anyone sees me, I'll die; but if anyone sees me, I'll live forever.

There's this old photo of me. I'm so deeply grateful to the whims of the universe and the gods of moving houses that I can't find it, otherwise

I'd be obligated to include it here. Forty years after its cursed snapping in the living room of our family's first home, this photo hangs in my memory, striking within me a gong of profound embarrassment that rings between my ears long after its disappearance. I can feel my brain blush just lighting up its details.

I'm seven and it's Christmas Day 1982. I know this because I'm modeling two of my most cherished presents: a fresh set of pristine canary yellow Pac-Man Underoos accessorized with a fetching plastic replica of He-Man's Power Sword. In the instant of the photo I am taking two forms at once: Like He-Man, I am holding my sword aloft, summoning the power of Grayskull to course through my body like static electricity from the shag carpet. And like the crudely anthropomorphized Pac-Man on my T-shirt, I am flexing, an imaginary bulging bicep stretching my short sleeve.

Meanwhile, I am serving some serious face: a wide, campy smile and a wry glimmer in my eye. And the flare of my legs is giving more Fosse than Conan, my knees locked and toes pointed. There's a legible irony, a self-awareness, even then, that any manly posture I could assume would be an affectation, a performance I could tilt toward comic or tragic but that would never scan as authentic. I am a boy alight with a queerness both unnamed and unchecked, all of the multitudes I would soon learn to contain bursting from my body like the garish light from the flashcube on my father's Instamatic.

But what was this pose I'd pieced together like the limbs of disparate action figures? Part barbarian, part pro wrestler (specifically, the briefs), and part supermodel—all condensed into the inherited pose of the flex.

In flexing, a man discards his indistinct body and assumes the form of a tried and tested metaphor for masculinity itself, a silhouette forged in the fires of mythology, branded into the male imagination, and carried through the centuries on everything from boxes of Wheaties to bottles of detergent, comic book covers to *Playgirl* spreads, end zones to iPhones (the "flex" emoji is my third most used).

In flexing, a man demonstrates his fluency in an unspoken language bestowed over the ages from father to son, coach to player, one generation to the next. Men learn early on that our bodies will do most of the talking for us; we handle the shouting.

But the flex is also a salute to fantasy, a pantomime of marble. It's a show of potential force, a display of membership. It's a metric of suffering, sleeve-stretching proof of "the work." It's an acknowledgment that manhood is a hardness that must be actively sustained. It's the flaring of plumage, meant to attract. It's also a pugnacious puffing, meant to repel.

The flex is a threat, but it's also a form of theater: beauty hinting at the beast, the shape of a man's dream of himself.

When Eugen Sandow arrived in New York City at the age of twenty-six in 1893—accompanied by his accompanist in several suspected senses, the pianist Martin Sieveking—he landed a gig as a slab of marble.

The strongman, as we know, had already made a name for himself in Europe, having defeated a sequence of growling wrestlers, having dazzled international audiences with his feats of strength. But Henry S. Abbey, the vaudeville agent who brought him stateside and secured the muscleman a six-week run at New York's Casino Theater, knew that Sandow's body was destined to be the main attraction.

The opener for Sandow's act at the Casino was William Gill's comic operetta *Adonis*, which featured the handsomely waify Henry Dixey, whose good looks and lithe form had earned him the soon-to-be-stolen nickname of "the perfect man."

The operetta was a gender-bending flip of the Pygmalion story, a mythological tale of an artist who falls in love with his creation, and the inspiration behind a string of adaptations including playwright George Bernard Shaw's 1913 *Pygmalion*, the 1956 musical *My Fair Lady*, and the 1999 American teen comedy *She's All That*. *Adonis* involved a young sculptress and an eccentric duchess whose four daughters are all endeared to the artist's latest enchanted creation: a statue of Adonis that springs to temporary and comically troubled life. Adonis is described in the program as "an accomplished young gentleman of undeniably good family, insomuch as he can trace his ancestry back through the Genozoic, Mesozoic, and Paleozoic period, until he finds it resting on the Archaean time. His family name, by the way, is 'Marble.'"

The show was a pleasantly irreverent romp and Dixey was sufficiently popular, but attendees who'd yet to behold Eugen Sandow in person could never have prepared for the transformation they were about to see next.

As the *New York World* described it: "Dixey, as Adonis, at the end of his performance takes his place on a pedestal and poses as a statue. The curtain goes down and rises again to reveal Sandow also posing. New York has come to look upon Dixey as a fairly well-made young man. When New York has seen Sandow after Dixey, however, New York will realize what a wretched, scrawny creature the usual well-built young gentleman is compared with a perfect man."

A review of the performance in the *New York Herald* concurred: "It was hard for the spectators, when a calcium light was turned on the figure standing on a pedestal in the back of the darkened stage, to believe that it was indeed flesh and blood that they beheld. Such knots and bunches and layers of muscle they had never before seen other than on the statue of an Achilles, a Discobolus, or the Fighting Gladiator."

Human statues, or *tableaux vivant*, were quite common as entertainment toward the end of the nineteenth century. But Sandow's body, in all its outlandish definition, blurred the line between fantasy and reality, flesh and stone.

Sandow's shows were also vastly different from the standard boorish vaudeville strongman fare. They were elegantly staged showcases of his physical virtues, demonstrated through dramatically choreographed feats like lifting two men hidden in a dumbbell above his head with one hand and allowing three horses to stand balanced on his chest (in a feat known as the "Tomb of Hercules"). But while his stunts were certainly the *act* of his act, Sandow's body—and the unfathomable reality of it—was unquestionably the star of the show.

The rising and falling of the curtain between "Adonis" and Sandow wasn't just a savvy special effect deployed as a partition between acts. It marked a significant shift in what "the perfect man" looked like. His nearly nude form—often clad only in a flimsy loincloth or strategically pinned fig leaf—also changed the place of the male body in the American erotic imagination, elevating a hunk of man to a work of art.

As the historian John F. Kasson put it, "even in the late 19th century, to display the unclad male figure, let alone the female one, bereft of divine allegorical or alien trappings—not as a god, virtue, ruler, hero, exotic figure, or scientific specimen but simply as a person—was to risk falling from the lofty plane of the nude to the shameful one of the merely naked."

Prior to his arrival in the States, Sandow had already lent his form to precisely these kinds of heroic depictions. Aubrey Hunt had painted him as a gladiator; Charles Van der Stappen had cast him as the devil in his sculpture, *St. Michael Vanquishing Satan*. But it was light, not bronze or marble, that gave Sandow's body his most enduring form. After his show at the Casino, on subsequent tours in the United States, Sandow took to employing a "posing cabinet" on stage, padded with velvet, strategically lit, and perfectly framing his form to match the aesthetic expectations one might bring to the Renaissance wing of an art museum.

The strongman and author Alan Calvert offered a detailed description of the standard-setting "posing cabinets" employed by Sandow in his 1911 book, *The Truth About Weight Lifting*:

> The lifter will have an iron framework about four feet square and seven feet high. On this framework he will hang curtains of black, or deep red, velvet. At various points on the framework will be fixed small electric lamps, and these lamps are so cunningly placed that when their light falls upon the lifter it greatly accentuates the shadows thrown by his highly developed muscles. The athlete stands on a revolving pedestal in this cabinet, and for the space of four or five minutes he will fall into various positions which throw the different sets of muscles in the highest possible relief period. I calculate that a properly lighted cabinet will exaggerate a man's development anywhere from 100 to 200%.

Sandow's rise also coincided with the emergence of photography, an intersection which meant his body was not just indelibly imprinted in the memories of those who saw him, but endlessly reprinted in newspapers, magazines, and "cabinet cards," simply mounted photographs popular in the late 1800s.

Sandow's body was a muse of several early photographers, including Henry Van der Weyde in London, Napoleon Sarony and B. J. Falk in New York, and George Steckel in Los Angeles. One of the most famous images of Sandow comes from his 1894 shoot with Sarony in which he effortlessly embodies the Farnese Hercules (both front and rear views) in rippling repose. Falk dressed Sandow in a fig leaf and strappy sandals that coiled around his calves for a depiction of "The Dying Gaul." Whenever his body ended up in front of the camera, the resulting image was a negotiation between the past and the present, the heroic and the erotic, the classical and the crass, the momentary and the eternal. But these photos also represent the earliest mobilization of a body standard that would dominate the American male consciousness for the next century and do so by mimicking Sandow's every move.

In 1894 Sandow posed for inventors Thomas Edison and William K. L. Dickson, who were testing out subjects for the former's Kinetoscope, an early motion picture device that allowed one viewer at a time to watch a short strip of film through a high-speed shutter. The footage (far more accessible now via YouTube than it was for the squinting audiences of Sandow's time, who had to cram into special viewing parlors) captures the strongman in perfect form—tilting and angling his body in poses that feel like a broad-shouldered bridge between eras. He pumps his biceps, flares his arms, squeezes his lats, and otherwise anticipates the choreography of bodybuilders and go-go boys for decades to come.

Sandow used posing as a way to distinguish himself from the rabble of his fellow strongmen and wrestlers (when he wasn't in a fig leaf, he was often ostentatiously dressed in luxurious suits custom-tailored to his form). His poses injected a sense of classicism to his act that would link his body with a lineage of de facto aesthetic perfection. And the insistent fascination surrounding Sandow's perfection did not emerge without an undercurrent of racist ideology. In 1901, for instance, a cast of his body was made for display at the British Museum as "the perfect type of a European man." Which is to say, the whiteness of Sandow's body was an unspoken but essential element of its purported *classicism*.

Posing was also a way for Sandow to move beyond merely aspiring to the forms he had adored as a boy. Through the eyes of artists and the lenses of cameras, he could now inhabit those forms, *become* them. Though the same desire that led Sandow to dominate his body would lead him to submit to an image, it would also grant him eternal life.

Some men aspired to Sandow's form with too deep a fervor. An article in New York City's *Sun* newspaper from September 1894 recounts the arrest of one James McCoy, a forty-one-year-old steamship engineer and "enthusiastic admirer of Sandow, the strong man."

Like Sandow, McCoy—no small fry himself, at 200 pounds—had a suite of elegant photos of himself dressed in gladiator garb, taken by the photographer Napoleon Sarony. Unlike Sandow, "gradually he became insane on the subject."

McCoy was beginning to concern his wife with calm requests that she cut off his head. "He had an idea that his decapitation would increase his strength and he was very much grieved when Mrs. McCoy refused to comply with his request," the article reads.

A week prior, McCoy had heaped all of their parlor furniture on top of the house piano, then forced his wife to climb on top. Once she was in position, he went underneath the piano and tried to balance the pile on his chest, imitating one of Sandow's standard feats. According to the *Sun:* "He failed to budge it, but when Mrs. McCoy was unwise enough to tell him so, and hint that he was a fool for trying the feat, he flew into a violent rage. More than once he proposed to break her in two across his knee and he also threatened to pull down the elevated railway structure on Flatbush Ave."

McCoy regaled the officers who arrested him with tales of his outsized strength, including one about the time his ship had stranded itself on the tip of an iceberg, forcing him to carry the vessel in his arms down the slope of the berg to the surface of the sea, where he "launched it so gently that passengers were entirely unconscious of any mishap."

Officer Thomas Moran of the Charities Department informed McCoy that Sandow was awaiting his visit in a Flatbush apartment, "and by means of this pious fraud the policeman managed to get him to the asylum without much trouble."

"McCoy was flattered at the idea that Sandow had sent for him," the article concludes, "and seemed particularly pleased with the additional suggestion that Sandow would cut off his head."

My Instagram feed is a never-ending procession of men. The algorithm knows more about me than I do at this point—my "recommended" page is a mirror perfectly shattered into little squares.

Some of them are powerlifters pulling their maxes on dead lifts, their necks strained with thick cords of veins. Some are bodybuilders, bronzed and shiny and smiling on some stage somewhere. Some are thirst traps posted by friends of friends, mugging for the camera with cute come-hither smirks and pushing their pecs together. Some are morphs—heavily enhanced digital manipulations of beefcake photos, engineered to push the bulge of the body beyond the bounds of the possible. All of them are men.

And this is not just because I'm a gay man who tends to click on gay things. (Though, that.) But because even the least savvy algorithm knows: Men want to see other men. Men want to be seen by other men. Men want adoration and envy from each other in equal measure; they want praise and pressure and presence. They want to be admired, acknowledged—if not loved, then at least double-tapped.

So they signal to each other across the silence of the grid. They flex, each square a little posing cabinet, each swipeable filter a palmful of the powder Sandow would use to shade and shadow his body. Like Sandow, they frame and light themselves for display, some of them caught in the loop of a GIF like one of Edison's experimental films, cycling into perpetuity.

One reason we flex is so that we fill the form that we imagine is expected of us. We flex to match the dotted outline we think hovers around us, the one that constantly indicates our insufficiency. We flex to feel ourselves pushing against the boundaries of our shirts and our skins. Flexing is a way of falling into the arms of a familiar shape, to be embraced by generations of heroes without having to say "no homo."

My feed replicates these poses into infinity—an endless gallery my thumb strolls through like a museum, past rows of flexing men cropped into headless torsos. They are forever on the Internet but last only the length of a glance in the inhospitable environment of my attention.

They are me and I am them: Men posing and flexing in our brand-new underwear. All grown up.

V

ARNOLD

I USED WADDED-UP TUBE SOCKS FOR BICEPS. They made substantial pecs too, stuffed into one of my mom's bras.

To thicken my legs I strapped on a set of my older brother's hockey guards. I used duct tape to girdle my torso with throw pillows. Then I stretched one of my dad's baggiest gray sweatsuits over my newly super-sized body, cinched my waist with an old tool belt, and voilà: *Ich bin Hans.* Or Franz. Whichever. No one but me ever saw our home movies anyway.

I would really love to be able to look back on my adolescence and do the Gen X thing where I say we were feral, outdoors all the time, unsu-pervised, living lives of juvenile adventure that could have been cut scenes from *The Goonies.* In reality we watched a lot of TV, and when we weren't watching TV, we were making our own little TV shows based on the TV shows we watched. My father got in on the camcorder craze a little bit too early, investing in a fifteen-pound VCR, the deck of which could be charged, detached, and carried around in a special bag to power a handheld camera with a wheezy auto zoom. We'd spend hours and hours videotaping low-rent parodies—fake *Saturday Night Live* "Weekend Update" segments, faux nature documentaries about my little brother (who was learning to walk), and imaginary episode after imaginary episode of "Hans and Franz," which had a special hold over me.

The two characters, debuted by Dana Carvey and Kevin Nealon during the thirteenth season of *Saturday Night Live* in 1987, were essentially in-distinguishable from each other but for a slight difference in height. But more importantly, they were both essentially indistinguishable from the public persona of Arnold Schwarzenegger. Through thick faux-Austrian accents and affectations ("Hear me now and believe me later . . .") and in matching overstuffed sweatsuits, Carvey and Nealon would sloppily synchronize their enduring co-catchphrase to the delighted applause of the studio audience: "I am Hans," "And I am Franz," "And we are here to PUMP" [clap] "YOU UP!"

From here (and in true *SNL* style) the skits would reliably draw from an incrementally less funny stash of trusty gags and one-liners along a given theme—they'd dole out ridiculous fitness tips, cajole their viewers as "fat pig losers" and "pathetic girly men," and abruptly grimace and freeze into various simulations of bodybuilding poses. The bit eventually reached a singularity of sorts in 1991 when Schwarzenegger (identified in the "Hans and Franz" universe as their cousin) made a dud of an appearance on the show-within-a-show as part of a promotional push for *Terminator 2: Judgment Day*. This was shortly after he'd been appointed by President George H. W. Bush as chairman of the President's Council on Physical Fitness and Sports, at a ceremony that involved Bush attempting, with assistance from Arnold, to hoist a barbell.

Hans and Franz were the prototypes of today's lambasted "lunks," who, in advertisements for the "judgment-free" gym chain Planet Fitness, are held responsible for impeding the comfort of other people's workouts. The gym has built its brand on filtering out those who clang too much or grunt too loud or try too hard; such behavior can trigger a (not kidding) "Lunk Alarm" that publicly shames the lunk in question. (In the ads, a thick-necked bodybuilder, oblivious to the world around him and to the visible chagrin of two "normal" onlookers, robotically repeats a single-minded mantra, again in a catchall Euro accent: "I lift zings up and put zem down.")

"At age 42, Arnold Schwarzenegger is so big," said Barbara Walters, before a 1990 interview with the star, "it takes two men to parody him."

But in their time, Hans and Franz weren't just send-ups of Schwarzenegger. They were icons of an entire emergent muscleman zeitgeist that took hold in America between, say, 1983 and 1993. Some might call this the Age of Arnold. Wrestling fans might more insistently suggest the Era of Hulkamania. Certainly, it was at least a Second Golden Age of Bodybuilding. (Consensus would situate the First squarely at the original Muscle Beach in Santa Monica, California, in the 1950s, an outdoor gym for acrobats and strongmen once described by the fitness guru Jack LaLanne as "a perfect place to show kids that anything was possible.") An injection of oversized muscle was pumping up every end of pop culture. Big was in the air: it was the Beefcake Belle Époque.

TV and the movies were overstuffed with oversized men. You couldn't have action without muscled stars like Dolph Lundgren, Sylvester Stallone, Carl Weathers, Mr. T, and "the Muscles from Brussels," Jean-Claude Van Damme.

At thirteen, I'd spend my Saturday afternoons downing bowls of Mr. T cereal (little crunchy Ts that left behind an addictively sweet milk) while watching the glistening flesh and occasional broken bone of WWF wrestlers, of whom I grew deeply fond. My classmate across the street had two posters: one of Hulk Hogan, straddling the limp body of a downed opponent and beating his chest, and one of Samantha Fox in a sort of companion pose, topless, kneeling and gazing out from the glossy paper at whoever might be looking. I'd sit and pretend to be gazing at one while memorizing the curves of the other.

I developed amorphous mini-crushes that I'd pass off as standard fan enthusiasm for giants in Lycra leggings with teased hair and spray tans. At various times I was obsessed with wrestlers like Jesse "The Body" Ventura, Jake "The Snake" Roberts, Bret "The Hit Man" Hart, Jim "The Anvil" Neidhart, and pretty much any other man over 250 pounds with a signature body slam and nickname fenced in by quotes. (There was even a standard brains-and-brawn tag-team in the form of Hercules and Bobby "The Brain" Heenan.)

As a budding theater kid, I loved the WWF for its over-the-top flamboyance and aggressive camp (though I recognized neither as such at the time). The parrot plumage of Koko B. Ware; the hot-pink zebra-print tights of Brutus "The Barber" Beefcake; the high glam of Gorgeous George, Ric Flair, and "Macho Man" Randy Savage (who'd reappear during commercial breaks to "Snap into a Slim Jim!"); the toy soldier come to life that was Sergeant Slaughter; the airborne skills of Jimmy "Superfly" Snuka (our imitations of whom wrecked several a couch in our house).

In between matches, ads would run for the Hulkamania Workout Set, aimed at preteen boys. The commercial featured a jacked and tanned Mr. Wonderful crashing Kool-Aid-Man style through a boy's bedroom wall, which was lacquered with wrestling posters. He pumps a quick flex and walks his pip-squeak protégée through the contents of the set: a headband and wristband set, a jump rope, a hand gripper, a set of blue prop plastic dumbbells, a workout poster illustrating all of the necessary exercises, and a cassette narrated by the Hulkster himself. Everything you'd need as a ten-year-old to get twenty-four-inch pythons.

In the cartoon fight-cloud of clownish masculinity, acrobatic violence, and actual athleticism that was pro wrestling, enough lines were blurred that a not very masculine gay kid could still find a place to belong in its periphery, shouting along with the others at the spectacle of men pretending to dominate each other. I remember the rush of having something, anything, in common with the other boys, and the instinctual fear of elaborating on my interest any further than necessary.

I was also a devoted fan, from its inception, of *American Gladiators*, a TV competition that challenged contestants selected from the country's growing pool of fitness enthusiasts to complete a regimen of obstacles against the titular team of uber-jacked professional combatants. The Gladiators all had massive muscles, bedazzled singlets, and little nicknames that hinted at semblances of personality: Malibu ("the cool laid-back surfer," according to the announcer), Lace ("feminine, sexy, but always a lady"), Gemini ("a split personality, calm one minute, violent the next"), Zap ("strong, silent, the terminator"), Nitro ("cocky, explosive and always aggressive"), and Sunny ("the all-American woman"). Tracksuited contestants would dive and dodge projectiles fired by the Gladiators. Or they'd "joust" each other with oversized Nerfy pugil sticks. Or they'd rope swing like a wrecking ball into a Gladiator on a tall pedestal. Or they'd play "Break Through and Conquer" (a tiny game of football).

American Gladiators was a predecessor for today's vast offering of obstacle-based challenges like *American Ninja Warrior* and ex-wrestler "Stone Cold" Steve Austin's *Broken Skull Challenge*. But its high-octane David-and-Goliath routine was more than just a Saturday morning spectacle.

If you think about the body as a reflection of the culture around it—in the same way that ocean waves shape the boulders on the shore—the Beefcake Belle Époque makes a practical sort of sense. Just as, at the beginning of the nineteenth century, pale white skin, lily soft hands, and a frail physique were physical indicators of privilege, refinement, and sophistication (signs of one's remove from physical labor), and just as the image of the rotund overstuffed "fat cat" banker emerged as the embodiment of American industrial wealth by the end of it (signs of one's wealth and indulgence), the shiny steroidal bodies of the late 1980s were glossy ambassadors of American values, extensions of Reagan-era consumption and a post-Vietnam reassertion of global dominance. The wispy hippies and rail-thin rebels of the 1970s had given way to a vision of bodily excess and indulgence that reveled in its novelty, the body an overbuilt temple to itself.

A parallel current in the pop culture of the time celebrated alternate extensions of American excess, like the low-stakes, high-on-everything follies of the young and super-rich in the 1987 film adaptation of Bret Easton Ellis's *Less Than Zero*. Or financial strongman Gordon Gekko's epigrammatic appraisal of American values in Oliver Stone's 1987 film *Wall Street*: "Greed—for lack of a better word—is good." Or Tom Wolfe's savage scratch at the New York aristocracy, the 1987 novel *The Bonfire of the Vanities*, which inspired the 1990 film starring Bruce Willis and Melanie Griffith.

These broader trends were reflected on the level of (increasingly) individual Americans, who, even in the context of global change—the fall of the Berlin Wall, the dissolution of the Soviet Union, revolutions across Eastern Europe, and demonstrations in Beijing—were far less interested in collective political action than hyper-individual expression.

Sports and fitness became one way for Americans to self-actualize, which was suddenly very important. Whether jogging against the resistance of one's own demons ("Just Do It," encouraged Nike for the first time in 1988) or lifting weights alone in one of the increasingly available commercial gyms—like 24 Hour Fitness (founded in 1983) and LA Fitness (1984)—the body was taking a central role in American consciousness, and the gym was becoming less a fringe space for athletes and muscleheads and more of a primary social space in American life. A 1987 Gallup poll showed that 69 percent of Americans were working out regularly (up from 24 percent in 1960). The number of gyms in the country more than tripled between 1977 and 1987.

Men and women alike gave in to one fitness craze, self-improvement scheme, fad diet, or weight-loss plan after the next—or at least pressed play on them. The rise of cardio as legitimate exercise (and national pastime) and the advent of the VCR opened the door for the growing fitness industry to turn American living rooms into home workout spaces. Celebrities like Richard Simmons and Jane Fonda led a largely VHS-based and mostly female aerobics revolution.

But studio-based fitness was also on the rise. The advent of the Nautilus machine—in which a weight is selected by positioning a pin in a discretely housed weight stack—made resistance training more accessible and less of a plate-lugging ordeal for gym novices. No more clunky barbells to load, no more heavy dumbbells to lug. Nautilus was hard work plus extreme convenience. (Even Reagan was shown working out on a Nautilus machine in a photo spread that also featured him chopping logs—or, as he put it, "Pumping firewood.") At the same time, aerobics classes and Jazzercise (in 1984, the second-fastest-growing franchise in America behind Domino's pizza) created space for women to gather in more safety than the average jogging path. It likely also triggered men to hit the gym.

It's difficult not to see the explosion of the male body in the media as a large-scale overcompensation by men against the rise of second-wave feminism, which between the 1960s and especially into the early 1990s trained its critical focus on the patriarchal structures that enshrined institutional male dominance. Feminism had moved beyond the assertion of particular rights and broadened into a critique of sexist systems in the home, the workplace, the economy, and the culture at large. As a movement, it was focused on equality, civil rights, and the intersections of personal identity and cultural power. The bodies that took over the big and small screens—oiled up wrestlers, vascular action heroes, *American Gladiators*—felt in part (and in parts) like cartoonish representations of the true source of brute male force: an overblown reminder of what "power" in America was supposed to look like.

You could argue that it was Schwarzenegger who opened the gates for the deluge of musclemen when *Conan the Barbarian* first stormed theaters in 1982. Two years later, his iconic turn in *The Terminator* ensconced his massive body as an action-movie standard for the decade: an impossible mix of brawn and beauty, sure, but more importantly, an icon of excess, an image of power.

In 1985, he played the perpetually sleeveless Colonel John Matrix in *Commando*—a seeming riposte to Stallone's 1982 *First Blood* and its more readily recognizable 1985 sequel, *Rambo*.

"Mr. Schwarzenegger first appears in *Commando* in parts," reads a review in the *New York Times*, "one huge bicep and then another; when the camera pulls back he is seen to be carrying an ax and the trunk of a large tree down a mountainside to his house." The reviewer, D. J. R. Bruckner, goes on to call the film ninety minutes of "mayhem unrelieved by humor and untouched by humanity."

Schwarzenegger's beefy form committing gory atrocities against bad guys (so many impalings!) was the main attraction. But the underlying charge of the narrative was the thrill of outlaw justice—that is, defining what's right and wrong on one's own unbending terms and rock-hard gut instinct. This was a theme that continued into subsequent Schwarzenegger roles, like Sheriff Mark Kaminski in *Raw Deal* (1985), paramilitary major Alan "Dutch" Schaefer in *Predator* (1987), and framed pilot and resistance agent Ben Richards in *The Running Man* (1987).

The one-two sci-fi punch of *Total Recall* (1990) and *Terminator 2: Judgment Day* (1991) represented Schwarzenegger at full force: a mountain of muscle, a fountain of catchphrases, a box-office colossus.

At his peak—and as though having completed his trials—Schwarzenegger made a turn to comedy (or return, if you count his unintentionally funny debut in *Hercules in New York*). Arnold's body was reconfigured into various punchlines: as a high-contrast foil to his diminutive costar (and, in the film, long-lost brother) Danny DeVito in 1988's *Twins*, as an undercover detective surrounded by mischievous munchkins in 1990's *Kindergarten Cop*, and as a parody of himself in 1993's *The Last Action Hero*. (The less said about 1994's *Junior*—in which Schwarzenegger's geneticist character gets pregnant from a dose of "Expectane"—the better.)

Key to Arnold's public profile and his Hollywood prowess was the same preternatural confidence he had brought to the stage in *Pumping Iron*—an ability to conquer the world with a shrug of the shoulders.

"It's no different than me taking bodybuilding seriously," he told the *New York Times* in 1993 on the set of *The Last Action Hero*—which ostensibly functions as a send-up of his entire cinematic career, but ends up feeling a lot like an Arnold movie nonetheless. "If somebody talks to me about bodybuilding in a very serious way, I say, 'Hey, wait a minute, what are you talking about?' Let's be honest. It's nonsense. Fifty guys standing around in their little posing trunks with oil slapped on their body. Showing off and posing in front of 5,000 people. It's a joke."

As America's primary visual export, Arnold's body was a stand-in for America on the world stage: the likable guy who could also very easily maul you and crown it with a winning catchphrase, whether strangling you with barbed wire ("What a pain in the neck!"), cutting you in half with a chainsaw ("He had to split"), or shooting you point-blank in the head ("Consider that a divorce").

That is, Arnold was America's favorite monster under control—and to the boys around me longing to be full-grown men, nothing could have been more relatable.

TO FAILURE

S PEND ENOUGH TIME clicking around the manosphere, and you'll quickly realize that few vague concepts are more important to men than *performance*. But what exactly does "performance" mean?

There's "performance apparel"—workwear designed specifically for a specific occupational purpose—which, over the past decade in menswear, has broadened into its widest possible interpretation and can now be understood as "clothes that men wear"—performance polos, performance boxer briefs, performance pants, performance ballcaps.

Performance clothes are close-fitting and often sport a subtle sheen but dodge the risk of being mistaken for fashion by foregrounding function. They're moisture wicking or self-ironing or odor-controlling, or offer optimal cooling. The entire category of spandex and Lycra garments, touted to promote circulatory benefits, has been rebranded as "compression gear," with "gear" doing the heavy lifting of ensuring one's tights are understood as mission-critical. The Instagram algorithm needs only the slightest whiff of your male scent to fill your feed with hundreds of flared-nostril man brands peddling "performance" or "tactical" gear, from Kevlar vests to boxer briefs with "targeted cool zones." The idea is to be ready for anything, even if most days involve nothing but browsing vests with an impractical abundance of pockets. The unofficial uniform of the Free American Man has resolved into a choppy sea of beige, khaki, and camo; tailoring aside, it could not be more fitting.

But, for all the "performance gear" that exists in the men's apparel space, just as many products marketed to men use "performance" as a daytime-TV-friendly byword for sexual prowess (or sexual basic function).

Male sexuality, far from being an extension of love or even pleasure, is largely understood as the performance of one's manhood, not to mention one's duty as a man. The use of *performance* in a sexual context also imbues the act with risk—the potential for the humiliation of poor reviews.

As part of the "Alex Jones Was Right Emergency Sale," at the far-right radio host's Infowars.com, men can keep such emasculation at bay by purchasing a "True Alpha Male Pack," which includes a vial of Super Male Vitality, a bottle of Alpha Power pills, or a "vital male androgen biosynthesis promoter" touted to boost "performance and energy levels" with its mix of niacin, zinc, and maca root. You'll forgive me if I didn't ingest any "horny goat weed" as part of my research for this book.

Meanwhile, in health food stores and supplement shops, dozens of similarly concocted over-the-counter "test-boosters" with names that sound like power-ups from video games (Alpha Boost! Andro Surge! Primal T!) promise "optimized physical performance" and improvements across several masculine-sounding parameters like stamina, endurance, and drive. While the FDA does not have the power to approve the vast array of "dietary supplements" on the market, the agency does periodically inspect and review supplements and regulates them through what amounts to a "pretty please" policy of asking very nicely to stay in compliance and not make outlandish claims about a supplement's ability to treat ailments.

In the gym and across professional sports, the term "performance enhancing drugs" serves as an enduring umbrella term for a vast range of athletic enhancers including anabolic steroids, HGH (human growth hormones), stimulants, and hormones like androstenedione and erythropoietin. Does "performance" mean on the field? In the mirror? Between the sheets? It hardly matters.

One thing "performance" never seems to refer to is the actual performance of masculinity itself, a role so all-encompassing, so unconsciously absorbed, so rote to its players that sometimes we forget we're playing, blinded by the glare of the footlights to anything beyond the edge of our stages.

But gaze into the opaque surface of "performance" and another image begins to form. Men's fetishization of performance becomes a mirror image of their fear of failure.

For as long as I've known men, the men I've known have maintained a fraught relationship with failure—they'd fly into a rage over a schoolyard game, a high school girlfriend, a round of *Tetris*, a college exam, a job interview. And more and more, it seems boys are raised to be men who understand winning as the only acceptable option and quitting as the ultimate feat of self-immolation. Failure is weakness, defeat, the shameful stamp of *can't*.

But in the gym, there's no succeeding without it.

In order to progress in the gym and to grow in the mirror, a lifter needs to continually approach and experience failure. The directive is short and to the point: You start a set and you take it *to failure*—the point at which another repetition becomes impossible. You fail. You rest. You add weight. You repeat. You fail. That's the drill.

This principle is known as *progressive resistance*, and it's the foundation of any workout program geared toward hypertrophy, the cultivation and growth of muscle tissue. Only by continually challenging one's muscles, by confronting one's very cells with impossible tasks and failing at them, can any growth occur.

When I tried lifting for the very first time in high school, my dread of failing was heavier than any of the weights I attempted. The fear of failing to lift the same weight the other boys in my gym class could was paralyzing every time Coach led us to the weight room in the underbelly of the basketball courts; the injuries I sustained from attempting weights for which I wasn't ready were enough to keep me out of the gym for years to come.

But the past two decades I've spent in the gym have completely recalibrated my own relationship with failure. Failure is now my workout buddy. We meet every morning, same time, same place. Without failure, it's impossible to assign meaning to anything I accomplish. In a world where anything is possible, lifting—ideally—trains one's focus, precisely, on what's not.

One of the founding fathers of progressive resistance training is Alan Calvert, who in 1902 founded the Milo Barbell Company, one of the very first commercial barbell companies at a time when fitness implements were hard to come by, limited to hand weights like dumbbells and "Indian" clubs (long-handled clubs with bulbed weighted ends). Calvert was a strength athlete, publisher (he founded *Strength* magazine in 1914), and prolific author. He devoted his life to legitimizing strength training in the eyes of Americans more accustomed to viewing strongmen as entertainers and the physical development of their oversized bodies as a novelty (if not an outright health risk).

Calvert's patented "Milo Adjustable Barbell" of 1902 featured a compartment that could be loaded with shot in order to incrementally increase its weight and came packaged with a workout program to guide novices through progressively heavier lifts.

"Progressive Weightlifting has developed all the famous Modern Samsons now exhibiting before the public," reads a 1902 newspaper ad for the apparatus, which retailed at $7.50.

These progressive techniques to muscle growth had roots in formative mail-order physical culturists at the turn of the century, like the German Theodor Siebert and the French Edmond Desbonnet. Eugen Sandow's mentor-turned-rival Ludwig Durlacher, a.k.a. Professor Attila, had schooled his strapping protégée in the tenets of progressive resistance, and Sandow, in turn, would build a vast mail-order training empire on its efficacy.

The principles of progressive resistance would undergird the success of a century-long lineage of mail-order muscle gurus, from magazine founder Bernarr Macfadden (*Physical Culture* in 1899) to authors Arthur Saxon (1905's *The Development of Physical Power*), Dudley Allen Sargent (1914's *Health, Strength & Power*), and Earle Liederman (1924's *Muscle Building*) and onward to magazine magnates Bob Hoffman (*Strength and Health* in 1932 and *Muscular Development* in 1964) and Joe Weider (*Your Physique, Muscle Builder, Mr. America, Muscle Power, Muscle & Fitness, Men's Fitness,* and *Flex*, several of which continue to grimace from newsstands today).

But the true roots of progressive resistance are the stuff of legend. The muse behind Calvert's barbell company was a sixth-century Grecian wrestler named Milo of Croton. A six-time Olympian wrestling champion who also enjoyed success at the Pythian, the Isthmian and the Nemean Games, Milo was known for his size, strength, and heroism. In addition to being a war hero, he once saved his buddy, the mathematician Pythagoras, by holding up the stone roof of a collapsing house.

And as indicated by that tale, like any strongman worth the salt of his sweat, Milo had a lore larger than life. He would dazzle onlookers with feats of strength, challenging them to bend one of his fingers or steal a pomegranate from his hand. His daily diet was rumored to be twenty pounds of bread, twenty pounds of meat, and eighteen pints of wine—plus the occasional snack of *alectoriae*, a.k.a. the gizzard stones of roosters, or "cock stones."

But the two most famous bits of Milo lore concern the big man's rise and his demise. We'll start with the latter, since it's the way Milo is most often depicted.

As a grown man well into his forties, Milo was walking alone through a forest when he came upon a tree trunk with a sizeable split, held open by wedges. Tempted by this irresistible test of strength in waiting, Milo attempted to pry the tree trunk apart. In the process he knocked the wedges out and the trunk closed on his hand like a trap.

And there, as dozens of paintings and sculptures show us, he squirmed and pulled and cried for help until he was discovered and devoured alive by wild beasts.

Sometimes they are wolves, as in *The Tragic End of Milo of Croton*, a 1750 painting by Jean-Jacques Bachelier. Sometimes it's a lion, as in *Milo of Croton, Attempting to Test His Strength, Is Caught and Devoured by a Lion*, a 1795 depiction by Charles Meynier. In painter Carlo Zatti's 1836 *Milo of Croton*, a single lion prowls hungrily in the background as a doomed Milo tugs at his own stuck hand, his toes curling in terror. In Pierre Puget's 1682 marble, Milo is suspended in a state of twisting agony as a lion snacks on his glutes.

The reliable centering of Milo's suffering in the moment of his doom always makes the "tragedy" of death seem more like a subdued celebration—a freeze-frame capture of comeuppance for Milo's reckless pride. The episode smacks of a "Take that!" from the gods, his ultimate failure a fitting end to a mortal man who fancied himself undefeated.

But as legacies go, Milo's death—and whatever lesson is insisted to lurk therein—has nothing on his growth.

The story goes that as a young man, eager to grow strong, Milo decided one day to pick up a calf and carry it across his shoulders. He did this every day for four years, and as the calf grew into a full-grown bull, Milo gained enough strength, day by day, to carry its weight.

In this way, Milo became the proverbial father of progressive training, complete with its own, less satisfying moral lesson about perseverance tucked somewhere within. And while depictions of Milo hauling bulls are harder to come by than images of his transition into lion food, the visual of Milo's beastly burden set the stage for strongmen over a millennium. Sandow, especially, may have taken the legend too literally, squaring off against a suspiciously yawning lion for a publicity stunt in 1894 and merely carrying it around, much to the chagrin of a crowd expecting something more . . . artful.

Sometimes I think of the bull on Milo's shoulders as masculinity itself: a growing burden we take on as boys and carry on our backs into manhood. Indeed, its weight is the only proof we have that we are becoming men and to fail would be to let it crush you.

In this context, the gym becomes a sacred space of sorts, one that gives men an allowance for failure that they seldom grant to each other. The gym offers men amnesty from their own rules, grants them the fleeting freedom to fail—loudly, proudly, repeatedly, and in front of each other.

We like to refer to what we do in the gym as "strength training," but when we go attempt to move immovable objects, all we're really doing is expanding the known frontiers of our weakness. (But try marketing that.)

Failure is an acceptance of the impossible, an embrace of what can't be done. To me, it's this experience—the relief and release of knowing what defeat feels like in your hands—that I believe men crave, perhaps even more than their "domination" of the weights they can manage. Failure can help to heal men who only know the expectations and demands of success.

It's failure that can help men forget our lines, our stage directions, our assigned roles. It's failure alone that can liberate us from performance.

VI

ANGELO

I NEVER FOUND OUT who punched me in the face in front of the arcade my freshman year, but I blame Dwight Eisenhower. If it hadn't been for him, there would have been no Presidential Council on Fitness since 1956, and if it hadn't been for that, there'd be no Presidential Fitness Test, and if it hadn't been for that, I wouldn't have been outed in front of the entire Fitchburg High School class of '94 as an easy mark.

The test was developed in the 1950s in response to a trove of research by Dr. Hans Kraus and Dr. Sonja Weber about the physical fitness of American kids (a project known as the Kraus-Weber Tests) versus their European counterparts. It found, among other dismal comparisons, 57.9 percent of US youth failing "one or more of six tests for muscular strength and flexibility," (compared to 8.7 percent of youngsters in Europe).

According to a 1955 *Sports Illustrated* article titled "The Report That Shocked the President," the cause for these comparative deficiencies boils down to "a number of factors ranging from the playpen to the school bus to television—in short, America's plush standard of living."

But Eisenhower's urgency to fix the problem recalls the consternation of Jahn as he brainstormed his Turnplatzes—the weakness of Americans was a national security threat.

"After hearing the report on the nation's youngsters at the White House luncheon, President Eisenhower was moved to recall some thoughts of his own," reads the account in *Sports Illustrated*. "During World War II, when he was a five-star general, the nation was facing the greatest crisis in its history. Men were never more needed to serve America's cause but, the President recalled, more than 50% of them were unable to serve because they were physically unfit. Dwight D. Eisenhower did not need to be reminded that a problem does exist."

The Presidential Fitness Test continued to be implemented in American schools into the Obama administration, which phased it out in 2012 and replaced it with the Presidential Youth Fitness Program—a voluntary "comprehensive school-based program that promotes health and regular physical activity for America's youth."

Coach Cosenza, the head football coach who doubled as our gym teacher, seemed very keen on getting the Presidential test out of the way for everyone early in the school year, not just so he could commence his own rigorous curriculum (which allowed his football players to train in the basement weight room rather than play kickball) but also so he could sort the rest of us into new recruits and hopeless cases.

The test made clear which camp I fell into. In addition to the test's one-mile run and a fifty-yard dash (neither of which went particularly well), we had to perform timed sets of sit-ups, push-ups, and, the great humiliator of them all, pull-ups.

It's hard to describe what it's like to hang like a drape from a pull-up bar in front of dozens of tetchy freshmen, quivering against the burden of your own body, absorbing the pointless encouragements being shouted in your ear by a large man in a crimson tracksuit. I guess I just described it, but it doesn't really capture the gravity-bending panic that sets in when one rep appears to be too much for you to make, when your brain is reduced to begging your arms to bend, but they just hang like hoses from the bar.

I remember the scrape of Coach's Bic on his clipboard as he drew an unambiguous zero on my chart—a number that felt like a weight I'd forever drag behind me. I remember his teacherly performance of kindness making the weight of his visible disappointment all the more heavy. And I remember the other boys taking their turns at the bar, hopping to grab the bar with both hands and popping reps like waffles in a toaster. I remember Coach's scowl arcing into a warm smile, once again given reason to be proud and growl "Atta boy!"

It was my first week in a new school, in front of a class of new peers and sneering upperclassmen, and I'd already self-sorted as Officially Scrawny— puny, even by Presidential standards. A 97-pound weakling.

That afternoon, I was walking home on my usual daily route—down the grand old front steps of the high school and across the park to Espresso Pizza (where they had a *Street Fighter* machine), down Main Street to the arcade (where they had *Pit-Fighter* and *Altered Beast*), straight on to the Corner Book Shop, and up Lunenburg Street to our house.

I'd made it only as far as the arcade when I noticed him: another boy, older than me, bigger than me, swaddled in a red and blue Starter jacket and a ratty pair of Jordans (the unofficial uniform for most boys at my school). I remember his eyes but not his face, as I caught them only for a moment before his fist smashed the side of my head.

I remember my head hitting the sidewalk and the taste of blood on my teeth. I remember a sucking sound in my ear canal and the rush of frigid air into the deepest part of my skull that I'd ever perceived. I remember the fast-vanishing scramble of boots on the salted sidewalk. I remember comparing the blur in my head to the TV scenes where someone gets punched in the face, the lens going foggy, the camera wobbling. I remember the ring of concerned passersby staring down at me, the slow unmuffling of street noise, the nice girl who rushed out of the pizza place to gather my books and blot my nose with a napkin.

The kid had sprinted around the block, but across the street, a group of smiling boys in Starter jackets sat watching the scene unfold, perched on the park fence like a row of crows. Unlike me, it appears that day my assailant had passed his test.

I started to wonder if I needed to take gym class more seriously.

Bullies have driven many a man—or boy, as it were—to the gym. One study on male muscle dysmorphia found that 21 percent of bodybuilders reported having been "regular victims of bullying" as children.

"I got into bodybuilding to defend myself," Lou Ferrigno once told an interviewer regarding the merciless bullying he faced as a hearing-impaired child. "It saved my life."

Dwayne "The Rock" Johnson, whose family moved often due to the career of his pro wrestler dad Rocky Johnson, reports being constantly targeted by bullies as the "new kid" wherever they landed. Ex-pro wrestler and actor John Cena was brutally picked on as a boy for being, in his words, "skinny and scrawny," not wearing the right clothes, or not listening to the right music. The young Sylvester Stallone faced so much bullying for his speech impediment that he fashioned his own weights and barbells from auto parts, cinder blocks, and poles.

In his autobiography, Robby Robinson—the champion bodybuilder known as "The Black Prince" who came to prominence in the 1970s—writes about how, as a young man in Damascus, Georgia, he used the gym to escape the abusive treatment he endured from his own family. He recalls gazing upon his *Superman* comics as a kid, wishing he could grow to protect his mother from danger, sending a quarter to Charles Atlas for the lifeline of lifting.

Years later in 1975, newly crowned Mr. America in his first year as a pro, Robinson experienced a far different reception when he returned to Damascus, explaining in *The Black Prince*: "In my hometown, there, I'm just like, you would say, the President of the United States, and everybody looks up to me, especially the kids."

But even that didn't end the bullying. When he first arrived in California in 1975, he was promptly told by white promoters that "Blacks don't get contracts" and regularly harassed by strangers and fellow competitors alike at local competitions. The abuse got so bad that by the 1980s, Robinson up and moved to Holland, where he spent most of his career and was treated "completely differently."

Like bodybuilders, bullies have been following essentially the same program for over a century.

In 1850, when George Barker Windship, who later became a renowned strongman known as the "American Samson" and the "Roxbury Hercules," was a freshman in Harvard University's class of 1854, he was immediately greeted with barbs from his more substantial classmates.

"There goes the smallest fellow in our class" is the traumatic taunt with which Windship opens his 1862 essay, "Autobiographical Sketches of a Strength-Seeker," published in the *Atlantic Monthly*.

Windship describes a sinister schoolmate who "had considerably the advantage of me both in inches and in years, and whose overflow of animal spirits required some object to vent itself upon, selected me as the victim of his ebullient vivacity."

"He began by tossing my book down stairs," writes Windship. "This seemed to me rather rough play, especially from one with whom I was not, at the time, on terms of intimacy . . . I subsequently found that it was merely the commencement of a series of similar annoyances."

Windship's subsequent career in strength was a powder keg sparked by "practical vengeance." "Wait two years," he told a friend, "and I promise you I will either make my tormentor apologize or give him such a thrashing as he will remember for the rest of his life."

Windship spent years studying the aesthetics and mechanics of muscle. As a student at Harvard Medical School, he went so far as to stress-test human bones in the dissecting room. A thigh bone, for instance, he discovered could "safely bear a strain of two or three thousand pounds," lending him confidence to proceed with lifting 500-pound barrels in his backyard for the entertainment of his neighbors—and the chagrin of his many strongman rivals.

He also spent a good amount of time wandering the halls of the Boston Athenaeum contemplating the forms of unbullied heroes in its collection of Grecian statuary, including a replica of the Farnese Hercules, the *Quoit-thrower* (the *Discobolus*, attributed to the fourth-century BCE ancient Greek sculptor Myron), and the *Dying Gladiator* (or the *Dying Gaul*, a third-century BCE bronze attributed to Epigonus)—forms that, decades later, Eugen Sandow would admire and assume. These sculptures would inspire Windship to articulate aspects of masculinity that now, in the Age of the Image, seem prescient. "The habitual contemplation of such works could not fail to have a good effect upon the physical bearing and development of the young," he wrote. "We are the creatures of imitation."

But perhaps the most well-known beanpole-to-brute story is that of Charles Atlas.

———

Long before a fifty-four-year-old Bernarr Macfadden dubbed the thirty-year-old Atlas "The World's Most Perfectly Developed Man" at a 1922 physical culture exhibition at Madison Square Garden, Atlas was the conspicuously scrawny Angelo Siciliano, an Italian immigrant who arrived in Brooklyn (from the town of Cosenza, oddly enough) at the age of ten in 1903.

A bullying episode in Coney Island in Atlas's teen years would prove formative not just for his body, but for the shape of his future fitness empire, as well as the course of American fitness for generations to come.

"One day I went to Coney Island and I had a very pretty girl with me," Atlas recounted. "We were sitting on the sand. A big, husky life-guard, maybe there were two of them, kicked sand in my face. I couldn't do anything and the girl felt funny. I told her that someday, if I meet this guy, I will lick him."

The lore goes that the dejected Angelo went on to begin looking more closely at the Coney Island strongmen on the boardwalk stages, as well as the eponymous titan atop the Atlas Hotel (the one that would inspire his new name). He also spent time gazing at the statues of Hercules, Apollo, and Zeus at the Brooklyn Museum.

While working as a janitor, Atlas started training at home, eventually getting gigs as a strongman in Coney Island and—as though following Sandow's blueprint to posterity—finding work as a model for various sculptors. Atlas's body became George Washington's for Alexander Stirling Calder's *Washington at Peace* in Manhattan's Washington Square Park. You can also still see him in Pietro Montana's *Dawn of Glory* in Brooklyn's Prospect Park, as Alexander Hamilton in James Earle Fraser's sculpture at the Treasury in DC, and as a sword-clutching warrior in Adolph A. Weinman's *Patriotism* at the Elks National Memorial in Chicago.

On a whim in 1921, Atlas entered a "World's Most Beautiful Man" competition sponsored by Bernarr Macfadden's popular magazine, *Physical Culture*, by sending in a photograph. Laying eyes on the image, Macfadden summoned Atlas to his office, where the latter stripped to leopard-print briefs and the former declared the contest over, handing Atlas a check for $1,000 as the two enjoyed a glass of carrot juice.

In 1929, Atlas founded Charles Atlas Ltd., a company built on his own "Dynamic Tension" system—a workout program one could perform entirely at home (much as young Angelo had), employing simple exercises designed to pit one's muscles against each other, and to which Atlas credited his own 47-inch chest and 32-inch waist. With the help of business partner Charles Roman, Atlas devised an ad campaign based on repeated revisitations to that fateful humiliation on the beach, targeting the weak spots of proverbial "97-pound weaklings" everywhere. (Enough so that three generations of men grew up discovering his ads on the back of their favorite comics, from *Archie* to *Zorro*.)

"Let Me Prove in 7 Days That I Can Make You a New Man!" his ads entreated with almost biblical assurance. Some taglines were less positive in their encouragement ("Hey, Skinny! Yer Ribs Are Showing!"), while others were meant simply to conjure common embarrassments experienced by men in the wild—or in the case of some (like "Battle Fought in Bed That Made Fred a He-Man!"), their own literal nightmares.

Most of the ads banked on the raw motivational fuel of humiliation and petty vengeance to sell the transformational power of Dynamic Tension. That is, it was never the work, but (as one 1934 ad was titled) the "*Insult That Made a Man Out of Mac.*"

After getting punched in the face, I remember standing up, thanking the girl who helped me with my books, gauging my options, and opting to waddle home. My ear still felt like the broken airlock of a spacecraft, and my head filled with a stinging pressure. I tasted blood, tangy and metallic. I thought if I kept the same walk home, I could shrink the aberration of the attack into a moment that just grew smaller and smaller as time passed. But really, the opposite happened—every passing person seemed like a potential attacker, every set of eyes could see right through me, every man could tell I wasn't one of them. And as the shock wore off and thickened into soreness across my brow and jaw, every flinch or twitch shot a reminder to my mind that I'd be hunted. That I needed to find another way home. Or out.

At the Corner Book Shop, often my last and longest stop on my walk home, I had a routine. I'd start with a benign, borderline performative perusal of video game magazines like *Nintendo Power* and *Electronic Gaming Monthly*. I'd gradually drift into the music section, browsing *Spin* or *Rolling Stone* for what I figured seemed like a normal amount of time.

And then, likely with the subtlety of a slamming screen door, I'd cross over to the end of the sports rack, where older gentlemen often picked up hunting magazines or issues of *Sports Illustrated* and where a sizable selection of bodybuilding magazines stuffed the shelves and shed subscription cards.

I'd page through copies of *Iron Man, Strength & Health, Muscle & Fitness*, and whatever others of the dozens of titles springing up in the exploding "fitness" category—many of them the handiwork of Joe Weider.

Born in 1919, Weider grew up in Montreal, a skinny kid who spent his teen years conscious of his slender body. He fixated on the Charles Atlas ads in the back of his comic books and issues of *Strength* magazine, published by the Milo Barbell Company. At 5 feet, 5 inches, and 115 pounds, Weider was (according to the official bio on his website) "easy prey for teenagers looking to score some quick change."

Young Joe fashioned a barbell out of an old axel and a pair of flywheels and started lifting on his own. "By the time he turned 15," his bio claims, "neighborhood bullies no longer bothered Joe."

In August 1940, Weider published the first issue of *Your Physique*, a body-centric magazine that he produced himself at night on a rented typewriter, hand-lettering the headlines, drawing the illustrations of musclemen, and mimeographing and stapling each issue.

Weider's labor of love not only expanded the field of weight training by focusing on muscle building over strength training, it pushed the envelope of how men were portrayed in mainstream magazines—a shameless celebration of good-looking, nearly nude men flexing spectacular muscles. *Your Physique* would develop into *Muscle Builder/Power* in 1966—now one of the most iconic muscle magazines in the history of the form and the platform where Arnold, Lou, and countless other titans of the stage got their start. By the time I got my twinky teenage hands on it, the magazine had rebranded to its current identity, *Muscle & Fitness*. Weider's empire would ultimately comprise over thirty different magazines over sixty years.

Weider had a singular presence (I'll admit, his moustache inspired mine) and an outsized influence on the burgeoning bodybuilding world. In 1942 he founded his own mail-order Weider Barbell Company. In 1946, with his brother Ben, he cofounded the International Federation of Bodybuilders (which still exists in over 170 countries). In 1965 he founded the Mr. Olympia contest—a title that would be held by legends of the sport like Larry Scott, Harold Poole, Sergio Oliva, Arnold Schwarzenegger, Franco

Columbu, Frank Zane, Ken Waller, and Robby Robinson. To this day, titans like Hadi Choopan, Mamdouh Elssbiay, Brandon Curry, Phil Heath, and Jay Cutler hoist the contest's signature miniature statues of Sandow upon winning the coveted international title. (The trophy, a replica of a full-sized Sandow statue created by Frederick W. Pomeroy in 1891, was first awarded in miniature to contestants at Sandow's "Great Competition" of 1901 and has reappeared as a fixture of the Mr. Olympia contest since 1977.)

Other muscle magazine publishers of Weider's time leaned their publications toward the functional aspects of weight training. Take York Barbell Company owner Bob Hoffman, for example, who founded his own magazine business in 1932, publishing titles like *Strength & Health*. A founding member of the President's Council on Sports, Fitness, and Nutrition and a decorated Olympic-level weight-lifting coach, Hoffman aligned his magazines with his lifelong talents as an athlete.

While Weider built his empire in part on his own line of exercise equipment (from doorknob-mounted resistance ropes to home weight benches), he was resolutely more concerned—in practice and in print—with aesthetics and beauty. Weider's eye for the perfect body made him a kingmaker among the biggest men on earth—and the epicenter of controversies concerning what it took to make the career-making pages of his beefcake bibles. Over his long career, Weider was accused of running the sport of bodybuilding like a monopoly.

A *Los Angeles Times* article from 1989 noted that because bodybuilding was such a niche unto itself, "the editorial voice of the sport and its primary source of news are Weider's magazines—publications that unabashedly exalt Joe Weider and hustle his wide range of barbells, amino acid tablets and other products."

John Balik, the publisher of the smaller Santa Monica-based *Iron Man* magazine, clarified the state of the business further: "He is the Hertz and there is no Avis."

The muscle mags of Weider's 1990s heyday offered pages and pages of glossy giants in the midst of intense workouts. Details of their muscles and movements were arranged in what were intended to be instructional sequences but read more like the walls of a gallery of ancient friezes. Photo spreads were interrupted by all-caps ads for various weight gain powders and mysterious supplements. Regular Joe bodybuilders with shiny perms posed in wide-neck sweatshirts and baggy neon pants in ads for the specialized regalia of early-1990s meatheads. Everyone looked happy, healthy, *huge.*

Within my magazine-browsing routine I had another ritual, and it had become more than a matter of daily discipline. Even the day of the punch, my ear pink and throbbing, my eye slowly swelling, and my nostril crusty with blood, I obeyed the pull of an uncanny gravity that drew me to the other end of the magazine rack—the one with the shelves obscured by long upright panels. Some of the magazines behind the barrier were packaged in an additional layer of security film. Others were unsheathed, ready to be thumbed through.

When the old man at the counter was busy stocking a shelf or helping a customer, I'd slip an issue of *Honcho* or *Inches* or *Mandate* in between the pages of *Flex* and browse my furtively collated hybrid by the literary journals, where no one ever went.

Here, in my hometown, down the block from my church, alone in the back of the bookstore with a split lip, I saw men coiled up in each other, lips open and touching, tongues tantalizingly dragging along each other's thick necks, hands pulling each other's jockstraps below their asses, and giant, expertly tended cocks leaping from the center of every spread. I'd never before seen men in love or lust. I'd never seen them in anything but like or hate. Each time I looked felt like the first time.

The sets in which these photos were taken all suggested proximity to reality—steam-filled locker rooms, a sparsely appointed "Coach's" office, a nondescript parking lot. And the "characters" were grown-up versions of archetypes that had populated my Legoland: cops, firemen, soldiers (no astronauts or pirates that I remember). It was as though part of the responsibility of gay porn was to provide a fantasy you could superimpose onto your daily life like a filter.

And while the muscles on these models were sized well beyond the specs of "classical" perfection, in the pages of *Honcho* they weren't carried as armor—they were gently lit, limned like oil paintings, inviting the eye to look and linger, an unthinkable way to know another man. The men gazed from the page, sometimes glancing out as though you'd interrupted them by looking, their cocks unbothered and crossed like benign swords. I remember my face turning as bright red as my ear as my eyes took mental photos of the photos. I remember my heart racing, my eyes darting around to make sure I wasn't browsing my way into another beating.

But as long as I kept flipping, the pages would return once again to the regularly scheduled programming of *Flex* and the turbulence would subside. The feast of steroidal flesh in *Flex* was somehow tame in comparison, somehow fully acceptable to any man who happened to walk past, but it was no different in its outrageously amplified male sexuality. If anything, it was more aggressive. Like the men of *Honcho*, the bodybuilders in the muscle mags grimaced as though mid-climax, their eyes rolled back in ecstasy, their veins bulging, their teeth bared, and the neon filament of a Lycra thong straining to remain intact around their twisting trunks.

Every scene was an explosion of testosterone, a tableau of pure masculine aggression. But each image also undeniably doubled as a celebration of male beauty, of bodily abundance, of erotic potential—none of which I'd found a trace of in myself. Each model was a monster and a miracle, a man and a god, a force of nature and a work of art.

I wondered how many of them had been bullied into their bodies.

THE ALPHAS

IKTOK TAMES the male gaze into something more like a catatonic stare. For those of us who grew up switching through channels with a "clicker," the TikTok experience—an endless stream down which one paddles with the oar of an index finger—reopens long-abandoned pathways in our brains, flooding them with fresh dopamine from an endless reservoir of fifteen-second video stimulations.

The algorithm knows what foods I enjoy watching be cooked, and that any ASMR tendencies I have are reserved for videos of the production and consumption of food. It knows I like cats, pandas, bulldogs, bears, owls, just about any animal that can lose itself in the act of munching. It seems to feed the flickering furnace of hope in my heart for the younger generation by offering a steady supply of cutting social critiques and critical self-examinations from the eighteen to twenty-five set. It also knows I like to get angry, and peppers my feed with know-nothing fuckfaces.

But the algo also knows how to capture with the most general of appeals—it is like the hand of a giant scooping up the land upon which I stand. I've found myself helpless to one particular stratum of content explicitly geared by its creators toward men, the clips often emblazoned with the caption "For my male audience."

What follows are videos of minor but impactful events: a bottle rocket getting fired below the surface of an iced-over pond, the flash of its muffled burst blooming into a smoking cobweb crack. A thick log of freshly dislodged muck flying from an unclogged sewer pipe in a sludgy column. A massive boulder pushed from its place of rest to tumble down a stony bluff and explode into pieces. A perfectly cylindrical shell of barely formed ice extracted from the inside of a barrel, carefully transported to a clearing of concrete, and casually tossed to the ground, exploding into sparkly shards. A glassy frozen puddle shattering beneath the weight of a boot.

Men love disturbing the undisturbed, breaking the unbroken—be it silence or ice. Making a mark, letting nothing be. It's proof of our purchase on Earth. We'll call it instinctual, but it's the result of millennia of conditioning assuring us that since we're here, we ought to make our presence known. Now, with so much of our experience mediated by the Internet, these small moments of collision with nature—the few bits of it we haven't already upended or erased—feel charged with significance. The disturbance of a long dormant boulder bestows upon the pusher a sense of control that might be compromised by the sight of, say, a crumbling glacier. The essentially masculine aspect of these clips isn't necessarily the climax—the boulder disintegrating, the ice cracking, the fireworks of whatever explosion—but the clip itself: the documenting of having done something that did something.

That's one stratum of so-called masculine TikTok content. Then, deep below it, coursing like an underground river of wastewater, runs another: the manosphere.

It's an Axe-scented world unto itself, led by a cadre of self-appointed "alphas," i.e., dominant males. Fun fact: "alpha" in this context is derived from the 1947 research of one Rudolph Schenkel, who deduced that aggressive "top dog" wolves asserted control of their packs. His conclusions were later amplified by Dr. L. David Mech's 1970 book *The Wolf: The Ecology and Behavior of an Endangered Species.* Mech has since, in a 1999 paper and in several subsequent interviews, distanced himself from the idea, calling it a misunderstanding. (Leaders within wolf packs, male and female, typically emerge simply through the act of breeding pups.)

Ironically, if there's one thing men secretly crave, it's other men telling them how to be men—from Walt Whitman posing as Mose to Charles Atlas counseling his fellow former beanpoles, from Robert Bly and his mythopoetic ilk helping men unearth their inner beasts to today's "Western chauvinists," "men's rights activists," "pick-up artists," and the exhausting bumper crop of contemporary manfluencers on social media. For something supposedly so instinctual, so hardwired into our manly cells, I'm sure some readers will join me in my disbelief that masculinity still requires a faculty of thousands to teach.

These days there's a guru waiting around every corner for young men to come clicking. They cover fitness, diet and nutrition, dating, politics, philosophy (however rudimentary), and, their favorite topic, masculinity—its dire state, its necessary preservation, its unlockable secrets, its bestowal of dominion. The difference between the manfluencers of old and today's glut is that, because white heterosexual men now perceive themselves as having (so generously!) ceded physical, financial, professional, and cultural ground to women, people of color, and LGBTQ folks (i.e., everyone else), they're doubling down on their occupation of virtual space. Unlike any other comparable Internet niche or eddy, the manosphere carries itself like it owns the place.

Manfluencers have ushered in a new era of rules, details, and suffocating boundaries of what "real men" are supposed to do, how they're supposed to behave, what and who they are supposed to prioritize—and they're as arbitrary and stringent as the finest and fanciest dining etiquette. Salad is carcinogenic. Straws are feminine. Washing your ass is gay. Manfluencers are selling a pinkies-out approach to perfecting the illusion of manhood.

Young men are especially vulnerable to these messages. Born into the chaotic marketplace of the Internet, staggered by its possibilities for self-definition and often opting for the path of least resistance, young men flock to their gurus like bugs to the indifferent glow of a zapper.

On his wildly popular podcast, *The Joe Rogan Experience*—which has accrued over two thousand episodes since launching in 2009—Rogan, the former *Fear Factor* host and sometime UFC commentator, has trafficked in anti-vaccination conspiracies, blurry anti-Semitic rhetoric, and heavy skepticism toward the trans community and virtually any other issue in which he's uninvolved and uninformed but interested in "just asking questions" about. Some of Rogan's more egregiously error-riddled ruminations find quick correction in his often smartly selected roster of guests, but most of his extemporaneous observations go unchallenged, quietly calling into question the true efficacy of the nootropic "Alpha-Brain" supplement he regularly hucks. In a January 2021 podcast, he cited an "amazing point" by British author Douglas Murray "about civilizations collapsing—and that when they start collapsing they become obsessed with gender, and he was saying that you could trace it back to the ancient Romans, the Greeks."

Never mind which exact entire era of antiquity he's referring to here, and never mind that the fifty-five-year-old Rogan's own admitted use of testosterone and human growth hormone suggests more than a passing concern of his own with his personal gender expression.

Rogan, who routinely performs a public struggle with the navigation of pronouns and other considerations of gender identity, still manages to summon rambling defenses against the term "toxic masculinity"—a descriptor he inexplicably expands to mean "anything men have ever done."

"That's a hilarious expression," Rogan says in one clip circulating around TikTok. "Because you need to thank 'toxic masculinity' for all the bridges all the fuckin' . . . all the jets, all the rockets. Toxic masculinity? You break down all the things that men have invented, and that all these 'toxic' men have prevented you from being murdered, war and protected the country, and all the different things that you could attribute to 'toxic masculinity'? Most of it is positive."

(A side note on the topic of toxic masculinity: I've never understood why it was considered an effective deterrent to label masculinity gone awry as "toxic." Branding corrosive ideas of masculinity as "toxic" is akin to pouring them into a gray plastic bodywash bottle—it makes them *more* appealing to men, not less. Among men, "toxic" has now become a byword for "badass." I propose the more straightforward "broken masculinity" as a potential replacement primarily because it accurately describes what we're dealing with—a model of masculinity that's completely broken—but also because it's less likely that men will walk around puffing their chests and declaring themselves "broken.")

Rogan's attempt at a point is an echo of a popular diatribe from recently decertified psychologist and ubiquitous manosphere fashion plate Jordan Peterson, who first tapped into the wild spirits of his expansive readership of disaffected men by giving them *12 Rules for Life: An Antidote to Chaos*—a seemingly well-intentioned and not a bit ironic rulebook that includes such guidance as "Stand up straight with your shoulders back" (a metaphor for the acceptance of "the terrible responsibility of life"); "Set your house in perfect order before you criticize the world" (a patently ridiculous request to make of anyone contending against actual injustice); "Do not let your children do anything that makes you dislike them" (to which no other response is possible but "OK, Boomer"); and "Assume that the person you are listening to might know something you don't"—actual sage advice that Peterson assiduously avoids taking himself. This is especially clear in his continued ascent as one of North America's leading (or at least most audible) anti-trans voices.

In a 2022 episode of his podcast dispatched in clipped form to TikTok, an earbudded and fastidiously outfitted Peterson winces with confusion when confronted with the imaginary prospect of freestyling social interaction with a hypothetical nonbinary person, and struggles aloud. "If I don't know whether you're male or female," he crows in with ear-curling disdain, "what the hell should I *do* with you? The simplest thing for me to do is go find someone else who is a hell of a lot less trouble. Who is willing to abide by the social norms enough so that they don't present a mass of indeterminate confusion on immediate confrontation."

The grammar strategy here is interesting—the installation of the other as the direct object, always the recipient of the action. Not *How do you prefer to be addressed?* (the only question trans and nonbinary folks would like to be asked) but *What should I do with you?* Peterson's solution does not follow his edict to "assume the person he is listening to knows something he doesn't," because he has no interest in listening—only responding.

The state of modern masculinity, to Peterson, is a human catastrophe and a financial jackpot, threatened at all times and from all sides by the tidal advances of inclusive language, politically correct rhetoric, and the ostensible Trojan horse of multiculturalism, which contains . . . I'm not sure what, exactly, apart from people of other cultures. The threat is real, and for Peterson, highly lucrative. (*12 Rules* has sold well over five million copies.)

In one highly clicked clip, a glassy-eyed Peterson, asked by an interviewer for a 2019 Dutch documentary if it's "OK to be a man," struggles against tears and embarks on a Trumpian slideshow of familiar man tropes: "It's not 'OK'! It's necessary!" he admonishes his questioner. "What the hell are we going to do without men? You look around the city here you see all these buildings go up. These men, they're doing impossible things. They're under the streets, working on the sewers. They're up on the power lines in the storms and the rain. They're keeping this impossible infrastructure functioning, and often literally. And the gratitude for that is solely lacking, especially among the people who should be most grateful."

Peterson's skill with cultivating grievance, refining it to what seems like a point is one of his greatest skills as a manfluencer, matched only by his ability to forget that people of all genders perform each of the presumably man-specific occupations he lists.

The sense of perpetual unfairness that he grooms into young men's understanding of their own place in the world is couched in a fraudulent nostalgia for a functioning but somehow abandoned order. He peddles an assurance of righteousness—that men's suffering isn't for nothing, that it's actually all part of the master plan of manhood, an essential cycle of masculine pain. Sorry, he suggests, we don't make the rules. (Except when we do, which is always.)

Peterson is correct when he asserts that the important and necessary role that men play in the world is not "toxic masculinity" ("that appalling phrase," he hisses). But the reality is that men, instructed to stunt each other's emotional growth, are routinely deprived of their ability to experience these roles as fully realized humans. Men learn to alienate themselves from their own feelings and turn their successes into subsets of vengeance.

Meanwhile, alpha charlatans like Peterson and Rogan, when taken together (as they often are), form a kind of brains-and-brawn team, chewing on current events with a numbing combination of obtuseness and obfuscation (Peterson) or blunted credulity (Rogan). Peterson, in ridiculous custom suits that looked pulled from the closet of a shelved Batman villain, plays the role in young men's minds of the firebrand public intellectual. Rogan, with his stoner chuckle, big cigars, and straining performance T's, represents the masculine urge to reduce complicated topics to insultingly simple terms, to deny reality in service of escaping "the matrix," to reserve their curiosity for aliens and ayahuasca and their cynicism for anyone who hasn't taken the "red pill."

"Red pill" masculinity is at the heart of many a manfluencer's core shtick. The term, a reference to the "red pill" in the 1999 sci-fi film *The Matrix*, denotes a man's moment of revelation in which classic misogynist tropes about the place of women in society and the home are understood to be correct after all. The red-pilled reassert traditional masculine roles and almost cartoonishly celebrate patriarchal values, in terms so explicit as to make the whole thing seem almost like unwitting satire. (That so many red-pilled young men find unironic heroes in the fictional antiheroes of the past quarter century—from *American Psycho*'s Patrick Bateman to *Fight Club*'s Tyler Durden to *The Sopranos*' Tony Soprano—lends credence to this theory.)

Perhaps the primary pharmacist in the red pill masculinity movement is former professional kickboxer and self-described "Top G" Andrew

Tate—who at the time of writing is sitting in a Romanian jail cell on charges of organized crime, human trafficking, and rape. Tate rose to prominence in the manosphere largely on the back of his "Hustlers University," a mail-order program for entrepreneurs that attracted over 100,000 subscribers at $49.99/month.

I have a whole stack of representative Andrew Tate quotes, but I only have room for him to park one Bugatti's worth of his bullshit, so we're going with this one: "When you're a G"—a gangster—"you're just accidentally like pimping hoes," Tate said in one widely circulated clip. "Like, you go somewhere, there's some bitch. She's like 'Hi,' you're like 'Yeah, hi, I'm the man.' Oops, you fuck her. Oops, now she's in love with you and shit. The real G's know what I'm saying. Like, you're pimpin' bitches, and you don't even *want* to. When you're pimpin' bitches like me, it's a full-time job."

Tate, whose lean body reflects his semi-successful kickboxing career but whose blank eyes betray an unknowable emptiness, has won thousands of impressionable acolytes over to his rank brand of unabashed dick-stroking rhetoric.

"You got convinced that being a strong man is toxic," manfluencer and full-time debate-bro Sneako says to one of his millions of young male followers. "That being a natural man, acting on your basic organic desires is 'problematic.' You got programmed. That's why your nails are painted. That's why you're 6'3", 230 lbs. but saying [in a mocking voice] *I think platforming these people is bad!* A man shouldn't sound like that. Why do you talk like that? What happened to you?"

It's the kind of blank-eyed soliloquy that gently reminds you that, while recording, these phones turn into little mirrors.

On just a single casual scroll/stroll through the manosphere, I was able to pluck this bouquet of beauties grown in the wild: "Every man has a warrior inside of him; it must be accessed through continual delayed gratification." "Do not give your strength unto women for those who ruin kings," which is actually Proverbs 31:3. "A woman having an Instagram is 100% cheating." "Chivalry is dead and women killed it." "Modern women like to be cheated on."

Another tried and true trope on TikTok is the "How did men go from This to This?" video, in which the first "This" is represented by grainy photos of troops in the trenches of World War II or furrow-faced cowboys squinting indifferently from a momentary pause in their grueling daily ranchwork, and the second "This" is, like, Harry Styles in a borrowed floral gown posing in a meadow or something. This simple juxtaposition makes an even simpler justification for rusty old arguments that "real masculinity" is facing (yawn) another existential crisis.

Why does this stuff work on men? For worse and for worse, the hole in men's souls doubles as a gap in the market. And while the business of selling men their own manhood is as old as time itself, the current climate of hyper-individualism has driven American men into an uncanny variation on isolation—a population of loners created in each other's image.

Manfluencers reinforce suspicions men have about themselves, hunches offered to them by their dads and older brothers and uncles and coaches and the men they see in public. They capitalize on men's low self-esteem in order to sell them heroic comebacks acquired through workout programs, intermittent fasting, and mental focus ("grindset"). Manfluencers tell men they are unlovable, that they are only valued when they are of use to others, that their status is equivalent to their "body count" (number of sexual partners). Because men derive so much of their self-worth from external validation from other men, they eagerly glom on to preconstructed value systems that keep their power in place, while still making their success seem against the odds.

With its supplements and sales pitches, hucksters and gurus, and suffocating conformity dressed up as individual discovery, manosphere masculinity is, at best, a multilevel marketing scheme, and at worst, a form of crypto. Those men it lures invest everything into it. Their idealized notion of what makes a "high value man"—financially independent, physically fit, sexually successful—rests upon the mastery of an unstable infrastructure built upon a foundation of insecurity. Women are rated like commodities, and the chemistry of attraction is externalized as a system of market factors rather than a personal portfolio of desires. "Game" is essentially a transposition of sexual politics into the language and dynamics of economics. Guys trade tips and tricks to optimize their SMV (Sexual Market Value), a thing I swear I did not just make up. One YouTube video calculates SMV as a factor of height, facial features, body type, IQ, location, and several other factors—all condensed to a convenient something-point-something metric.

But masculinity as it is currently marketed to men—as a commodity, a program, a regimen of behaviors and attitudes, a pricey myth—runs counter to the true nature of the stuff, which can be inexpensively expressed through confidence, compassion, strength, and through the values we inherit from and bestow to one another. Indeed, the way each man defines our own masculinity may be the only truly individual thing about us—which sounds like an unbelievable idea.

This may be why guys consume manfluencer content with an attention level somewhere between oblivion and fervor. Certain men's allegiance to outdated strictures of gender is ultimately an expression of fear, a clinging to the edge of the pool for lack of knowing how not to sink. Men follow men who followed men. Together we continue to cultivate a tradition of undoing each other, all of us shoveling coal into the same old engines of traditional masculinity that blacken our lungs and shorten our breath.

Men can reconnect with our true selves, but so much of who we are is frozen under the surface. Maybe this is why we love to hoist a boulder over our heads, throw it as hard as we can, smash the ice so it knows we were there.

VII

HENRY

I N 1993, I wanted out.

That meant everything. I wanted out of my room, out of my house. I wanted out of my classes and my school. I wanted out of Fitchburg and Worcester County. I wanted out of my homework and my job. I wanted out of my future.

It was my cranky punk phase, swirled together with a standard-issue honors student insouciance and some real-time gay repression. I wrote angsty letters to myself in smudgy journals and read a lot of books I didn't understand (at my dishwashing job at Slattery's, I kept a copy of Sartre's *Existentialism and Human Emotions* and Camus's *The Myth of Sisyphus* on a shelf for "light reading" between rushes). I kept thinking I could think my way out of my dire teenage situation, find some college far enough away that I could let my guard down and see who I might become when I wasn't performing the person I wasn't. In the meantime, I found means of fleeting escape.

I became a theater kid, which anyone could have seen coming. My entire fascination with professional wrestling, for instance, was more founded on the internecine drama than any of the simulated combat. And in another outbreak of the least surprising news ever, I was developing a taste for the show tunes my parents would bring back from their theater dates in Boston. I would wait for the house to be empty so I could absolutely flame out over the balcony of our staircase like the Evita of Fitchburg. At school I auditioned for every play, every skit, any opportunity to become someone else.

But most of my solo time I spent playing video games. I'd pass hours sunk into a dusty beanbag in front of the shitty old TV relegated to our basement, shoving cartridge after cartridge into a Sega Genesis. The console was a marked upgrade from the Nintendo Entertainment System my brothers and I had spent close to a decade beating up—Sega's then-advanced 16-bit resolution an eye-popping upgrade, allowing graphics with then-unprecedented richness of color, depth, and texture.

These attributes were put to full use by game designers adapting stand-up arcade titles for home use, putting every available pixel into robust renderings of hyper-muscular heroes. When selecting my character in any of the dozens of side-scrollers or button-masher fighting games, I reliably chose the biggest virtual bodies: If it was *Street Fighter II*, I chose the mohawked musclebeast Zangief. If it was *Golden Axe*, I was the Arnold-inspired barbarian Ax Battler. If it was *Final Fight*, I opted for the barrel-chested, pipe-swinging Mayor Mike Haggar. If it was the *Bloodsport*-inspired *Pit-Fighter* (which I've since learned was nearly titled *Masters of Buffness*), I'd pick the flexing ex-pro wrestler Buzz—whose body was a digitized version of bodybuilder Bill Chase's. (A year later, *Mortal Kombat* would vastly improve upon this high-res recruitment of real bodies into the gaming realm.)

I still remember the temporary buzz I'd get playing *Pit-Fighter* when Buzz would get his hands on an intermittently appearing power pill—emblazoned with a *P*—that would send him into a rage of temporary invincibility and lend his body a pulsating green glow. I also recall the unsettling feeling I'd experience every third round, when Buzz was forced to fight an identically beefy doppelganger of himself in a "grudge match." It had a Lynchian creep factor before I knew what that was.

The photo-realism of *Pit-Fighter* was the brainchild of creator and Atari star Gary Stark, something of a fitness buff himself, who recruited beefcake game models from his gym. In front of a green screen, the musclebound models performed the signature moves of various characters like Southside Jim (James Thompson), Chainman Eddie (Eddie Venancio), and the Masked Warrior (a husky harnessed harbinger of the leather daddies I'd encounter in real life a decade later, played by bodybuilder Bill McAleenan).

The virtual reality of their bodies transposed into such a realistic digital palette was something I'd never encountered. Buzz's finely formed bulging body on the glassy curve of the screen held for me an erotic charge—not to mention a pre-echo of the tech-enhanced images of bodies that would soon dominate the Internet.

Nowhere was this high-resolution revolution on fuller-bodied display than in my favorite game, Sega's *Altered Beast*, which came as a pack-in with the Genesis. Set in a nonspecific but seemingly ancient Grecian otherworld, the game pits an unnamed hero against several slow-scrolling levels' worth of decrepit but persistent zombies. Your character—a former warrior freshly resurrected by Zeus, who intones "RISE FROM YOUR GRAVE" at the game's outset—punches his way through a graveyard teeming with lunging blue wolves and slowly advancing undead. The wolves, when kicked, release a blue orb that, once nabbed by your character, summoned another scratchy voice sample of Zeus: "POWER UP!" And in a sexually charged update of Mario's magic mushroom (which traditionally doubles the size of the adventurous plumber), the already strapping hero would undergo a sudden steroidal growth spurt—his tunic splitting, his arms swelling, his strength boosted. A second orb takes our hero to further extremes—his shirt tears off completely as his body plumps into a Michelin-man of muscle with oversized pecs, washboard abs, and a loincloth shrunken into a Speedo.

The final available dose of wolf juice in each round transforms the hero into one of four possible therianthropic manbeasts—a ripped werewolf, a burly-bodied grizzly bear, a super-swole tiger, and a shredded dragon, each capable of different forms of zapping, all wreaking greater doses of havoc.

In each of these games, I found myself less wrapped up in the challenges the games presented, less driven by a desire to win, then I was taken by the opportunity to occupy a body that wasn't mine, however virtual. *Altered Beast* in particular offered me a playable metaphor of my own inner demons and my longing to release them—a feeling that I contained something far bigger and more powerful than what I'd come into the world with. And a desire to punch my way through a swarm of zombies.

On that note, I was also immersing myself in music. After befriending some of the skaters at my school and putting in some initiation hours loitering at the Leominster Denny's, I started going to local punk shows. Though most of the music that made it to my Walkman reflected a budding queer sensibility—mixtape after mixtape of woozy, chorus-drenched Cocteau Twins, steely-sexy Depeche Mode, maudlin Morrissey—when it came to live shows, my tastes took a plunge into the basement.

Every weekend there was a different set of hardcore bands turning some
VFW hall, Unitarian function room, or unlucky suburban basement upside
down. I learned to navigate entirely new subcategories of my fellow kids.
There were straight-edge boys with giant *X*'s Sharpie'd on the backs of their
hands—they'd slap a cigarette out of your mouth or throw your snuck-in
beer on the ground just to start shit. There were the punk girls with black
lipstick, claws of neon pink bangs, pristine white Doc Martens, and tongue
bars. There were buzz-cutted skinheads, bruisers whose politics (and relative
threat to your personal safety) were allegedly coded into their bootlaces.
(I was too scared to inquire further.) There were skaters and stoners and
goths and gays, each bearing their own identifying markings and behaviors.

Just as I would do in the halls of my high school, I learned to drift
around and among these extracurricular factions like a ghost, haunting
their spaces from the periphery. When I felt brave or anonymous enough,
I'd throw my body into the pit at the edge of the stage—a whirling vortex
of swinging fists and kicking steel-toes. I'd get my glasses punched off. I'd
get footprints on my back. I'd get clocked in the ear and savor the heat
on my head and the sudden thud of swollen silence. Different bands drew
different factions of (mostly) boys to climb over and collide with each other.
Dive, Entropy, Opposition.

I actually loved the scream and scrape and violence of the music. My
tinnitus today reminds me of how I'd vanish into its volume, the wash of
distortion screaming from stacks of amps, the smallest stray sound resulting
in howling feedback through the hot microphones strewn around the stage,
the smash of crash cymbals and the chest-clearing pummel of a double-kick
drum—the sounds penetrated my body, excited a buried instinct, resonated
through my bones.

All around me were other disaffected, angry, emotionally mute, and by
vast majority white young men, each releasing his respective rage, all putting
our individual alienation to collective use, unleashing on each other through
the omnidirectional vengeance of the pit, shouting the same chorus like a
cannon into the same sour-smelling microphone thrust into the throng.

To survive in the pit was to savor its abuse: each time I got punched
in the face, I felt newly initiated, baptized—like I belonged. How was this
possible? In attempting to abandon the tropes, trends, and trials of traditional masculinity, I'd somehow gone voluntarily kicking and screaming
into a more feral model, one that somehow excused itself under the banner

of self-expression. I'm reminded of a 1984 image by the artist Barbara Kruger depicting a pair of hands bound by chains, superimposed with three bars of text:

You construct intricate rituals / which allow you to touch / the skin of other men

For years I was intoxicated by this intersection of art and violence, as though the latter were deployed specifically to obscure the former. The circular swirl of the pit was an ouroboros of urges, the fight devouring the dance, young men knocking each other out, then picking each other up.

It wasn't common at the time for the basement sounds of punk and hardcore to scratch the surface of the mainstream. In 1993, Nirvana was still leading a surge of heavily distorted grunge, with bands like Smashing Pumpkins, the Melvins, Tool, and Stone Temple Pilots laying it on thick. But that year I also found myself secretly smitten with an unlikely American folk hero—one who knew how to growl my language and seemed to embody a part of myself that I didn't.

Henry Rollins, whose years as the vocalist in the legendary punk band Black Flag were before my time and whom I'd only seen in videos on MTV, had a body like the ones from the Soloflex ads I'd stay up past *SNL* by myself to watch. (I would also devotedly tape them.) A master storyteller in his own right, Rollins followed his work in Black Flag with a name-making run in the "spoken word" scene (a term he loathed), but he was also a prolific writer, turning up often with fiery tour diaries, diatribes, and dispatches from the front lines of American punk. His throat-straining 1992 single with the Rollins Band, "Low Self Opinion," felt like a reprimand against my own self-imposed isolation. But I was more struck by the messenger than the message.

An inextricable part of Rollins's persona was his body. Shortly before the band's 1984 tour, Rollins had started hitting the weights hard, his body thickening around him. It was a move that some read as regressive and macho—a bad look for an anarcho-punk outfit presumably fighting the power. Others thought the beefening was a physical and emotional shield against angry Black Flag fans—their distaste for Rollins (who had replaced original singer Keith Morris) had occasionally turned violent, with people punching and stabbing the singer at shows.

But as out of place as Rollins's body was in the punk milieu of 1993, it was very much of its time: a crossover from the new generation of action stars led by Jean-Claude Van Damme, a more road-weathered take on the hardbody sexplosion in pop culture led by Mark Wahlberg and his tight white Calvins, and a reclamation of raw male aggression in service of psychological introspection. Rollins's muscles felt like an extension of his ethos: the products of a strict and sober DIY approach to the body, reclaiming the physical vocabulary of the jocks who had tormented him in his youth and using it to articulate a politics of the body—his life itself as a form of resistance training.

In 1993, Rollins published an article about his journey in the gym for the men's fashion magazine *Details*—the sartorial outlet an unlikely platform for Rollins, seldom seen in this era wearing much more than shorts. His piece "Rollins on Working Out" (later retitled "The Iron" for his 1997 collection of essays) was far from the usual celebrity profile instructing readers to emulate his abs or achieve his signature stage squat. Instead, it was a probing piece of self-examination, a consideration of the body.

"I believe that one defines oneself by reinvention," he writes. "To not be like your parents. To not be like your friends. To be yourself. To cut yourself out of stone."

He recounts in the essay his experience at the age I was reading it. He describes himself as having been a "skinny and spastic" kid who was "there to be antagonized," yet consumed by a "rage that filled my every waking moment" and made him "wild and unpredictable." He recalls hating what he saw in the mirror and envying the well-manicured ease with which his fellow students carried themselves.

He also recalls the intervention of one Mr. Pepperman, a powerfully built Vietnam veteran who taught history and gave the young beanpole Rollins a stern wake-up call. "You're a skinny little faggot," his teacher said. "This weekend, have your mommy take you to Sears and buy one of those one-hundred-pound sand-filled weight sets and drag it home. I'll show you how to use it."

Pepperman put Rollins on a training program and offered to periodically punch the teen in the solar plexus as a means of charting his progress. Rollins trained devotedly, never missing a workout and progressively getting stronger, adding more and more weight to the bar. "My body had a shape," he writes. "You couldn't say *shit* to me."

From here the essay turns into a gym bag of philosophical tidbits derived from Rollins's success under the weights. He advises novice lifters to work with the iron and not against it ("The material you work with is that which you come to resemble") and assures them that the iron is an antidote for not just weakness, but loneliness. He cautions readers not to become separated from their bodies—as I had—that in the consistency of weights there was great power to be unlocked.

"Always there like a beacon in pitch black," Rollins writes of his weights. "I have found the iron to be my greatest friend. It never freaks out on me, never runs, never lies."

Rollins, now in his early sixties, continues to do speaking gigs, podcasts, TV, and radio shows as well as occasional appearances in films; in 2019's *Dreamland*, he played an extra lean, extra mean child-trafficking crime boss named Hercules.

"I *hate* men," he told the *Daily Beast* in 2020 when asked how his history as a survivor of sexual abuse influenced his portrayal of Hercules. "I go case-by-case but by and large . . . and including me. I am part of the reason why the world sucks at times. I don't think women are starting wars. Men are part of the reason why you don't get to have nice things."

Despite the crowd of musclemen fighting for my teenage attention on TV, movies, and video games, it was Rollins who made me realize I wanted out of my body. I hated it. I hated that I was stuck in it. Hated that it was how I was seen by others. Loathed its hard lines and ugly paunches, my bunchy dick and gangly legs, my slim arms and boyish neck.

I wanted his tree trunk neck, his volcanic traps (extra so in the video for "Liar," slathered in red paint). I coveted the breadth of his back and the rocking horsepower of his legs. But mostly I just wanted to feel like he looked like he felt. Forged out of something molten, hardened into something formidable.

An attempt to ingratiate myself to my own Mr. Pepperman, i.e., Coach Cosenza, didn't go as successfully as Henry's experience. Coach had returned from some coach-conference thing with a fat white three-ring binder emblazoned with the logo of some program he'd just signed on to: BIGGER, FASTER, STRONGER. He'd just gotten what he considered his own gym finished in the basement locker room below the basketball court—a fully appointed spread of free weights and plate-loaded machines, caged into a corner of the renovated locker room with a wall of chain-link fence.

To his brow-furrowing surprise, I volunteered to join his weekly lifting unit, dedicating myself to four hours of training through the week on all the primary lifts—bench, squat, dead lift. The thicker boys from the football and hockey teams exchanged puzzled glances at my sudden interest but quietly accepted me among their ranks. Coach taught us the basics of how to lower the barbell for our bench press, how to situate the bar for our squats, how to lift with the legs, not the back. And I was doing OK at it; got a couple of "Atta boys!" that made me feel momentarily present.

But one thing Coach did not teach us was proper handling of weight plates. This was a lesson I instead learned in the flush-faced instant when a forty-five-pound plate I'd set down on the floor casually rolled (seemingly of its own volition) right into the brand-new mirrored wall Coach had just finished installing. Moments after the plate kissed the corner of the glass, a long crack searched upward and split the mirror into a thousand pieces, sending large jagged shards sliding down the length of the gym. A ghastly silence stalled the gym's relentless clanging. Our school colors were red and gray, and Coach C. turned both of those that day.

Humiliated and officially banned from the high school gym (and condemned to running miles for the rest of the semester), I resumed my weight training at home in the attic, where the small Weider weight bench my older brother had received years before as a Christmas gift had been laid in limbo.

The bench sat in the center of the unfinished room, sealed off behind a serious-looking door. It sat beneath a single dramatically hung light bulb, and between lolling pink tongues of insulation drooping from the ceiling. It was a crimson padded bench with a slight sparkle like the seat of my Huffy. Its rack cradled a slim steel barbell that fit a corresponding set of black iron weight plates—about one hundred pounds total, just like Henry's. In a cardboard box, we had a grip exerciser and one of those chest expanders Charles Atlas had peddled—two handles attached by a trio of springs. There was a curl bar and a leg extension that could be pinned to the edge of the bench.

And, most importantly, there was a beam. It ran across the A-frame of the attic and was just sturdy enough to support my weight. Night after night I'd hang there, my memory still haunted by my spectacular failure years before in the Presidential Fitness Test but metabolized into something like fresh motivation. I'd tense up and pull, my arms bowing into rigid L's, my wimpy lats straining to raise me. One . . . Two . . . Three . . . .

And then I'd fall into the arms of failure.

As I reached senior year, and as the prospect of truly escaping from Fitchburg and potentially finding myself became a possibility I could barely make out on the horizon, I started to feel myself struggling against a different type of resistance—a grudge match between myself and myself.

Sometimes after my dishwashing shift, after I'd dragged out the mats and sprayed out the trash cans, after I'd changed out of my wet clothes and into dry sweats that still reeked of fishy water and trap grease, I'd get in the car, put on something loud—Helmet, Quicksand, Drive Like Jehu—and I'd drive, past my driveway, past the park, past the city limit, and past where the streetlamps ceased on the winding woodland Ashby State Road. I'd drive until I could only see the two cones of my headlights slicing the darkness.

About two miles up Ashby State, a small clearing opened up on the left—a modest parking lot for a small red roadhouse of a bar. An unlit Miller High Life sign hung by the road, a panel of Western lettering softly announcing the joint's given name: The Country Lounge.

In Fitchburg parlance, the only known (or suspected) gay bar in a twenty-mile radius was referred to as the Goody Goody—a nickname I could tell was as old as homophobia itself—and I only knew of it because our cross-country team was forced to run this road, and a reliable exchange of gay jokes among my teammates always greeted our passing like a mile marker.

I felt drawn to the place like one of the moths fluttering around its blinking neon signs. I'd drive slowly past, U-turn a ways up the road, come back just as slowly on the closer side of the road. I'd squint to see if I could see anything through the windows. I dared not pull in, for fear of my Nissan getting clocked by god knows who was in there.

But who was in there? Whose cars were these? Unassuming brown sedans. An Oldsmobile. A pickup truck like the ones I'd see at the hardware store. A bumper sticker touting an honors student. I remember scaring the shit out of some poor man who stepped furtively outside the bar and did a double take at my drive-by—the two of us terrified of knowing each other. I remember dimming my lights and seeing pairs of men walk into the woods, unaware I was watching.

I remember accelerating away when another car would eventually come down the road, paralyzed by the fear that someone could tail me, trail me home, expose me to my folks, or beat the fuck out of me on the street. I remember my heart pounding, both in fear and in thrall of the thrill of my fear.

Here, on the periphery of everything, I watched men and their bodies collide and vanish behind closed doors. I wanted in. I wanted out.

THE DRAG OF BIG

O N MY WALK TO THE GYM TODAY, some bad news buzzed my phone: a small riot had erupted a few miles away in Silver Spring, where an independent bookstore had been attempting to host its Drag Story Hour. A local drag queen named Charlemagne Chateau would read books to children that, according to the Story Hour chapter president, would "highlight the values of kindness and being inclusive."

Naturally, this incited violence.

A small mob of assorted assholes and Proud Boys showed up in matching masks and embroidered caps, hoisting signs and menacing anyone who dared approach the bookstore. Their numbers were dwarfed by an ad hoc opposition group, the Parasol Patrol, who blocked the bookstore doors and shielded incoming patrons with a barrier of downturned rainbow umbrellas.

The throng of masked dweebs forced their voices lower and louder to berate any parents who dared bring their kids to the event: they were *pedophiles*, they were *predators*, they were *groomers*, they were *child abusers*. Police tried and failed to keep the factions separated. No one was arrested, but somehow the leader of the Parasol Patrol got his nose busted open.

What else is news?

In 2022, drag events faced over 141 protests and significant threats in a bizarrely belated backlash, including the November 19 shooting at Club Q in Colorado Springs, which left five people dead and at least seventeen others injured. One report from GLAAD found that threats against drag events in 2022 happened every 2.5 days. A loosely aligned coalition of neo-Nazis, Proud Boys, Patriot Front, Christian nationalists, and assorted militiamen and rando-Rambos have targeted drag storytime events at children's libraries and drag brunches at cafés and restaurants.

In practice, this swell of anti-drag activism has less to do with any good-faith protest against the family-friendliness of certain drag performers or even the art form itself. The surge of drag's mainstream popularity— made most visible via the success of the multiple-Emmy–winning *RuPaul's Drag Race*—has been weaponized and employed as a Trojan horse within which to package broader, more toxic political ideologies that are explicitly hostile to the existence of transgender, nonbinary, and queer people, and anyone else who dares move more freely about the gender spectrum (or even suggests one exists).

Thus, participants and attendees of drag events can now expect to be heckled, harassed, and worse by these ad hoc gangs of anonymous aggressors. Meanwhile, Republican politicians have introduced bills in eleven states to outlaw drag performances in specious service of children's safety, with legislatures in Tennessee and Texas successfully passing laws that explicitly and implicitly target drag performances.

Worse, many of these bills use language vague enough to target not just drag performances but transgender individuals. A bill in West Virginia, for instance, proposes to prohibit "any transvestite and/or transgender exposure, performances or display." Other bills define drag performers as any who exhibit "a gender identity that is different from the performer's gender assigned at birth"—extremely (and likely intentionally) dangerous language that makes clear that real target is the increasing cultural acceptance of fluid, nonbinary, and nontraditional expressions of gender.

"When you take one of these little kids and put them in front of drag queens that are men dressed like women, do you think that helps them or confuses them in regard to their own gender?" asked (Republican) Arkansas state senator Gary Stubblefield from the floor, tipping his hand.

The claim that anti-drag legislation protects children poorly cloaks the reality that these laws only protect patriarchal insecurities concerning the liberation of gender, particularly from those straight men who find themselves cowardly masking their faces before rolling up to harmless bottomless brunches with long guns, cryptic flags, and angry Cookie Monster voices.

What's going on? What's got men's performance briefs in such a twist over drag? Even before *RuPaul's Drag Race*, drag had entered the mainstream through RuPaul's own pop songs—"Supermodel (You Better Work)"—as well as big-screen features like 1994's *The Adventures of Priscilla, Queen of the Desert* and 1995's *To Wong Foo, Thanks for Everything! Julie Newmar.* To borrow a question from Bey: Why the sudden change?

For one thing, the intensified strictures of today's broken masculinity demand men abhor the very ambiguity that defines drag. This deeply programmed male repulsion by the feminine is why drag exists to begin with—it draws its transgressive force from the brazen violation of cross-dressing: men breaking uniform. The body of a drag queen—her big hair, her fierce paint, her rhinestones, her padded curves, her impossible heels, her tuck—is a defiance of the gravity of masculinity, a bursting of its seams.

Men are protective of their gender roles precisely because their gender roles are so protective of them. These roles provide lines, blocking, costumes, and direction—not to mention privilege. Gender roles are a foundation of rules upon which men can construct their identities, and they require a watertight seal. If gender becomes fluid, the fortress becomes porous. The guard is down, the gates are open.

The acute revulsion to drag among heterosexual men may also be due to its deceptively effortless subversion of masculinity's chronic *seriousness.* As much as drag inflates certain features of femininity, it also deflates core concepts of masculinity, puncturing its power with well-placed pinpricks of camp. Drag dismantles binaries of gender (masculine/feminine, hard/soft), celebrity (star/impersonator), and performance (tragic/comic), and in doing so, undermines the authority of those binaries, smudges them into a blur, blends them into a smoky eye, as it were. Broken masculinity relies on the girding of these binaries to derive its value, which is always comparative, always relative to the perceived weakness of others.

When, a year or so ago, my husband came out as nonbinary, their repositioning on the gender spectrum—their free movement about the cabin of our bodied journey together—made me suddenly hyper-conscious of my own assigned seat. When I consider my own personal misalignments with my gender—my own resting state of physical, sexual, and emotional asynchrony with the enforced march of "manhood"—I usually return to my state of relative comfort with not quite fitting in, and have learned (at long last) that the guidelines of manhood are mine to define. But I do wonder how many men long to wander, even if just to stretch their legs.

Binaries put far too much pressure on the joint between our bodies and our identities; they presuppose a casual symmetry, a semiotic seesaw, a this and a that. But if men truly sought balance, we would grapple with gender like the irregular object it is: we would bring our full understanding to the particular shape of our gender roles, the burden we force ourselves to carry, as well as those carried by others. As men we need to tune more faithfully into our own bodies, examine what inhibits us from inhabiting them more fully and freely. We need to become conscious of how our bodies contain us.

Why is the breaking of binaries so difficult for some men? After all, it's not like we're incapable of understanding the nuances of a spectrum. Men are capable of rating their sexual conquests and experiences on precisely calibrated numerical scales. They can assemble fantasy football teams based on granular analyses of sprawling datasets. They can engineer their own avatars in video games down to the finest parameter and faintest whisker. They can go on and on about the miniscule distinctions that differentiate types of craft beers, guns, and UFC fighters. They maintain a comprehensive purview over the possibilities of tit shape. Yet, confronted with the now universally understood (or at least entertained) idea that gender itself comprises a continuum of identities, many men freak out: NOPE. THERE CAN ONLY BE TWO.

Much of this is because we've invested so much time and effort into playing our parts as men—the rehearsals, the memorization, the soliloquys into the mirror. But another reason is the perception among men, handed down over several generations of us now, that we—particularly us white men—have collectively ceded our cultural cache and political power to the steady erosion of feminism, multiculturalism, and social justice (the other climate change). For many men, their masculinity is akin to a kind of nationalism, a compulsion to champion and defend one's turf, even if one's turf is a prison cell.

It would be easy to suppose that men who are consumed with the upkeep of their own machismo are repulsed by drag simply for its aggressive pursuit of the feminine, its inherent queerness, its dissolution of social and sexual norms, its hyperbolic beauty standards, or the sheer amount of Cher. And certainly, all of these play a part.

But sometimes I suspect men's aversion to drag also stems from a deep understanding of it. Sometimes I think drag, in all of its outsized presence, overperformance of gender, and overinflation of its signifiers—hits men a little too close to home.

After all, what are big muscles but drag?

Decades spent being not quite one of the boys drove me to consciously overcompensate by growing muscles like massive protective pads. When I started building my body I wanted to take everything about myself that I'd once struggled to hide—my waify arms, my weak back, my absent ass—and make them impossible to miss. I wanted to build a new me atop the old one, I wanted to poof it with beef, contour its curves. I wanted to present anew, be noticed upon entrance, project beauty and power and confidence just by showing up differently, making more of what made me less. I wanted my body to be commitment to the bit. I wanted to become a real man by becoming an unreal one—a form in submission to a fantasy.

You hear a lot about Hercules and his twelve labors, but seldom do you hear about the demigod in semiretirement.

Not long after Herc successfully abducted Cerberus, the three-headed dog guard of the underworld, to satisfy the twelfth and final trial in Eurystheus's purportedly impossible scavenger hunt, Hercules entered an archery contest. The prize was Iole, the daughter of King Eurytus of Oechalia.

Predictably, Hercules smoked everyone in the competition. He had learned well from his former teacher, Eurytus himself (ouch!). But Eurytus feared for the safety of his daughter in the hands of Hercules. These were the same hands that, in a fit of murderous rage induced by the embittered goddess Hera, had killed his first wife, Megara, as well as their boys. Rather than risk Iole to one of Herc's legendary murderous rages, the king hit our hero with a resounding nope and rescinded the prize.

Only one person, Prince Iphytus—an alleged part-time lover of Herc's—cried foul at the withdrawal and came to his defense, to no avail. Hercules left Oechalia enraged and empty-handed. It's safe to say he didn't properly process his anger, because shortly after, he killed Iphytus, tossing him to his death from the top of the walls of Tiryns. (Another murderous rage.)

Long saga short, the Delphic oracle Xenoclea declared that Hercules could only atone for his crime by submitting to a year of slavery and was thus sold to Omphale, the queen of Lydia.

Under Omphale's eye, Hercules performed several mini-trials—he captured the trolly forest creatures, the Kerkopes; he killed an abusive vineyard owner (and his daughter) with the former's own hoe; he defeated the raiding Itoni mobs; and he slaughtered a monstrous snake-beast-thing.

But his year of service to Omphale is best known for the "women's work" assigned to the hero—attending to Omphale's needs, spinning wool with her maidens, and dressing in the queen's silken gowns (if anything at all). The queen, meanwhile, had taken to toting around Herc's giant club and draping herself in the trophy of his first trial, the pelt of the Nemean lion.

Artists have long fascinated over the reversal of these roles: Bartholomeus Spranger's painting *Hercules and Omphale* (c. 1585) delights in Hercules's humiliation in a flouncy gown, as well as the Herculean stature of the club-wielding Omphale. Around 1602, Peter Paul Rubens painted a voluptuous near-nude Herc wincing, pinching a thread, and holding a spinner's distaff as Omphale tugs at his ear. Antonio Bellucci's 1698 painting *Hercules in the Palace of Omphale* finds the hero clutching a spindle like his surrendered club as maidens thread flowers into his hair. In Luigi Garzi's *Hercules and Omphale* (c. 1700) he shyly taps at a tambourine as cherubim flutter and giggling ladies gawk. Charles Gleyre's *Hercules and Omphale* plays up the comedy of a sausage-fingered Herc attempting to spin delicate threads of wool as Omphale and her coterie look on with a blend of desire and pity.

But my favorite image of Herc's year of relative rest and relaxation is *Hercules at the Feet of Omphale*, a lustrous painting by Belle Époque artist Gustave-Claude-Étienne Courtois.

Courtois had an eye, and a hand, for beautiful men. For his Hercules model, he selected strongman and Greco-Roman wrestler Maurice Deriaz. The 5-foot, 6-inch, 200-pound Deriaz—known as *Le lion Suisse*—was one of seven athletic Swiss-born brothers living in France, and between 1907 and 1913, he was Courtois's most muscular muse.

In Deriaz, Courtois saw the body of a demigod—so much so that he cast him as two, in addition to painting a striking, sensual portrait of the wrestler as himself. As the Grecian hero Perseus in 1913's *Persée délivrant Andromède*, Deriaz's glowing body stands astride the freshly harpooned sea monster Cetus. He extends his meaty arm and an indifferent gaze toward the comparably nondescript Andromeda, and there's more detectable attraction between painter and model than hero and princess.

But there's a magic about Deriaz as Hercules in *Hercule aux pieds d'Omphale*. How at peace he looks, down on one knee, gazing obediently up at Omphale, guiding a golden thread through his fingers on to a big beefy bobbin for her pleasure. He is captive to the queen, scantily clad in pelts and ribbons, and seemingly at ease with an eternity in Omphale's service and Courtois's adoration.

Technically, it's supposed to be Hercules at his lowest point. But at the feet of Omphale, his big body hits different. He's a gentle giant, a monster under control, sure, but here, liberated from his labors, stripped of his trophies and triumphs, relieved of his myth, we see Hercules happy—most himself when allowed to be someone entirely different.

VIII

TOUKO

T HE FIRST PART OF ME to come out of the closet was my voice. The rest of me wasn't ready. I was terrified of myself, of growing further implicated with everything I knew I wasn't supposed to be. I dreaded my self-realization as a gay man with each day that made that realization clearer. I knew from the news anchors and their grim numbers that my sexuality was a pending death sentence. I was raised to parse the gay body as a grave, a vessel of doom, property of AIDS.

When I arrived in Boston for my freshman year of college in 1994, the first HIV protease inhibitor, saquinavir, was still a year away from FDA approval. Over two million people had been newly infected with the virus the prior year, with AIDS cases peaking at just over 106,000. AIDS remained the looming second shoe to drop after any HIV+ diagnosis, and the young gay men I'd never meet in the cities I didn't live in concocted their own cocktails of optimistic hope and nihilistic abandon in order to smother their anguish and blur the uncertain days.

Still, arriving in Boston with a suitcase instead of the backpack I'd take on weekend trips into the city as a high schooler felt significant, like landing on a new planet with new air, a civilization full of foreign bodies where I'd learn a new language, choose a new name, join a people. The commuter rail from Fitchburg had been a lifeline late in my high school tenure. I'd bike down to the depot ass-early and ride the ninety minutes and dozen or so stops to Harvard Square, where I'd spend entire days slumming around the "Pit," watching the crust punks and the law students shoot each other dirty looks. I'd buy records from bands I'd never heard at Newbury Comics. I'd buy giant Dickies and electric blue Doc Martens at Allston Beat. I'd try on versions of myself and see what fit. Not knowing who I was was an addictive form of freedom.

As scared as I was of myself, I still longed to see myself reflected back in others. I wondered if I'd hate my awkward body less if somebody else might love it. But I couldn't bring my body to be me.

So instead, I sent out my voice. In the 1990s, gay virtuality was the province of print and the phone. In the backs of the men's magazines I'd continue to page through, in the back of Boston's now-shuttered and then-stowed-away gay bookstores (like Glad Day and Calamus), I'd read the boxy little classified ads printed in the closing pages like clues transmitted in a code I'd yet to decipher: "MWM, 45, 5'9", 230, 8 cut, dom top for serv btm no fats or fems"; "GWM, 23, 5'10", 160, blond blue physical smooth discreet jock 4 coach"; "GBM, 30, 5'8", 140, ddf ex-mil for same."

The personals in the porns were dead ends for me—they required an SASE sent through the mail with a written response and the idea of leaving a paper trail of my unspoken desires terrified me. But the local alt-weekly, the *Boston Phoenix*, printed its own adult section, segregated from the rest of the paper, with a grid of gay personals fenced in by quarter-page ads for dozens of niche-specific 976 premium-rate phone-sex lines. Each phone service promised hot uncensored man-on-man action with "real local guys"—an assurance that, despite my isolation from any sign of community, there were more of us, living life and searching for traces of each other. The ads were illustrated with studs in torn-open shirts showing lusciously shaded pecs—images abducted from old drawings by the Finnish homoerotic artist Touko Laaksonen, a.k.a. Tom of Finland, or amateurishly rendered in the artist's voluptuous style.

The personals ads in the *Phoenix* were tied to voicemail boxes, where you could tap in a four-digit mailbox number and hear a short prerecorded message from one of the "men seeking men." I remember scanning the listings for men whose stats I could fathom into some sort of parasocial attraction. Every man was self-proclaimed as "masculine"—back then, it was common to sell yourself as "straight-acting" as well—so I scanned the weights for men whose stated forms fit the outline I'd drawn in my head: I wanted one of the men from the magazine covers, crossing his thick arms, creasing his macho brow, a beefcake, a bruiser, a bully. There was something about the body of a bully that I wanted to love. It was as though I craved a man who could physically force me into myself.

From the isolation, darkness, and silence of the closet, I simply wanted to hear what another gay man sounded like. I'd listen to their greetings, repeat them by pressing the pound key, sculpt an imaginary body around the wire frame of their voices: Some of them you could tell were pushing themselves into a lower, darker register to sound more manly. Others dwelled in silken treble, feathery and feminine, helpless to hide their softness, or uninterested in such effort—i.e., actually proud.

Even when I found a voice I liked, one that I could imagine curling up in my ear as a whisper before bed, I never crossed the line of the beep, never left a response. I'd close my eyes and listen to the crowd of strangers' voices assembled in my memory. A party in the darkness where no one meets.

Once these one-way conversations led me back to hopelessness, I branched out into the 976 lines. Most were one dollar for the first minute and a dime or two for every additional minute—way out of my student budget. I stuck to the free group chat lines, which were accessible through toll-free local numbers and predictably free-for-alls. Like an analog version of the bathhouses I would years later be bold enough to enter, the group chat lines felt like virtual labyrinths. Callers would start out in a "lobby" where multiple connections would shade the line with breaths—you could feel the presence of a dozen absent bodies.

You could also opt to move through a queue of callers sorted by what they were searching for into "rooms" that sounded like virtual gay bars: The Dungeon, The Locker Room, The Man Hole. Free of the fear and loathing of my body, I converted myself into pure energy, a signal searching for a connection. An automated voice would growl *You're being connected* and another voice would appear on the line.

I quickly learned that my wispy "Hello?" was a nonstarter—men would hear it and immediately hit pound to advance to the next caller. I started adding some gravel to the edges of my voice, weighing it down to a lower octave, or relying on a raspy whisper to suggest my imaginary wife was sleeping upstairs. If my roommate was out partying, I'd go hours into the night talking with dozens of men until they were done and hung up. And when I was done and hung up, the crowd vaporized, my dorm room returned to a quiet prison, my body my cell.

It wasn't until the tail end of my college years that I fully accepted myself. I treated school as a way for me to retreat into my mind, my work, my lousy poems, and whatever other distractions on paper could keep me safe from the truth in real life. My life of the mind was really just an escape from my body—a physicality that felt too dangerous to fully engage. My waify form felt like a receipt for my bookish devotion, a way of exempting myself from notice. I was an idea of myself that hadn't yet been expressed.

Coming out meant going out, and with the small crew of queer friends I'd made at school, I eventually summoned enough confidence to cross the thresholds of Boston's then-many gay bars.

There were chummy pubs like Buddies and Sporters and Chaps. There were dark dance bars like the Loft, Man Ray, and Machine. Some were unmarked, like the 119 Merrimack—a bear bar full of men who had strayed from their Bruins game, or the Napoleon Club, where the senior set of tweed-clad dads in three-piece suits would croon Cole Porter songs around an out-of-tune Steinway. Some were sketchy and occasionally stabby, like Playland—a bucket of blood that was a favorite of hustlers and queens.

At Luxor, walls of screens would loop Madonna videos or heavily edited clean cuts of highly stylized porn tapes. At Ramrod, I'd tremble at the sight of beefy cigar-chomping leather daddies in full regalia and tall boots, leaning against the walls and surveying the room behind opaque aviators. At Quest, hunky go-go boys in jockstraps and G-strings gyrated atop black plywood pedestals, the disco balls and spinning lights throwing illuminated confetti over their oiled bodies as they flexed and posed.

At every bar I entered, I was surrounded by the men from the *Honcho* magazines stashed under the mattress in my dorm. It was as though they'd sprung from the construction sites, biker gangs, and football teams so tenderly simulated in the pages of *Inches*, *Torso*, and *Mandate*. They wore high-and-tight military crew cuts, tank tops, tight jeans, and tighter moustaches. They wore leather vests over studded harnesses with worn chaps hugging ancient Levi's. Or they wore nothing but the legally defined minimum of clothing (for example, a jockstrap adapted with a bar towel into an ersatz loincloth), letting the ripples and heaves of their physiques speak for themselves in the form of a freshly attained pump from the gym. I'd push through the packed dance floors, between throngs of sweating, moving bodies, a tangle of groping hands, a bramble of stubble, a mélange of musk and muscle.

It was as though a grand inversion had flipped everything I'd known about manhood. Here, the muscles were meant to invite contact rather than conflict—they attracted those who knew how to read them and repelled those who didn't. Here, men's bodies were meant to be looked at, gazed up, fawned over. Here, men held each other close and nibbled on each other's necks. They tugged each other's nipples, and they pressed their hips together in a swaying slow dance held together by magnetism. They smiled and kissed, sang the chorus to "Express Yourself" at the top of their lungs, they sweated and cried and restored what they'd lost with vodka and club soda.

I was naive and tipsy enough, in the 1990s, to have thoughts like: *On the dance floor we are all one body!* The reality was that I was completely overwhelmed by bodies, the variety of them, all more attractive to me than my own. Bodies longing to be looked at, noticed, seen after however long in hiding. If we weren't exactly one, we were at least united in fate and mission: to confirm our existence through presence and pleasure, to embrace ourselves by embracing each other, to make of our bodies our lives, to make our way by force.

It being the 1990s, one could also sense in the air (and in the bars) the insidious arrival of a paradigm shift, downloading as slowly as a lurid JPEG over a dial-up connection. The Internet—or the World Wide Web as we understood it—was starting to open up massive channels of queer infrastructure.

The rise of AOL chat rooms, primordial online dating hubs like Gay. com, and the proliferation of niche-specific "web rings" and newsgroups all signaled a migration of queer culture to the virtual, and with it, a trend toward disembodied sociality that would come to characterize gay social life in the twenty-first century, when cruising apps like Grindr and Scruff assemble thousands of men into a grid of cropped bodies—a hyperclassical exhibition of headless torsos.

I remember dancing at the 119 one night. Shitfaced on Snapple mixed with my roommate's peach schnapps. Just a mess. CeCe Peniston was growling "Fiiiiiii-nally!" through a partially blown speaker and I was twirling around a fake palm tree that had somehow managed its way into the décor. I was halted in my twirl by the stare and smile of an older man leaning against the bar—a look that felt like a lasso. I felt like I had seen him before, and I had; he looked like all of the men in the ads for the group chat lines—one of Tom's men. That was on purpose.

His eyes were shadowed under the ridge of his brow. His hair was cropped in a cop-like crew cut. His stubble was perfectly manicured so as not to appear perfectly manicured. His unbuttoned flannel framed a chiseled furry chest, and his hairy shoulders stretched the holes that had once been sleeves. His thumbs were tucked behind his belt, and when he noticed he'd caught my gaze, he tugged up on the waist to display what he had to offer. I was so fucked up, couldn't believe it was happening, that this man was real, that his eyes could really see me.

I wandered nervously over to him and his hands found my waist. He asked what my name was and I told him, but I don't think he heard it because I don't think I made a sound and I don't think he cared. I don't think it mattered anymore. In his arms I was a body, not a voice, not a word.

BEAUTY AND
THE BEEF

I N FEBRUARY 1976, just a couple of weeks before I was born, the Whitney Museum of Art staged "Articulate Muscle: The Male Body in Art,"
a one-night "symposium, demonstration and film" (also billed as a "live
exhibition") of massive bodies, namely those of Frank Zane, Ed Corney,
and Arnold Schwarzenegger—the very trio of bodybuilders trailed by
novelist/ex-lifter Charles Gaines (pun not intended but appreciated) and
filmmaker George Butler for their book-turned-documentary, *Pumping Iron.*

"It was rather ironic that body building, a sport with a low repute in
this country, was the one to bridge the gap between art and athletics,"
wrote Katherine Lowry, covering the event for *Sports Illustrated*, "and that
its classical implications were substantial enough to be celebrated in a
world-famous and highly respected museum."

This irony did not prevent nearly three thousand people from cram-
ming into the galleries and sitting cross-legged on the floor like school-
children awaiting storytime (as well as a screening of a segment of *Pumping
Iron*). Writing for the *New Yorker*, Ian Frazier noted that "the crowd had
about three sophisticates for every two bodybuilders."

To set the scene for the exhibition, Lowry pulled a quote from Gaines's
own book: "The body itself is an art medium: malleable, capable of being
aesthetically dominated and formed the way clay is by a potter." As such,
the men on display weren't discussed, observed, or appreciated as physical
specimens or avatars of athletics, but rather, as "artists living inside their

own creations"—a perspective the men themselves may have been surprised to learn they held.

The artworks of the evening—Zane, Corney, and Schwarzenegger—each took the stage, a small revolving circular platform as might befit a tremendous cake. Zane was introduced as "the most classically symmetrical man in the history of bodybuilders" and impressed Lowry with a form "that looks as if someone had magic-wanded a perfect marble statue into flesh."

Frazier noted that "under the lights, [Zane's] skin looked like very expensive tan suede, and his face had the rapt, Madonna-like expression appropriate to great works of art." His tensed body, he wrote, was "trembling like a tuning fork."

The compact Corney (5 feet, 7 inches, 195 pounds) may not have struck as imposing a form as his more towering counterparts, but Lowry noted his fluidity, "style and grace." "If one doesn't accept bodybuilding as fine art," she wrote, "posing should at least be considered a performing art."

Schwarzenegger was last to step upon the pedestal. At the time, the six-time Mr. Olympia had only a single pseudonymous film credit—as "Arnold Strong" in the charmingly atrocious *Hercules in New York*. But his spot atop the esoteric Olympus of bodybuilding was prominent enough that his appearance on the platform inspired wild applause from the aesthetically inclined audience—especially when he pumped irony in the pose of Rodin's famous *Thinker*.

Not everybody was impressed. One art professor on the discussion panel with Schwarzenegger remarked that the bodybuilding poses on display reminded him of "some of the worst excesses of the Victorian era."

"That's just something somebody thinks," Arnold replied with the disdain Zeus might hold for noisy mortals. "For me, being here tonight is like going to heaven." Which I suppose must be something like the top of Mount Olympus.

———

Contemporary bodybuilding competitions for men break down into three main categories: bodybuilding, classic physique, and men's physique. The latter two focus on the attainment of an "old school" or "classic" bodybuilder look—a range of physiques that might run from Steve Reeves circa *Hercules* to Arnold circa *Pumping Iron*. The proportions (small waist, wide lats, thick thighs) as well as the poses (front double bicep, side chest, back double bicep) all hail from the fantasies of the past, all made real at sacred sites like Muscle Beach and Gold's Gym.

And then there's capital-B bodybuilding. While the aesthetic criteria by which bodybuilders are judged in competition also include mass, definition, symmetry, and proper proportions, the animating drive of the sport is simple: *Bigger*.

Those in the crowd at the Whitney who crumpled their noses at the ostentatious presentation of Zane, Corney, and Schwarzenegger's beefy bodies as icons of male beauty might feel faint at the sight of the more contemporary colossi of bodybuilding, like eight-time Mr. Olympia Ronnie Coleman (1998–2005) or four-time winner Jay Cutler (2006–7, 2009–10).

Though representing distinct and immediately subsequent eras of bodybuilding champions, Coleman and Cutler each embodied the forward thrusts of the sport into impossible-seeming extremes of growth. Both men hovered in the 310-pound range in the off-season (between competitions) with arms that measured just under two feet around.

To watch either man work through his posing routine on stage is to watch an alchemy of sculpture, modern dance, and theater of the absurd. The tiniest details can break the largest men or make the difference between a posing routine that is genuinely thrilling or aggressively preposterous.

Coleman in his prime was one of the first bodybuilders who enthralled me. When he competed for Mr. Olympia in 1997, I had only seen photo coverage in muscle magazines; now, going back to watch it on YouTube animates a sequence of stills in my memory, restokes the awe. Coleman posed to Rome's "I Belong to You (Every Time I See Your Face)," a slow jam as slick and supple as Coleman's oiled body.

This was on purpose—Coleman's routine moved with unreasonable ease between titanic classicism and mind-bending eroticism. His movements are slow, exacting, meticulous, turning from flesh to stone to liquid and back, then flipping vibes at the finish to the pumping beat of Notorious B.I.G.'s "Going Back to Cali." The following year, at Coleman's first Olympia win, he collapsed with shock to the floor at the sound of his name—his massive body heaped like a mound of cannonballs.

Cutler at his peak had a body like a glossy mountain of granite and leather. At his 2006 win—finally besting Coleman after eight years—he took the stage to a voice-over that introduced him as "the all-new 2006 Cutler Supreme [sporting a] special edition deep brown finish" (a nod to his spray tan that earned a laugh from the audience). When the voice-over got to "precision detailing," he flexed a 22" bicep, at "all-wheel drive," he tensed his 30" thigh into a crag. In the 2009 competition he introduced his signature "quad-stomp"—a dramatic wag-and-flex of his blimpy upper thigh that floored audiences and still makes the rounds on Instagram.

Today's bodybuilders, closer in form to (and more closely informed by) Coleman and Cutler than Zane or Schwarzenegger, are marvels of engineered muscle, optimized size, and hyper-realized hypertrophy, but you almost never hear bodybuilders referred to as beautiful—or even considered in proximity to beauty. In a 1975 article on bodybuilding for the *New York Times*, art historian Vicki Goldberg went so far as to refer to the inhabitants of the Venice Beach Gold's Gym as "grotesques."

"The men who frequent Gold's are serious body builders, who compete in an increasingly popular sport (some would call it an art, and others would tail it a form of exhibitionism)," she writes. "Their work on the machines, along with heroic, protein-rich diets, is designed to develop their bodies into the perfectly flared shapes they consider a mark of beauty."

Consider Goldberg unconvinced, as she goes on to observe in the burgeoning sport "an obsession with exaggerated masculinity at a time when traditional concepts of masculinity are under heavy assault."

Popular sentiment toward bodybuilding remains generally unflattering, with oversized muscles often coming across like a clown suit or a punchline at best, and fleshy evidence of untreated trauma at worst. Big muscles have come to be parsed as the uniform of toxic masculinity. Even contemporary beefcake celebrities like John Cena, Dave Bautista, and The Rock all vibe more ex-wrestler than bodybuilder, constantly undercutting their brutish bodies through comedy and camp.

For many, the body of the bodybuilder represents a garish vision of self-preening hyper-masculine egotism, capitalist excess, and slicked up sexual domination, spray-tanned and strung up in a straining thong. With the stakes physiologically, chemically, and hormonally raised to never-before-seen standards (and the range of available performance enhancing drugs reaching new levels of potency), the impetus to bodybuild has transcended the achievement of mere "peak" humanity and is now almost exclusively concerned with *superhumanity*.

In the twenty-first century, fantasy is no barrier to reality, the perfect man is no match for a freak of nature, and beauty has been devoured by the beast.

——

It wasn't always this way. In 1858, Walt Whitman, writing as his fitness influencer alter ego Mose Velsor, declared "manly beauty" the "true ambition" of men, an essential consideration in any earnest endeavor "to be a man, hearty, active, muscular, handsome—yes, *handsome.*"

"To the one who has no such feeling," he writes, "the electricity has gone out of that man; there is little hope for him." Whitman roundly rejected the idea that "personal beauty" was the exclusive province of women. "It is a germ, implanted by nature, that you should make grow."

"Nor is there anything to be ashamed of in the ambition of a man to have a handsome physique, a fine body, clear complexion, nimble movements, and be full of manly vigor," a clearly worked-up Whitman writes. "Only let it be the ambition that realizes a masculine and robust style of beauty, not the beauty of parlor elegance, of too much refinement, or of the mere fop."

A few decades later, in his 1894 book *Sandow on Physical Training*, Sandow himself laments the fallen role of beauty in the development of modern men, having only understood beauty and strength as one and the same—the *arete* of the Greeks. "With the higher knowledge that modern science has brought us," Sandow wrote, "how indifferent has been our approach to the consummate beauty of physical form for which the Greek—especially the Athenian athlete—was famed."

With the subsequent rise through the early twentieth century of mail-order fitness gurus like Bernarr Macfadden, Earle Liederman, and Charles Atlas, the trajectory of muscular development reached a crossroads. As an increasingly conservative post-WWII society grappled with an emergent image-driven mass media, men were increasingly compelled to show their hands: Was this pursuit of the perfect physique a matter of form or function? Aesthetics or performance? What, exactly, was the nature of men's desire for the perfect body?

This split was most evident in the advent of the beefcake magazine—a physique-specific offshoot of the formative physical culture publications of Macfadden and Sandow, geared far more overtly toward an eroticized vision of male beauty, and arguably launched in the home studio of one Bob Mizer.

Born in 1922, Mizer moved at the age of five with his widowed mother from Hailey, Idaho, to Los Angeles. There, he grew up snapping pictures, snipping muscle magazines, collecting any images he could find of defined male physiques, and hoarding them away in his attic bedroom.

As "Bobby" grew more confident with his camera, he started shooting photos of the bodybuilders who gathered and exercised at the famed Muscle Beach in Santa Monica, California. Gradually he earned trust among the tight-knit coteries of musclebound beefcakes, who spurned the disposable interest of shutterbug tourists but fancied Mizer's knack for capturing the best assets for posterity.

Before long, the bodybuilders who haunted the gyms and flophouses of Venice started requesting Mizer's time rather than the other way around. And if this all sounds a little gay, it wasn't. It was a lot gay.

Mizer's photography was elegant, classically conceptualized, plainly homoerotic, possibly heteroerotic, yet barely plausibly deniably erotic-erotic. With a steady influx of young bodybuilders literally showing up on his doorstep to be cast into perpetuity through his lens, Mizer established the Athletic Model Guild out of his mother's house in 1945.

Eventually Mizer expanded his operation to his own AMG Studios, sourcing his models from ads placed in the back of *Strength & Health* magazine. Business was bulging until 1947, when Mizer was arrested and charged by prosecutors for distribution of obscene material. His entire body of work was considered prohibited under the Comstock Law of 1873, an Act for the Suppression of Trade in, and Circulation of, Obscene Literature and Articles of Immoral Use, which made materials like Mizer's illegal to send through the mail. Defiant and poorly defended, Mizer pleaded not guilty and was swiftly convicted and sentenced to serve six months in a Saugus, California, prison farm. (This conviction would be overturned by the Supreme Court, who found in 1953 that lower courts had incorrectly instructed the jury about the definition of "obscene.")

If the goal was to frighten Mizer out of testing American censorship laws, it failed spectacularly. In 1950, when *Strength & Health* caved to threats from the US Post Office to yank the magazine's permits if it didn't drop ads like Mizer's, he took matters into his own hands. In May 1951,

Mizer launched his own small-run quarterly titled *Physique Photo News*, soon to be rebranded as the daddy of all beefcake magazines—*Physique Pictorial*. For the next thirty-nine years, *PP*'s covers were guarded by muscle-bound gladiators, visited by shore leave sailors, and frequented by leather-and-denim-clad rebels without causes (or undershirts), beefy beach bums and bullies, cowboys and come-hither ranchers, cops, and criminals. Near-nude musclemen peered from its pages in classical poses, testing a line as thin as a posing strap between pure athletics and impure aesthetics. They flexed, they wrestled (boy, did they wrestle) and engaged in lovingly documented episodes of horseplay. The bodies of *Physique Pictorial* were meant to pass idle hours and fuel daydreams, but I'm certain the simple sight of beautiful men being beautiful with other beautiful men also saved generations of men's lives.

Over his fifty-year career, Mizer photographed and filmed over ten thousand men at an estimated sixty shots a day. (Even Schwarzenegger posed for AMG in 1975.) But as comprehensive a catalog of men as that may seem, Mizer excluded Black models from his pages until the mid-1970s, and even then, he presented them as "specialized" features in all-Black collections.

Through the articles that Mizer wrote in his magazine, *Physique* doubled as a chronicle of Mizer's tastes, predilections, passions, and politics. Unavoidably *Physique* also offers a long-exposure of not just Mizer's biases but of the racial divides that penetrated the deepest of American subcultures. *Physique*'s archives are a compendium of beautiful bodies, but also an ugly reminder of the ways beauty and power reinforce each other in American culture.

Physique was followed by an explosion of beefcake magazines that sought to emulate it—line-blurring celebrations of male beauty like *Tomorrow's Man, VIM, Grecian Guild Pictorial, Apollo, Vulcan, Young Adonis, Strive,* and Joe Weider's *Demi-Gods*.

These beefcake magazines attracted the vitriol of the burgeoning strength-training community. A 1959 article in *Sports Illustrated* titled "For the Love of Muscle" described the growing "Body Beautiful cult" of muscle-admiring men as a "lunatic fringe." Targeting the proliferation of unsubtly erotic "little magazines," writer Stephen Birmingham questioned the motives of Mizer, Weider, and others banking on beauty to sell subscriptions—as well as their degenerate view of masculinity.

"When accused, as some of them have been, of catering only to homosexuals, they act shocked," Birmingham writes. "Editorially they protest they are eminently 'cultural,' devoted to 'esthetic appreciation of the male figure,' no naughtier than *The Atlantic Monthly.*"

Birmingham even dragged then-sixty-six-year-old Charles Atlas into the fray, gently implicating him in the inadvertent creation, "with his emphasis on strength and muscle, of a few Frankensteins"—a.k.a. monsters: "When it was pointed out to him recently that bodybuilding, which in his hands had been advertised as a way to get yourself a girl, had become, in the hands of others, a way to get something quite the opposite, Mr. Atlas reddened beyond his usual healthful ruddiness and said 'Some of those people—why, why they're not *normal!*'"

In the same story, Atlas's longtime business partner, Charles Roman, chimed in to clarify further: "We wish to have absolutely no connection drawn between Charles Atlas Limited and the publishers of the male physical-culture magazines. We do not wish to be associated with them in any way whatsoever. Charlie Atlas has done too much good for his country to worry about people like that."

While coy about admitting to their gay gaze, these publications offered enough potatoes to balance out all the meat—potentially salacious pictures were balanced by equal portions of diet advice and exercise guidance. It's a familiar model that continues to aid ab-studded men's magazines in justifying their not-so-subtle homoerotic appeals to men at large.

Still, beefcake magazines (the "so-called bodybuilding publications . . . peddling outright homosexual pornography in text and illustration" as the *New York Times* sneered) launched an associative link between bodybuilding and "homosexual" culture that has never been severed.

In addition to immortalizing thousands of young hunks, Mizer also launched the careers of gay illustrators like George Quaintance, Dom Orejudos (a.k.a. Etienne), Harry Bush, Spartacus, Art-Bob, and Touko Laaksonen, a.k.a. Tom of Finland.

Born in the small town of Kaarina, Finland, in 1920, young Touko spent solitary hours playing piano, penning comic strips, and fantasizing about Urho (or Hero), the beefy farm boy next door. One fantasy started shaping and shading the next, and before long, Touko's comics had taken a turn into dirty pictures, each explicit scene a private defiance of his strict Lutheran father.

In 1940, Laaksonen was conscripted into the Finnish Army and sent to an antiaircraft unit in Helsinki until 1944, earning the rank of lieutenant. Frequent blackouts plunged the streets into complete darkness, setting the scene for Laaksonen to find dozens of sexual encounters with Finnish, Russian, and German soldiers that would shape and shade his art for decades to come. Laaksonen was intoxicated by the men's regalia, their anonymity, their brute force, their buried tenderness.

After the war, Laaksonen took up work in design and advertising while playing music on the side, studying piano at the Sibelius Academy. But he also took to quietly producing a secret trove of explicit illustrations. One after the next, he sketched skillfully rendered visions of officers in leather uniforms working patrol, roughneck men laboring by the harbors, hard-knuckled farmhands and woodsmen.

In the spring of 1956, a friend encouraged Laaksonen to send a handful of his drawings to *Physique Pictorial*, with which the young artist was already smitten. Mizer responded to Laaksonen immediately, offering "Tom" (as he had signed his work) a new nom de plume as well as a career-launching cover of *Physique* in the spring of 1957.

The cover illustration captures a hunky blond shirtless lumberjack balancing on a log as it floats down a choppy river. Half a furlong or so back, a dark-haired companion gazes upstream in a freshly blown-open shirt. It was the first in a long journey together; Mizer would go on to publish over one hundred of Tom's drawings.

Slackening obscenity laws around Europe through the 1960s (and, by 1969, in the US) opened a new market for Tom's work, which descended deeper into S&M and fetish territory. His favorite recurring character, the steely-eyed leatherman Kake, debuted in 1967 and grew to be Tom's most iconic ambassador. Kake was the leather-clad protagonist of what seemed like a ceaseless sexual awakening. Sometimes a trooper, sometimes a biker, always the center of attention, Kake was at once instantly recognizable and unknowably general. He was a man cast out of molten masculine forms into a new archetype that would provide a center of gravity to gay male visual culture for the rest of the century: the clone.

"The absence of individuality and his characters made them not so much real human beings, but rather icons of masculinity, onto which viewers could project their own fantasies," writes Tom scholar Micha Ramakers. "Moreover, the cultural specificity of the characters was downplayed by the absence of language in most of Tom's work. This crucial tactic not only facilitated international distribution of his work, but ensured that Tom's characters were types instantly recognizable to gay men throughout the western world."

Tom's men continue to shape the men I meet to this day—the muscleboys and leatherdads, the bears and the silver foxes, the jocks and the coaches. But more than the eroticism, more than the classically composed gang-bangs, more than the fearless sexuality of Tom's men, I was drawn to their pleasure, their pride, their confident occupation of fantasy—all of which added up to a kind of beauty I'd never known.

Touko's claim on manhood allowed gay men around the world to feel at home in their imaginations, rather than at war with them. And his sweet-faced, stone-silent men reclaimed heavily guarded archetypes of machismo, softening the hard lines of masculinity into something more relatable, a sensuous gray area.

IX

BIG LITTLE

THE FIRST TIME I saw Big Little, I was sitting at the Au Bon Pain on Newbury Street reading manuscripts for my college internship. He rolled past on his way somewhere like a 1953 Mercedes-Benz Ponton. I say this not because I know anything about cars, but because after some Googling, it's the model that most closely captures the uniquely distributed bulk of his boxy body—the impossible curves of his torso that looked like inflated steel, the art deco arcs of his traps and pecs that stretched his shirt, the generous shelf of his epic butt.

Big Little was a short, stout, auspiciously swole Atlas of a man, and he carried his amplitude with the waddling gait of a gorilla, his thick arms flared out and resting atop cushiony lats that tested the stretch of his polo, his eyes fixed in a steely forward glare, determined to never be the one looking.

Such a spectacle was Big Little's body that it seemed to tow its own gravity behind it, slowing time through the seized attentions of a wake of rubberneckers who turned to watch him pass like a parade float.

I was one of them. Up until this moment I had known Big Little only by his screen name on several of the burgeoning selection of gay dating websites springing up in the late 1990s and early 2000s. I'd spotted him on Bear411, an online hub geared specifically toward the "bear" subculture of bigger, hairier, and purportedly more masculine gay men, and on Big MuscleBears.com, a far more rigidly curated platform for semi-separatist "musclebears" (for whom size matters on multiple levels).

And I'd only known his body as a suite of scruffy JPEGs—a snap of him at a pool party, coyly peeking through his Oakley sunglasses over his pumped trap; a supple black-and-white studio shot, Big Little twisting and flexing like a young Sandow; the requisite perspective shot from the viewer's hypothetical knees, a furrow-browed Big Little glaring disdainfully down over the massive crag of his chest. His were the first pictures I ever dragged into a misleadingly titled folder on my shitty Compaq.

But here he was, materialized before me as a mountain of muscle. Seeing him in three full dimensions was something else entirely. Since starting college, I'd joined a gym—a fusty Gold's in the shadow of Fenway Park—but working out alone sucked. I hated the bony body that followed me around in the mirror, and I felt relentlessly defeated by my own ignorance of what I was supposed to do. (It would be another three years or so before YouTube and its deluge of virtual trainers would arrive.)

I found myself returning solely to pantomime exercise while stealing clumsy glances at the reliable crew of titans that assembled there each morning. They were a trusty trio of bodybuilders in full throwback regalia: baggy zebra-print Zubaz tucked into red high-tops reserved for gym use; neon shredders (i.e., T-shirts reduced to torso-baring rags) and string tanks emblazoned with flexing avatars of other gyms; headbands and du-rags and knee wraps and wrist straps. They stalked the dumbbell area, guarding benches and spotting each other, chugging gulps of bright pink pre-workout formulas from repurposed gallon jugs (meant to give lifters a high-octane kick of caffeination before exercising). I watched them from what felt like a safe distance, trying to piece their routines together into something I understood, but it was like learning a language from across the room.

Hence my awed silence when Big Little rolled by—an event I soon realized took place every weekday afternoon while I was reading manuscripts at the Au Bon Pain, and which kept me faithful to my internship. I claimed a sidewalk table each day simply for the promise of the passing of his celestial body—and the brute force of his indifference.

The second place I saw Big Little he was for sale: Contestant #11 at the New England Bears' Bear Bachelor Auction at the 119. Unmarked and tucked behind Boston Garden, the 119 was the only gay bar I felt remotely comfortable dragging my barely decloseted body into. At twenty-three, I moved through these spaces like a ghost, visible only to a select few who didn't require me to have a built body—which, at the 119, was exactly nobody.

The bar was teeming with men in Bruins hats, leather vests, and stone-washed jeans. Big Little took the stage to wild applause, a last-minute entry to the auction. He'd grown and tightly cropped a little goatee that seemed to function in tandem with a precisely selected trucker cap. He was shirtless, the wedge of his torso in stark contrast to the more amply bellied bachelor contestants and regulars, their guts and fur an ostensible fuck-you to the dominant glossy muscleboy mold of 1990s gay culture.

Some have speculated that bear culture fully emerged in the 1980s as a bodily response to the AIDS crisis—the big, burly body appearing as a tacit assurance of health. Others credit its origins to a broader reclamation of traditional masculinity by gay men who didn't align with the stereotypically feminine tropes associated with gay life, or who sought to actively sub-vert the heterosexual monopoly on masculinity. The aesthetically specific dress-coded "leather and Levi's" bars that gained popularity through the 1980s evolved into an intricate global network of bear and leather clubs and organizations, complete with chapters and bylaws. Imagine a much sluttier Elks.

It was this fraternal aspect of beardom that made me feel—even as a terrified, trembling baby gay—that even I could find a place within its extensive taxonomy of subcategories. By the 119's presiding "bear" stan-dards, and in the nomenclature of capital-B Bear culture, I was somewhere between a "cub" and an "otter," but barely much of either.

On the auction block of the stage, Big Little was visibly bigger than he been had the last time I'd spotted him just a few weeks prior. His pecs were more pert, his nipples almost comically conic, the meat of his arms more articulated. The top edge of a fresh jockstrap artfully peeked over the waistband of his Silver Tabs—a discontinued cut that, I'd come to learn, were the only Levi's capable of accommodating his ass.

He tried to restrain a smile as the men around me held up bills and hollered bids. He waved appreciatively as he earned the night's highest price (a hundred something) and the winner claimed a dinner date with him—along with the responsibility of covering whatever overage the gift certificate inevitably wouldn't.

For the rest of the night, Big Little and his body were surrounded—a god lost in a throng of adorers, each reaching for a touch of his flesh like the figures in some horny fresco, and me gazing from across the gallery, fantasizing over what it must be like to be looked at.

The third time I met Big Little, he picked me up.

It was Pride and I was twenty-five, tipsy, stoned, and braver than usual, stumbling homeward from the oonst-oonst thump of the festival through the Boston Common. Big Little was by himself, crossing the park in a full rugby kit after having marched in the parade with the local gay rugby league—the Ironsides—for which he served as a prop, a detail he'd volunteer with veganesque enthusiasm.

He caught me staring and gave an "I see you" type of wave—*fuck!* I sheepishly returned the wave with my own and Big Little bounded over like a charging bull, gathering me up in a hug. Gay men have a long tradition of pretending to already know each other to avoid the humiliations of having to meet, but this felt different—like Courteney Cox getting pulled up on stage by Bruce Springsteen in the video for "Dancin' in the Dark." I felt both hand-selected and cast in a stunt he'd pulled before.

Caught in his bearhug, I suddenly understood Big Little's screen name, or so I thought. Once again, he was bigger than the last time I'd seen him—a pattern was emerging—and I couldn't quite get my arms all the way around him. But on his vertical axis he was a modest 5 feet, 7 inches, or so—his muscles densely packed into his body like poured iron. His hug was a dominant cuddle, designed to both embrace and bear down on you. And as he dragged his stubbly chin across my neck, leaving a pink skid, I felt marked—smudged by the smell of his sweat (tinny from whatever stack of steroids he was on).

"Hey big boy!" he said. "You're looking huge!"

These words, I would learn, were the terms through which Big Little opened every conversation with every man he met: an affirmation of the presumably agreed-upon value of big, whether the recipient appreciated it or not. It was a compliment flung like a medicine ball into the arms of an unsuspecting trainee, with the intention that it be thrown back even harder.

"You too! Bigger every time I see you!"

He slid a hand behind my head and guided me into the huddle of a deep, scratchy kiss that tasted like the wet iron of his sweat and the synthetic coconut of his sunscreen.

"Need a ride home?"

Big Little's brownstone studio apartment, where he took me instead, was like a diorama of his multitudes. The lace curtains in his bay windows were light enough to dance in a breeze, but were also, I would learn, heavy with symbolism—tattered battle flags from a repressive Irish Catholic upbringing that had pushed him into silent excellence and enduring suffering. An Ivy League–trained architect, he filled his modest parlor with bulky Victorian furnishings and its walls with large framed lithographs—antique maps of Rome, detailed studies of various palazzi, even some of his own drawings of the sturdy Colonial homes that were his specialty.

The floor, meanwhile, was strewn with damp tank tops and threadbare jockstraps from his twice-daily workouts. Big Little loved donning the roughneck regalia of the guys who had probably pushed him around as a kid in Worcester in the 1980s, appropriating their shredder Ts, branded bandanas, and tacky sunglasses. His kitchen was cluttered with funky-smelling shaker cups left unrinsed from his thrice-daily protein shakes. The fridge had nothing but a Brita, a gallon of milk, some pizza, and a few fresh vials of Trenbolone neatly lined up in the butter caddy.

The most prominent feature of the apartment were the mirrors. A full-length was propped against a wall, facing a lushly upholstered chaise; another leaned on the opposite wall by the bed, the headboard of which, I discovered as he threw me on the mattress, was a mirror too.

At first I imagined this array was part of a sensible strategy to add an illusory dimension of grandeur to the tight space of his studio. But within a few minutes of him crawling on top of me, I realized that the mirror was where Big Little actually lived.

Sex with Big Little was, in fact, an elaborately staged performance—complete with sets, costumes, lines, and the unbroken attention of his reflection, an audience of one. While I was blissfully buried under his 275 pounds, which he liked to rest on top of me as dead weight until I had to "tap out," he'd watch the scene in the mirror. ("Am I crushing you with my weight?" he'd ask, out of caution for my sake and confirmation for his.) Or he'd sit up, straddle me at the waist, and flex for his own admiration, my slim arms reaching up, pale references for him to gauge the swell of his own. Or he'd hold me by the back of the neck and drag my face around his body like a gym towel. Or he'd stand us both up and pose us in the standing mirror in the living room: "Look how fucking tiny you are compared to me," he'd say. "You ever think a big fuck like me would pick you up?"

"No."

I remember a little crease cracking his brow when I said that, as though he'd spotted someone else in our reflection, but only for a second.

"That's right, you didn't."

The next few dozen times I saw Big Little were split pretty evenly between eating, lifting, and fucking. Sometimes he wanted a companion to watch him clean the plates of the breakfast special at Mike's, where piles of salty thick-cut ham came atop an oversized heap of home fries and extra eggs. The act of eating for Big Little was intended as a public spectacle, an intentional distraction for his fellow diners, a display of his animal appetite. (And I'm certain he savored the irony of his comparably waify brunch date, barely able to finish my western omelet.)

Other times, Big Little wanted me to tag along to the gym with him. In exchange for him playing coach, I'd snap shirtless beefcake shots of him under the good light when he was sufficiently shiny and the basement barbell room was empty.

Other times he just wanted to hook up, which felt less like sex than an essential component of his workout—a posing performance, proof of his pump. We'd fuck to Bach and he'd flex as he finished, hardening into marble for a moment, striking a classical pose for the headboard. Or we'd fuck to Bowie, "Boys Keep Swinging" on repeat: *Life is a pop of the cherry / When you're a boy.*

"Don't you love being a boy?" he'd say, mashing my head into the pillow and glaring at himself.

He took to texting me video clips from YouTube—his new addiction— of off-season bodybuilders posing in their gym mirrors, deep into their "bulking phases," the curves of their bodies plumped and pumped.

"WANT," he'd offer as caption, with the understanding that "want" was used in the most general and all-encompassing sense.

Or he'd send me videos of himself working out, glossy with sweat, doing sets of heavy shrugs, his traps as big as softballs, the column of his neck compressing like a pack of hot dogs on the back of his head. The gym would always be pumping some awful peak-hour club anthem, but he'd have his earbuds in and an iPod shuffle clipped to the strap of his tank top, blasting angsty misspelled mid-aughts nu metal like Korn and Staind.

Every time I saw Big Little, he looked bigger and I felt smaller. One time he summoned me to his apartment a few days shy of Halloween to see the makings of his costume. He'd shaved his head and trimmed his beard down to a little moustache, its tips tapered into waxy curlicues. He'd found a vintage one-piece swimsuit that he'd slashed into a singlet and that strained to contain his nearly 300 pounds. He'd even fashioned a stunt chain for breaking as a party trick. He was, all at once, Sandow and Schwarzenegger, Atlas and Cutler, the Farnese Hercules and some anonymous trick from one of Tom's orgiastic sketches—a body built from generations of archetypes, bursting at the seams.

And while Big Little was the rugby player, after a while our encounters started to leave me feeling more like the prop: the 150-pound weakling volunteering for the kicked sand of semi-regular sex so that the bully could feel bigger. And, to be clear, this wasn't a dynamic I resisted—I'd fib to my boss at the office where I worked and cross town in the middle of a busy workday to experience the thrill ride of Big Little's body for a few fleeting minutes, fortified by an unconscious assurance that I wasn't entirely powerless in the arrangement. Our bodies gave each other fleeting flashes of meaning. It was only through me that Big Little could see himself. (And only with my assistance that he could reach his ass with the needle.)

I was too young to understand how deeply Big Little suffered from body dysmorphia. Too young to even know what it was—or that a germ of it was starting to glaze my own eyes as well, would keep me for years from seeing my body as it really was.

It's almost impossible to find meaningfully accurate estimates of the number of men who suffer from muscle dysmorphia—though it's possible to triangulate an idea based on other metrics. An estimated one in fifty Americans, regardless of gender, experience general symptoms of body dysmorphic disorder (a diagnosis introduced to the *DSM III-R* in 1987). Another study found that 22 percent of men aged eighteen to twenty-four reported muscularity-oriented disordered eating. (Not for nothing, muscle dysmorphia is often referred to inside and outside of muscle-building communities as "bigorexia.") Men, already more prone than women to avoid seeking help for mental health issues, are extremely unlikely to self-identify as dysmorphic, especially given the Internet's illusion of consensus that men should be as big as possible, as strong as possible, as soon as possible.

Though he hardly ever spoke the words aloud, Big Little displayed all of the symptoms of muscle dysphoria—and seemed to indulge them as guilty pleasures. Missed workouts and disruptions to his gym regimen drove him into fits of rage and resentment, often triggering mood swings that could arc through months—a symptom of his dysphoria, but also the by-product of the stack of steroids he was cycling. Big Little would train through injuries and sickness. He'd miss parties and skip dinners with friends if either impinged on the sanctity of his workout schedule. The simplest of plans were wholly dictated by the state of his post-gym pump.

Big Little was obsessed with men who made him feel tiny: bodybuilders like Cutler, Dorian Yates, and Lee Haney and wrestlers like Goldberg, Big E Langston, and Ryback. Their mere existence on the same earth confirmed within Big Little a sense of insignificance that fueled a rage he kept stoked like a furnace. He was desperate to be the biggest man at every gym he went to—and if he wasn't, he found a different gym. He mistrusted compliments, convinced they were disingenuous and designed to subtly mock him.

But more than the perceived disdain from others, what weighed most heavily on Big Little was his own pain. One time when we were wrestling around, I somehow managed to pin him by the arms and he howled in terror and threw me off. After we'd caught our breath, he confided that he'd been sexually assaulted, held down by a member of a rival rugby team who'd only befriended him for a steroid hookup.

It was part of why he gave up the sport shortly after I saw him in uniform at the park, part of why he vanished into the depths of the weight room, part of why he was coming up on 310 pounds and finding it hard to breathe.

"No one is ever going to make me that small again," he once told me in a text message.

The last time I talked to Big Little he had just come from a stay at the hospital after a hypoglycemic episode and feeling flutters in his heart. It had been a few years since we'd last seen each other. I'd gotten hitched to my husband and we'd moved to Texas. But Big Little and I still kept tabs on each other, him offering compliments on pieces I continued to write for the *Boston Globe* and me offering reassurance that he continued to look large in his social media pics. He said he was most relieved to be out of the hospital because it meant he could resume his cycle of Tren, Dianobol, and growth hormone in time for summer.

"Starting tomorrow," he texted, "WOOHOO!" This was accompanied by a picture of him in the hospital, his shaven body splitting a hospital johnny, his torso a tangle of white wires and electrodes.

His enthusiasm was a put-on. The truth is he was drained. His pool of architectural clients had started to dry up. He could no longer afford the membership at his gym and someone had stolen his $300 Dave Draper squat bar from the storage closet where he'd kept it ostensibly locked away. No one was messaging him back on the apps.

"Why bother going to the gym and expending a huge amount of time and pain if you're never going to hook up with another guy?" he texted me once in the middle of the night. "Rhetorical question."

He started working the door as a bouncer at the gay bar down the street, stocking his fridge with sandwiches on the brink of expiration foraged from the 7-Eleven on his walk home from work. He stopped going to the bars, the clubs, Happy Hour, Tea Dance, and Bear Week. He stopped having sex. ("I'm as chaste as the maidens of Dionysus," he remarked.) He started getting sick and eating like shit, pigging out on Oreos, Chinese takeout, McDonald's, diner breakfasts, cookies, potato chips, and boxed protein drinks he'd buy in bulk from BJ's.

He'd been in and out of the hospital, his doctors repeatedly warning him about the pressure his growing layers of hard visceral fat were putting on his internal organs. But the "bad fat" was, to him, the "sexy fat," and no doctor could reach him. They could barely examine him—his arms were too big for the blood pressure cuffs, his neck was too big for immobilization collars, his ass was too big for the 2XL surgical scrubs. On one visit, the doctors declined to give him a turn in the "special" MRI reserved for professional athletes and "really big guys," which he took as insult to injury.

Deprived of his former body—which now drooped here, sagged there and betrayed his weakening grip on his self-control—Big Little considered himself irrevocably relegated to D-list status in the local gay scene. A novelty past its prime like a punctured parade float. An "old never-was."

He'd send me photos of the men who used to invite him to parties but no longer did, and screenshots of the radio silence he'd receive in response to his texts. Men who had once lusted after him, watched him from afar, or pursued him at the bars had since defriended him on Facebook, unfollowed him on Instagram, unliked his photos, blocked his number.

"I will never be even a shadow of these men," he texted me. "Perhaps I'm just mourning my death as an attractive man, an object of desire or even envy. Perhaps I don't know what my life will be without those things."

Like Hercules, who built his myth upon the atonement he served for crises he created, Big Little wielded his rejection like a bludgeon, bore the burden of his body like a punishment.

I would tell him over and over that he was still impossible not to notice, that he was never not the biggest guy in the room, that he was a tank, but because he was, my praise would ping off his thick shell. He couldn't see himself in the mirror—still a handsome, broad-shouldered, thick-armed bull of a man. He couldn't hear himself described. He could only feel trapped in his own inadequacy, constantly exposed by his own imperfection.

"I am about to spend over $5,000 on steroids, growth hormones, IGF-3, and Insulin," he texted me. "Putting order in tomorrow. I hope this finally makes me big. I hate my body."

This hatred of his body went beyond some cosmetic fixation. From the time when he was a beanpole teenager to his adult categorization of "muscledaddy," Big Little felt captive in his body—a windowless prison that was starting to collapse.

"I'd rather be big and dead than emaciated and alive. LOL. :-)"

A week later, I got the call from a mutual friend that he had dropped dead of a massive heart attack in the parking lot of a bar. I read our last conversation over and over, hoping for a different result. "I don't want to die, or become really sick . . . but WHO am I gonna be if I lose what little size I have? It's existential. . . . Either way I cease to BE."

It's been five years since he died, and I still see Big Little all the time.

Sometimes snippets of video that strayed from his phone make their way to mine—a friend sent me a clip he found of Big filming himself eating at Mike's, our former breakfast spot. The camera is sitting where I used to be, my former space at the table overtaken by extra sides of potatoes and bacon. He's got the ham special and he's groaning with satisfaction as he clears his plate by the overloaded forkful, gulping his water and coffee, chomping on a side of onion rings and loudly belching—likely a video made for one of his "encouragers," members of a gay fetish subculture of "gainers" who now and then sent him donations in exchange for documentation of his many feedings.

Sometimes those old photos I snapped of him during our workouts together find their way back to me through my feed, posted to various muscle admirer accounts on Instagram. But like my own memories of Big Little and his body, they've been warped.

Passed down through the years from one muscle-worship Tumblr account to the next on Twitter, reposted to porn sites, admirer hubs, and "gainer" websites, Big Little's body has been digitally morphed and distorted beyond the humanly possible. Sometimes an amateur artist uses his pics as templates for elaborate fantasy scenes. There's one where he's rendered as a giant, smirking down at the camera and flexing as he stomps a crumbling city block in white spandex leggings. There's another from the perspective of a human-sized man standing at his feet, Big peering down hungrily, eyeing the viewer as a snack.

But most of the time when I see pics of Big Little now, his body has been clumsily inflated by amateur Photoshoppers. The morphers thicken his neck and his wrists (both of which he loathed), they widen his belly and chest, they beef up his thighs and add bulging calves. A friend recently texted me a morph they'd found of Big perched on the edge of his bed. He's mean-mugging for the camera and sporting an extra fifty or sixty virtual pounds of Photoshopped mass. He's also flaunting an admittedly impressive but unconvincing ten-inch dick, dragged and dropped from some anonymous porn star and hanging between his plumped-up thighs. "He would not have wanted this," my friend wrote.

I wasn't so sure. I still don't know if Big Little died from his consumption of fantasy, or from fantasy's consumption of him. Like his screen name, it was probably both at once.

My favorite way to remember Big Little is through the animated GIFs of him that still circulate online—scruffy little snatches of the gym videos he had faithfully posted, now trimmed and looped by unknown admirers to capture him squatting a barbell or squeezing out a set of cable flys into perpetuity. He looks happy, forever pumped, never at rest, finally at peace.

THE PUMP

A SK A MAN WHY HE LIFTS, and that man will lie to your face. He will assert and insist that his "training" is purely in service of health, fitness, strength, endurance, stamina, and whatever other buzzwords he can throw in to throw you off the trail. He will go on and on about the spirit of competition one develops with oneself in the gym, the thrill of pushing one's limits and testing one's abilities. He'll cite the enhanced heart health, regulated blood pressure, and lowered cholesterol that come from regular visits to the gym, and he'll point to the strengthening of bones and joints, the boosting of immunity and energy. He might even say that he *enjoys* it. That it relieves the built-up stresses of every day, offers escape from his main routine in the form of another, more taxing routine. I know men for whom the gym has provided critical support in times of dire mental health, men who report to the gym the way some go to church or a fairy pond in Zelda—for a sense of spiritual replenishment. I would join these men in affirming each of these sentiments as true. But I'd also call bullshit.

The real reason men bring the devotion of an addict to the gym is that iron is an addictive substance—and the pump is the high.

Available to veteran meatheads and newbies alike, this basic biological response of one's muscle tissue—muscles engorging and visually swelling with an influx of nutrient- and oxygen-rich blood as well as intracellular fluid retained due to the production of lactic acid—is an uncanny source of motivation and an unmatchable physical buzz. And the visual stimulus of the pump is perhaps for men the most intoxicating (and immediate) payoff of lifting weights.

No more potent proponent of the pump exists than Arnold Schwarz-enegger himself, a youthful iteration of whom famously sang its praises in a particularly rapturous passage of *Pumping Iron*, describing it as "the most satisfying feeling you can get in the gym."

"It feels fantastic," a beaming Arnold says. "It's as satisfying to me as having sex with a woman and coming. Can you believe how much I am in heaven?! I'm getting the feeling of coming in the gym, I'm getting the feeling of coming at home, I'm getting the feeling of coming backstage when I pump up, when I pose out in front of 5,000 people, I get the same feeling. So I am coming day and night. I mean, it's terrific, right?"

Schwarzenegger elaborated further in his 1985 *Encyclopedia of Modern Bodybuilding*, writing that the pump's "combination of the physical and the psychological can have a tremendous effect on how you feel and how hard you can train."

"When you are pumped, you feel better and stronger, and it is easier to motivate yourself to train hard, to achieve a higher level of intensity," he writes. "Sometimes you think you're King Kong walking around the gym!"

Many lifters have long attested that the pump is productive in itself. Consistently "chasing the pump," increasing blood flow, and thus regularly stretching the fascia surrounding the muscles is no vain indulgence (pun seriously not intended), they argue, but actually integral to helping muscles grow, as though nudging outward the outlines of the body's imagination.

"When you look into the mirror you are seeing the future of your body," three-time Mr. Olympia Frank Zane told *Muscle & Strength* in 2010. "That is the line your body is taking because you pump up to that look you are acquiring over time. You pump up, it goes down, a little bit stays. You pump up next time, a little more stays. And gradually that accumulates over time and that creates your look."

Whether transient hypertrophy (a.k.a. muscle pump) actually enhances or improves one's chances of long-term hypertrophy (a.k.a. muscle growth) remains fodder for ongoing speculation and heated bickering in comment sections across social media, where such things don't matter. Whatever the long-term benefits may or may not be, the moment of the pump is undoubtedly among the most documented in American culture. Put another way, every gym selfie you've ever seen is a direct product of the pump—evidence of the moment of expended effort captured on camera because it couldn't be sustained any other way. For men attempting to make something out of their bodies, the pump is proof of purchase.

Every contemporary staple of "serious about the gym" gymwear—the short-shorts and string tanks and compression shorts and yoga pants—is stitched (or torn) in anticipation of the pump. I have at least twenty tattered tank tops that make no contextual sense unless my body broadcasts a semi-recent visit to the gym. I have one shredder bequeathed to me years ago that features the engine of a Harley Davidson sandwiched between two hamburger buns: "HERE'S THE BEEF," it announces. It's among my most treasured possessions. Another of my favorite stringers sports some muscle-dude striking the pose of Rodin's *The Thinker*. "THINK BIG," it suggests. Only a pump can authorize this level of cheese. I have another stringer that Big Little sent me as part of a shipment of gym clothes he'd outgrown but couldn't bear to throw out: a Powerhouse Gym XL tank, heather gray because he liked his sweat to show, featuring a little Michelin-man of a bodybuilder struggling against a bending barbell. He reminds me of Big Little. And when I wear the shirt to work out, a decent pump is just enough to fill the space he left behind.

There were times when I depended on the pump to pay the bills. During a summerlong stint working at a Houston leather bar, I had to factor in a trip to the gym before each shift. Without a pre-shift pump, my harness wouldn't quite hug me right, my armbands would plummet into bangles, my chaps would hang loose, the whole fantasy would slump—and my tips would suffer.

Like the fleeting, pulsing power of a supercharged Mario after a meal of stars and mushrooms, or like a real-life version of the orb I used to grab in *Altered Beast*, the pump offers a temporary puffing to mythic proportions. A good pump feels a long-delayed realization of my childhood *Incredible Hulk* fantasies, my suddenly powered-up form presenting an unexpected threat to the seams of my shirts. And it's hard not to parse another thrust of meaning from the freshly pumped body and its jacked-up vascularity—the whole body is supersized and phallusized, fully engorged and engaged in the performance of masculinity.

In the mirror, in my shirt, in my eyes, the pump feels like more than just an amplifier of presence or a fluffing of plumage à la "Hans and Franz"— though it feels like both of those things. The pump reminds me that I'm a machine made of blood and breath and electricity, my life a matter of meat.

X

ZEUS

FELT WEAK when they sawed off the casts. Two of them, one on each arm, freshly split and cracked open like some crusty seashell, revealing at long last the pale noodles of my withered arms.

Two months earlier in July 2011, I'd been pedaling my bike back to the rental shack on the last day of summer vacation, enjoying Bear Week in Provincetown with my soon-to-be-husband. Get your gay jokes ready because as I was coming down a particularly steep stretch of Bradford Street, my front tire hit a dew-slickened and nonfigurative manhole, the wheel slipped and twisted, and I went flying face-first over the handlebars into the street. I managed to break my fall with my hands, snapping the radius of my right arm and cracking the wrist of the left. My front tooth cracked against the pavement; a gash in my forehead dribbling a river of hot blood down my face that tasted like salt, copper, and sunscreen. A spike of broken bone poked and pitched the skin of my forearm like a tent. A little crowd of worried daddies formed in front of the leather bar. A passing cop fell off his Segway at the scene. I was rolling around in the road, every cell in my body freaking out, trying to determine which fuckup to fix first.

After a blast of morphine from the EMTs, an ambulance ride to Hyannis, and an emergency surgery, I was outfitted with a pair of casts that turned my arms to logs of plaster and allowed only the tips of my fingers to touch fresh air. Back home in Boston, I devised an outfit that allowed me to dress myself—wide-pocketed cargo shorts with suspenders and a carabiner for my house keys paired with a short-sleeve shirt with two pockets for my bank card and bus pass, attracting the ostensibly sympathetic stares of passers-by and fellow passengers on the bus and subway, each of whom wanted extensive recaps of what the fuck had happened to me.

I spent most of that month at home popping pills, wasting away, weeping through marathons of *What Not to Wear*, and somewhere, within the fog of blurred pain and crust of plaster, healing. I started becoming hyper-aware of my body in a new way—my fresh helplessness within it, the equation I'd never made between my body and my experience of the world. So much I had taken for granted. Each morning my eyes shot open and I'd gasp my first waking breath, snapping out of whatever dream into the reality of the casts, and I'd calm myself with the solace of cellular faith, a belief in the body to build itself back from the brink.

Once the casts came off I started visiting a physical therapist, squeezing various brightly colored putties and pulling at big rubber bands of increasing resistance. I started bending my wrists and fingers over the edges of tables, reacquainting myself with the petrified sinews of my own body, the stiff ache of each stubborn joint. Over time I worked my way up to a set of small teal dumbbells, a pound a piece, rotating and curling them with my wrists. After about a week I graduated to the five pounders, relearning to grip, my hand trembling less with each demand. I could feel the tenderness around the plates of titanium now bolted into my bones. I could still feel the screws that had sturdied my wrist even though they'd pulled them out weeks ago. I could sense the seams in my bones, the breaks that every doctor had downplayed with the same refrain. It'll grow back stronger.

It was a couple of months after the casts came off and our wedding rings were exchanged before I attempted a return to the gym. At the time I was at the South End location of the local gay chain, where Big Little had urged me to sign up but which he himself eventually abandoned, convinced he was a laughingstock among the locals. Over the course of a month I made a slow ascent back up the dumbbell rack—progressively handling 10s, 12.5s, 15s, 20s in my trembling arms. I followed my doctor's orders and eased my way through the circuits of resistance machines, carefully controlling each movement and taking every motion slow and steady. I was terrified of pushing too hard and snapping something, wrecking myself anew. I was getting back to normal but normal felt soft, vulnerable, weak. Normal was just on the verge of broken.

At the time I had a couple of friends from the bear bar who were into traditional Scottish highland games, for which there was a circuit of competitions all around the region through the spring and the summer. Kilted giants from across New England (mostly straight family men who enjoyed throwing things) would converge to toss telephone-pole-sized cabers in open fields, fling iron hammers and chunky stones, run up steep hills, hurl heavy weights over tall bars, and dig their heels into the turf for fierce tugs-of-war. Then they'd stomp their muddy cleats into some pub, drink too much, sing, dance, and drift into an affectionate manly blur. I think this is the part my friends liked the most.

They'd gotten into highland games after training at what could only be described as a "hardcore gym" situated on the edge on an industrial zone in Everett, a mile or so from the very end of the Orange Line. They swore by the place, a five-floor facility that overtook the better part of a large brick former furniture factory, filling its massive space with squat racks and deadlift platforms, a long stretch of artificial turf, a gallery of refurbished Hammer Strength machines and rusty dumbbells, a boxing ring and fighting studio, and a range of implements beloved only to strongmen: heavy sandbags and anvils, weighted yokes and harness-drawn sleds, tractor tires for flipping and "Prowlers" for pushing. Notably, there were no mirrors.

But more than any single piece of specialized equipment—like the rows of "monolifts," able to suspend heavily loaded barbells for super-heavy squats—the main draw of this gym for the men who trained there was each other.

Once I'd worked up a base layer of strength, $300 for the fee, and nerve enough to show my face, I visited the gym, which required a five-flight ascent to the front desk. A room of normal-looking exercise bikes and elliptical machines sat empty to the side of the check-in station—a Potemkin cardio room that nobody seemed to use, conspicuously placed to give the illusion of familiarity. This suspended disbelief, however, was disrupted at regular intervals by the thunderous boom of barbells dropped on the deadlift platforms directly upstairs. A faint snow of drywall dust landed on my head as I signed my membership form and safety waivers for the gym, and more specifically, for "Awesome Camp"—a ten-week introduction to powerlifting and advanced strength training that met four times a week and started the next day.

Our coach was Anthony, a steely-eyed, highly caffeinated self-described meathead with deep Jersey roots. Everything about him—from the clip of his speech to the pistonesque execution of his bench press—was an exercise in control. He wore the same set of sweats every day, lending him a sour aura of authority that hung in the air like his orders. Anthony was also ridiculously strong, his top bench in the 500s, his best squat in the mid-600s, his dead lift edging into the 700s. In powerlifting, the sum of one's "max" lift in each of these core lifts amounts to a "total"—a numerical expression of one's dominance in the sport. Super heavyweight powerlifters—which Anthony, lean and mean, was not—must total over a ton to be considered "elite."

Our first three weeks were spent training myself to forget every bad habit I'd picked up since the weight room at Fitchburg High. Corrective attention was given to every aspect of every lift. For my squat he moved the bar into a natural notch below my neck and fixed my stance, the point of my toes, the spread of my shoulders, the push of my chest, the torque of my knees, the drive of my feet, the thrust of my hips, the storage and release of my breath. He dismantled my bench press and rebuilt it into a suspension bridge, my shoulder blades pinched to hold an imaginary pencil, my back arched and butt planted, my legs driven down through flat heels, my bar path clear and straight and smooth as though opening the drawer of a flat file, my press quick and controlled, pushed like a feather in the updraft of my exhale. He taught me to deadlift, the most caveman move of the trinity of powerlifting exercises, forbidden in commercial gyms uninterested in subsidizing chiropractors, and ridiculed by "norms" for its silly-seeming minimalism—i.e., I lift zings up and put zem down. Under Anthony, I learned the dead lift's elegance—the intimate choreography of intention and impulse, tension and tissue, precision and power that enables each rep, and more importantly, the rep after that.

A typical workout at Awesome Camp would find me and my small group—each cycle started with around ten people and typically winnowed down to four or five—gathered around the bench or the monolift or the deadlift platform, taking turns under progressively heavier bars, toggling between competitive taunts and supportive cheers. (Week by week the number of reps of each exercise would go down as the weight loaded on the bars went up, until we reached a "test week" measuring our one-rep-maxes, and thus, our "totals.") After a rigorous hour or so on the core exercise of the evening, Anthony would dispatch us to the turf to carry sandbags, flip tires, pull heavy sleds with thick ropes, or push them fifty feet only to turn them around and push them back. Or he'd bring us to the training floor and send us through a circuit of pull-ups, push-ups, dumbbell presses, and barbell rows. If the push-ups looked too easy, he'd drape chains over our backs. If the pull-ups seemed too effortless, he'd strap us into weighted harnesses until we hung, trembled, and dropped. The young cop in my group would curl up on the floor to catch his breath. An older man named Moose sometimes puked in the trash can at the edge of the turf. I'd hang half my body out the window, letting the winter air fill my spent lungs and steam rise from my shoulders, the city's sleepy skyline blinking in the distance. Lazy fucks. Anthony's whistle. One more set.

Men love to act like weight lifting is about some expression of domi-nance—reasoning that one who budges the immovable object must thus be an unstoppable force. But men who have spent decades lifting heavy shit might beg to differ. It's hard to imagine an act more submissive than lifting weights. For one thing, the ten weeks I had initially intended to spend pushing myself past the threshold of normal turned into three years of dutifully taking orders from Anthony—doing whatever he asked, how-ever he specified.

But more fundamentally, the act of lifting itself is really just a precisely managed pursuit of failure. One might jot down in one's gym journal the weight of the heaviest lift they were able to perform, but the more import-ant number is the weight they couldn't budge. The drive for success, the fleeting high of dominance may be what brings men to the weight room, but it's the promise of failure and pure vengeance against gravity that forges the discipline of the true meathead. Further, performance in the gym re-quires compliance, not defiance. Success in the gym is merely a measure of one's dedication to finding failure, not one's ability to feign freedom from it. Muscles may look like the trophies of triumphs, but they're really the receipts of defeats.

It could be this dynamic that explains the men I met at Olympus—my nickname for the gym, due to its five-flight climb and its roving populace of superhuman figures. These men behaved in ways to which I was wholly unaccustomed: They helped each other, praised each other, failed freely in front of each other with something like enthusiasm. They kept diaries and confided their goals to each other. They protected each other from harm and leapt to rescue each other from danger (e.g., getting "stapled" by the bar). They complimented each other's form and progress, confessed their mutual envy, expressed their mutual respect.

As I made my way through the Awesome Camp program, and the next, and the next, and as my T-shirts shed their sleeves and my traps started to eat my neck, as my butt began to bulge and my pecs began to pop, and as the scale started its lurch into the 200s as I stepped onto it, something unexpected happened: I became visible.

"Looking thick, buddy!" CJ the owner barked at me on my way out after squats one night, making me turn extra pink. "There we go, hoss!" shouted a coach watching from across the gym as I struggled through the lock out of a dead lift. "Beast! I see you!" said Zeus, instantly killing me.

Zeus was the name I'd given to the biggest man at Olympus. He was always there with his lady, the two of them entirely mapped in tattoos and completely immersed in whatever ridiculously heavy lift they were in the middle of. Zeus was 6 feet or so, easily 300 pounds of solid muscle topped with a shaven head and a Herculean beard. Oftentimes I'd walk into the gym to find a crowd of men gathered around him at the monolift, all of them hollering at the top of their lungs as Zeus lowered himself into "the hole" of a heavy squat below a bending barbell. They'd howl as he drove up, rattling the plates and roaring, his thick neck hardening into a column of cords as he re-racked the weight to a set of hanging hooks. Then they'd cheer and slap his big back, leaving handprints and a hovering cloud of chalk dust.

The men I met came to the gym for different reasons—some were small trying to get big; some were big trying to lean down; some were out of jail and trying to straighten up; some were out of rehab and trying to settle down; some were replacing one addiction with another; some were trying to find somewhere to put their anger, their grief, their bitterness, their loneliness; some had too much free time, others couldn't bear any of it. All of them, myself included, were looking for a different relationship with difficulty, the ruse of volition making our suffering feel more like a choice—a delusion of Herculean proportions.

For the big men I met at Olympus, getting massive and terrifying was a way to authorize a level of affection and support that might otherwise be impossible—as though ferocity were a path to fraternity. It was as though the standing threat of their powerful bodies was insurance enough to allow small violations of the cold codes of masculinity. Despite the growling heavy metal soundtrack of Cannibal Corpse, Pantera, and whatever Ozzy's Boneyard was streaming, despite the grunts and groans and chains and ropes and sweat and blood, despite the dogged pursuit of difficulty these men sought out here each day, the lifestyle of the meathead seemed to me almost entirely in service of achieving a kind of benevolent ease with the world.

The week after Zeus first acknowledged my existence, he passed by as I was struggling to stand up beneath a load of 405 pounds, the heaviest squat I'd ever attempted. I'd walked it successfully out from the monolift, sturdied it across my shoulders, gripped the bar and drew in a big breath. Zeus stood facing me, giving me a slow sturdy nod, and I lowered my body, smooth and certain in the hole. Zeus's eyes widened and his brow bent into an expectant arch, as though awaiting an answer. I responded with the hardest push I'd ever given, driving the soles of my feet through the five stories of the building, a wake of flames trailing the plates on the barbell's ends as they thrust upward, a burst of energy radiating out across the gym floor, and a surge of lightning shooting up my spine and down the length of the bar. My body was vibrating, my blood coursing with endorphins, I felt power-pilled, superhuman. I racked the weight and a hail of congratulatory slaps hit my back.

Zeus smiled upon me and strolled off. I felt chosen.

It's wild how much strength men could find in each other's affection if only we allowed ourselves to share it, if friendship and love and support between men didn't have to be disclaimed and no-homo'd to death. At Olympus, our work let us disappear into a mythic performance of manhood: Sisyphus interminably pushing the sled down the turf, Atlas struggling to carry the boulder of Earth on his shoulders, Milo hauling progressively heavier sandbags.

But joining the fold of meatheads also allowed me to understand their devotion to difficulty, the use of hard work against impossible weights and inevitable defeats. I started to understand why men at large default to the language of their bodies to express that for which words were too brittle. Our workouts weren't so much routine as ritual: a collective performance of our shared struggles—the barbell an icon of our private burdens. It was as though lifting all of this heavy weight was just a way of making the world feel lighter.

MEMBERSHIP

"**N**O ONE is coming to save you."
Ever since the pandemic, this line—which seems shaken from the liner notes of some mediocre nu-metal band—has become something like a mantra across the manosphere. You find it scrawled across memes and tucked into captions, printed on T-shirts, and intoned in growly soliloquies over grainy footage of brutal workouts.

The sentiment, I suppose, is that you're on your own. Your weight is yours alone to pull. Your actions have consequences. You reap what you sow. And the entire range of similar clichés to this effect, all the way up to the passive-aggressive "Pull yourself up by your bootstraps."

Self-sufficiency being one of the primary principles of broken masculinity, its promotion and enforcement has been delegated to the manosphere, which spreads the gospel of hyper-individualism to literal millions of idly clicking young men, who are convinced beyond a doubt that they have no need for each other, and thus, that no one is coming to save them.

What these men presume to need saving from is left conspicuously unsaid, but the pandemic gave rise to another refrain—the unrhetorical question "Are men OK?"

Right now, men are at the core of another pandemic—an unaddressed mental health crisis in America. Studies estimate that each year more than six million American men suffer from depression, a number that remains foggy due to men being statistically less likely than others to seek help or receive diagnoses.

According to the Anxiety and Depression Association of America, an estimated three million men suffer from anxiety and panic disorders. Ninety percent of patients diagnosed with schizophrenia before age thirty are men. One in five men develops substance abuse problems. In 2021, men accounted for 80 percent of suicides, four times that of women.

Men also make up 70 percent of the nation's unhoused population—many of them veterans and the formerly incarcerated. To that end, men are nine times more likely than women to be imprisoned and make up 90 percent of incarcerated folks, with Black men representing 33 percent, almost triple their share of the national population.

Online, these statistics—which only seem to worsen with time—are swiftly cited as ironclad evidence against the existence of patriarchal privilege by men's rights activists, or MRAs, defined by the Anti-Defamation League as "a subset of extremist misogynist culture" that "emerged as a reaction to second-wave feminism and the belief that men are being victimized by employment and family law, among other things." And yet, so much of what pains and plagues men stems directly from the patriarchal ways in which we learn to become men. So much of what poisons men has roots in manhood.

When hurt, men are encouraged to "man up" and keep emotions hidden from sight, to heal fast or siphon the ache in activities like sports or work. The act of reaching out to others can be interpreted as an expression of need—which is also forbidden. Men are raised to be self-sufficient, stony, and stoic. To acknowledge need is to acknowledge lack; to acknowledge lack is to acknowledge weakness. To acknowledge weakness is to cede manhood.

Broken masculinity cultivates isolation. One recent study showed that only 27 percent of men have six or more close friends, with 15 percent of men reporting no close friendships at all—the latter a jump representing a fivefold spike since 1990. The pandemic exacerbated and accelerated the shrinking of men's social circles, cutting them off from offices, bars, gyms, and sports—all of the physical social spaces where their closest connections with other men were made.

Over the past decade, straight white men led by a squad of manfluencers and podcasters like Matt Walsh, Ben Shapiro, and Steven Crowder have staged a virtual turf war over the once relatively quiet meadow of gender variance that stretches between the binaries. The spectrum is now a battlefield, with hard-drawn boundaries and borders. To compensate for a perceived loss of cultural dominance, they've ramped up their occupation of virtual space, launching thousands of podcasts and talk shows whining about the erosion of "traditional" masculinity. And there's no shortage of an audience for these complaints: the manosphere is powered by the anxiety of men desperately in search of a sense of belonging, and there's no resource more renewable than male grievance.

Despite their hyper-individualist, "no one is coming to save you" crowing, men long to belong, to feel part of something bigger than their own bodies, to feel required and integral—as producer or protector, definer or defender, coach or quarterback. It's why we join sports teams and gentlemen's clubs, college fraternities and secret societies; it's why every town has its Eagles and Elks and Shriners and Masons. Men love a code, a creed, a secret handshake, a password, an initiation, a vow of secrecy, a clubhouse, a world unto themselves.

But the parasocial pull of the Internet has not only made it difficult for a growing percentage of young men to physically and socially connect with other people in the real world, it's forced many of them to double down on virtuality as a way to actualize their presence, diffusing themselves ever further into language, avatars, comments, and replies. Online, men can operate liberated of their bodies, but still in possession of all the privilege and social dominance they feel entitled to because of that body.

Thus, the Extremely Online Man is propelled forward by the combustion of contradiction: a desperate need to connect and belong, driven by a bitter alienation from everything and everyone around him; a confidence that seems wielded with the security of a genetic inheritance, deployed all over social media from behind a screen of empty threats, acronyms, pseudonyms, and blank profile pictures.

Online, this pain point of male isolation has become a sweet spot for marketing that targets their clicks and cash. Click on enough fitness influencers and the algorithm will quickly serve up cadres of "alpha" entrepreneurs selling elaborate multiday conferences geared toward men looking to activate their true potential or some shit. An entire industry of conferences, classes, clubs, camps, and crucibles geared toward maximizing male potential and building vague infrastructures of "brotherhood" has sprung up seemingly overnight.

In Florida, the annual "21 Convention" bills itself on its website as "the world's ultimate convention for men featuring 100% toxic masculinity and non-stop masculine self-improvement," promises to "make men alpha again," and invites participants to "stop navigating the War on Men alone" with their purchase of a "standard" ticket at $2,499.

Another organization called The Powerful Man touts its "Alpha Reset" retreat on its website: "During these 4-days, you will understand at a core level what it means to be activated and be the Powerful Man that you've always known yourself deep inside to be."

Other gatherings take a more overtly man-camp approach. There's the "Wake Up Warrior" program, catering to "married businessmen" with gatherings like "Warrior Week" (for $10K) where each participant is "embedded with a Code that becomes his compass, and he finds the association and connection with a brotherhood of men, just like him."

Another, the Modern Day Knight Project, offers an intensive seventy-five-hour program (for $12K) that instructs men in the killing of their "Inner Bitch" in order to make room for their "Inner Beast."

And yet another, the Men of War Crucible, bills itself as a "rite of passage" designed to "weaponize businessmen, CEO's, leaders and warrior minded men with high level strategies, philosophies and tactics utilized by elite ancient warrior cultures." Its Instagram account is regularly updated with footage from undisclosed locations, where men in matching fatigues crawl on their bellies through creek mud, carrying giant logs or their fellow campmates on their backs, sparring with each other in the woods, and marching in formation down the beach.

A questionnaire attached to the program screens applicants through a series of probing inquiries: "Do you consider yourself an Alpha?" "Does your wife support you attending the Crucible?" "Who do you feel has disrespected you in your life?" "Are you an honorable man?" and, slyly, "Are you ready now to financially invest in yourself?"

Grifters, as they say, are gonna grift. But this emergent wave of alienated American men is particularly vulnerable to such schemes, and their frustrated energy presents a standing threat to others. We've seen a marked rise in gender-based violence over the past five years, and a steady clip of mass shootings in schools, churches, and other public spaces, overwhelmingly carried out by young white men who are often posthumously vocal about the isolation that drove them to the brink. See, for instance, the YouTube video left behind by twenty-two-year-old Elliot Rodger, who in 2014 killed six people and injured fourteen others in Isla Vista, California, before taking his own life. Titled "Elliot Rodger's Retribution," the video features Rodger detailing his plans and motivations, decrying sexually attractive men, lamenting his virginity, and vowing revenge on women who rejected him.

"College is the time when everyone experiences those things such as sex and fun and pleasure," he says in the video. "Within those years, I've had to rot in loneliness. It's not fair. You girls have never been attracted to me. I don't know why you girls aren't attracted to me, but I will punish you all for it."

Since then, Rodger has risen as a martyr of sorts among the incel community, i.e., involuntary celibates. These are misogynist men who violently decry contemporary feminism as a corrosive force against their inherent entitlement to sex with women. Essentially, they can't get laid.

Rodger's regressively violent rhetoric has replicated itself in the musings of one mass shooter after the next, like Mauricio Garcia, who in 2023 killed eight and injured seven in a shooting spree at an Allen, Texas, shopping mall before he was fatally shot by police. Posthumous examination of his social media found that he was a member of several radical right-wing organizations, including several incel forums. "I hate women. Their [sic] I've said it," he posted to one of them.

We've also seen the rise of "male separatist" and "male supremacist" movements. "Male supremacists see the world as a matriarchy propped up by 'cultural Marxism' meant to eradicate or subjugate men," reads an explainer from the Southern Poverty Law Center, a progressive advocacy group. "It is driven by the belief that men are entitled to a place in society that is superior to women, who are biologically and intellectually inferior. As a result, any advancement that women might have obtained is nothing more than a usurpation."

We've seen subcultures of men form like factions in a gathering war. The vanguard line is PUAs—pick-up artists—specialize in the seduction (i.e., manipulation) of women into sex, closely following guidelines and lore traceable to Neil Strauss's 2005 book *The Game*, which sold nearly three million copies. Their techniques are designed to turn the AFC (Average Frustrated Chump)—a twenty-first-century descendent of the 97-pound weaking—into the AMOG (Alpha Male of the Group) by increasing the odds of success with one's "target" through perfection of "the game." Their strategies include "negging" (a backhanded compliment or outright insult crafted to elicit interest from a woman), "peacocking" (flaunting garish fashion or accessories as a way to draw attention), scanning for IOIs (Indicators of Interest), isolating her from her group, and presenting her with a false time constraint to force her decisions.

PUA tactics extend into neurolinguistic programming, psychological manipulation, and coercion, all softened by terms like "speed seduction," and those are all on the less scummy end of the PUA spectrum. At its worst, PUA culture is tantamount to rape culture—a cynical and antagonistic approach to women that commodifies their bodies in service of a man's sexual clout, or "body count."

On the opposite end of the male supremacist spectrum are MGTOWs (Men Going Their Own Way), a separatist faction of men who have sworn off interactions with women as a whole. Hundreds of thousands of men populate Reddit forums and MGTOW-specific websites devoted to "going monk."

An archive of the movement's defunct online headquarters lays out its ethos: "It is saying that, as a man I will not surrender my will to the social expectations of women and society, because both have become hostile against masculinity."

It goes on to criticize "gynocentrism" as "the main religion that rules mankind" and, in a turn that seems to inadvertently take the scenic route to the fringes of feminism, declares that "men deserve to live for themselves."

"There is no need to live as a free servant for someone else because of your gender," the website reads. "The slave days of traditional gender roles are over. Keep your right to decide for yourself and let others do the same, whatever their decisions might be. Live for yourself and let others do the same."

These online communities of men are a far cry from the campsite of the original mythopoetic "men's movement" of the 1970s and '80s. They are distinct, too, from the "men's rights" iterations that have sprung up in the digital age.

The disembodiment of the Internet and the separation of men from their own physical realities has had a pernicious effect on interpersonal empathy and connection (visit any "Call of Duty" lobby for quick confirmation). The priority placed by incel culture on the preservation (and enforcement) of strict gender norms places it precariously close to even more toxic ideologies. Clumsily coded "Western chauvinist" movements can and do serve as on-ramps to white supremacy, Christian nationalism, and violent extremism, and these movements online serve as gateways to discrimination and violence in the real world.

What does it mean to belong to a community bound by isolation? What kind of connection springs from disconnection? What does it mean that more and more men experience dejection as a mark of membership, rejection as brotherhood, loneliness as belonging? How do we collectively pull the next generation back from the brink of catastrophe? Who is coming to save them—and how?

XI

GREG

MY FRIEND GOT MORPHED. He's OK—no one got hurt. He was actually kind of flattered.

Greg, a sixty-three-year-old personal trainer from Knoxville, sent me the pic on Messenger. It was the kind of pic I'd seen countless of iterations of: him, shirtless and flexing at his desk where he films most of his flexing videos, his arms freshly pumped from a workout in the home gym that takes up most of the background, his body bathed in the light of his strategically angled desk lamp. One detail does stand out—or two, technically. His pecs are the size of volleyballs.

Someone has digitally selected them, swollen them up to three times their human size, thickened the chest hair a bit, jacked up the contrast, and rereleased the photo into a network of pec-worship pages.

Getting morphed is the process of having your image altered to the specific sexual specification of a given fetish community, often without any consent. Morphing communities attract hundreds of thousands of followers online, posting heavily altered beasts from the worlds of professional wrestling, bodybuilding, mixed martial arts, strongmen, and that endless well of beefcake source material, social media.

Morphers use photo editing software to inflate their subjects, add inches to their arms and asses, impart imposing bulk to once inauspicious curves, and turn already big men into unreasonable behemoths.

Some men see morphs as a form of motivation. One particularly burly friend of mine found a morph of himself online in 2017 and spent the next five years attempting to mold his body to match the image and lend it some truth.

"When you're looking at a morph, you're looking at an image of someone who has attained the unattainable goal," he told me, "truly shocking, overwhelming size and power, along with the satisfaction and security those things appear to bring. It's like a kid who grew up in a trailer watching the Kardashians or the Housewives and fantasizing about what it would be like to have everything you always wanted most."

For others, the impossible standards set by morphs promote unrealistic body standards and unhealthy means of attaining those standards. To be the muse for a morph is a backhanded compliment: your body is merely the basis for its own improvement.

For Greg, whose modest apartment doubles as a fully equipped gym, the morph was bittersweet. In part it was a punch in the nuts—an overwrought reminder of a time when his objectively hefty pecs were perceptibly perkier and his shoulders popped a little harder. He's been an online muscle model for the last fifteen years, so his pics and videos are everywhere: muscle Tumblrs, lifting forums, flexing fetish sites, and his own OnlyFans, Just4Fans, and Clips4sale pages.

So as much as the morph hinted at a body beyond his own, it was also a reminder of his audience of thousands of admirers (and his hundred or so paying subscribers).

"I was and still am always amazed that people pay money to look at me," he says.

Greg grew up mostly in Mobile, Alabama, getting teased for his lanky "spaghetti arms" and immersing himself in comic books. Around the time he turned nine, he was also obsessed with the Saturday night pro wrestling matches that broadcast from a local Florida affiliate in the late 1960s, when the matches were a bit rougher around the edges and the wrestlers looked more like your roughneck neighbor than a glossy Malibu bodybuilder. Pro wrestling in the middle of the twentieth century was a lot closer to the crude (and often staged) matches of Attila, Cyclops, Eugen Sandow, and George Hackenschmidt than the multimillion-dollar federations of today. But common to all eras of professional wrestling is an unspoken commitment to theater.

Greg loved wrestlers like Ken Lucas, Cowboy Bob Kelly, the three Fields Brothers, and Jerry Stubbs, who wrestled at various times as Mr.

Olympia and Mr. Perfect. He liked how they walked in, commanded attention, kicked ass, and left. He loved how their show of force made him feel.

And though naysayer friends often decried wrestling as fake and wrestlers as frauds, it did nothing to dent Greg's interest. The core of what's known as kayfabe, pro wrestling's cherished code of presenting staged events as real, was immediate and intoxicating. He was fascinated by the way these men could fight and not get hurt—there was a tenderness in this assurance of safety, an affection within the illusion. Something about the violence of their big bodies authorized their ultimate harmlessness.

Watching matches in private on a thirteen-inch TV in his bedroom, Greg found himself getting aroused—but he didn't want to touch or wrestle or fuck the men he saw in the ring. He wanted to have what they had; he wanted to *be* them.

As a young teen he'd clip photos of wrestlers that would run in the *Mobile Press Register* after the matches that would roll through town, carefully trimming out the body of each big brute—and then lopping their heads off. The decapitated beefcakes could then be topped with the heads of his choice: other wrestlers from his stack of magazines, beefy jocks from his school yearbook, his brother-in-law.

When he finally made it to a live pro wrestling match decades later in the 1990s, he remembers feeling let down—his heroes shrunken by the distance between seat and ring, the intimacy of his bedroom viewing suddenly drowned out by the din of the crowd, the privacy of his dream exploded into a public spectacle. It was what he'd come to see, but it also wasn't. Reality was no match for fantasy.

Like me, Greg was a late bloomer and didn't start lifting weights until he was nineteen, doing it at home on a small spread of equipment he'd managed to piece together from local sporting goods stores. By the time he was married in his mid-twenties, he had enough of a gym to fill a garage. He workouts grew obsessive and he started honing his diet to maximize intake of protein and carbs. On double dates, he'd catch the other man's eyes straying to stare at his arms. At church, he could feel the eyes of his fellow husbands. When men learned he had his own home gym, they wanted in. Suddenly Greg's body, once invisible to all, was becoming a topic of discussion, a magnet for attention, a center of gravity that drew other men toward him.

"When it comes from strangers, that's when you know," he told me when I asked him about the first time he felt big. "When it's someone in an elevator, or someone on the street asks if you're a bouncer or a wrestler. I wasn't, but I was becoming the person I wanted to be when I was little."

By the time Greg was in his late thirties he was up around 220 pounds of solid muscle, training in the sprawling basement gym of the rural Tennessee home that he shared with his wife. This is how I met him. Or "met." In 2006, he uploaded a video to YouTube titled "Hungry Muscle Bear," the last two words carrying enough algorithmic weight that the relatively ramshackle Google of the time managed to cough it up on one of my horny, unemployed search binges. The video was what it said on the tin: Greg, shirtless and stacked, clearly freshly pumped, standing in his kitchen and bulging under a strategically chosen overhead light, eating an entire container of leftover spaghetti. It was super hot.

At this point I was only a year or so out of grad school, unemployed but working the door at a Cambridge rock club for some part-time hours. I spent most days fucking around in a South Boston loft I shared with three other musician friends. The guy who I'd replaced when I moved in had left his weight bench stacked up in the entryway—a well-equipped Weider with a set of iron plates and some dumbbells.

"He'll be back for it," my housemate said.

"Tell him to take his time," I growled, Rambo-style. "I'll be here . . . getting *jacked*."

We laughed because I was kidding, but I also kind of wasn't. That night I dragged the bench into my room and started filling my spare time with sets. I did pull-ups in my doorframe and push-ups with my toes on the bench. I hugged plates and squatted. I loaded the barbell and squirmed through sloppy bench presses. And I watched Greg's videos. Lots of them.

Greg's eating video was linked to a training site he'd just launched. It was an aggressively HTML 1.0 operation he'd hand coded at home and split up into separate pages, each devoted to a different body part and featuring short scruffy video clips of him demonstrating various exercises. He was shirtless in all of these ostensibly educational clips, his hair a spiky shock of Guy Fieri blond, his body clean shaven and perfectly proportioned. He'd offer vaguely provocative angles in his tutorials, which promoted good form by taking the exercises at an enjoyably slow tempo.

I was taking notes, both as a remote pupil with no coach of my own, but also as an overwhelmed admirer. It's difficult to convey the rush of interpersonal access the early Internet ushered into our lives. Suddenly strangers could be spoken to. The hard lines of our social circles were dissolved into an entirely new parasocial landscape. Men I'd never dream of speaking to, who I only knew as images, could now be clicked on, emailed, IM'd.

Greg started offering choppy webcasts of his workouts over Yahoo! Messenger, and I started sending him *hi*'s and *hey*'s and asking him workout questions that I only kind of cared about the answers to. I could tell through his stubbornly short but reliably volleyed responses that he found me equal parts annoying and endearing, likely detecting an echo of his beanpole self in my persistent tugging at his proverbial sleeve. Eventually the topics of conversations got deeper: his budding exhibitionist streak, his crumbling marriage, his longing for personal independence.

He'd send me little wrestling clips he'd download from amateur sites—men stomping on each other's groins, gagging each other in headlocks, pinning each other, and pulling one "dirty tactic" after the next—the ease with which he found them telling me that entire audiences existed for such simulated bullying. He'd send me clips ripped from porns he liked—always one guy roughing up a smaller one. He'd send me short videos of himself flexing in wrestling singlets and boots, and he'd send pics of the guys who contacted him through his secret profile on GlobalFight.com, where masked male wrestling fans could connect with each other for matches on garage mats or motel beds.

More than anything, he wanted a wrestling buddy, someone to grapple and gut-punch and pin and dominate. He longed to connect and conquer.

Meanwhile, Greg's audience was growing. He and his wife divorced a few years after I met him, whereupon he packed up and moved an hour east to his own place in Knoxville, where he still lives today. It's a modest ground-level apartment almost entirely filled with gym equipment. When he's not training clients, he's filming content for his OnlyFans—lifting, flexing, now and then beating off because some guys would cancel their subscriptions if he didn't. On weekends he makes videos for private clients.

Some guys sent him outfits: wrestling singlets and masks, leather harnesses and jockstraps, Make America Great Again hats. He's been paid to play a redneck bully, an evil henchman, a rampaging giant, and a guy at the gym who just caught you staring at him. In a way, he's embodying the "heels" (bad guys) played by his favorite wrestlers.

Between his OnlyFans subscribers, download sales, and custom videos for private clients, a good month for Greg nets about $1,500—a figure that helps sustain him from month to month, but that he can't help but feel would be higher if he were comfortable being, for lack of a better term, a huge slut. His competitors on OnlyFans are thousands of younger, beefier muscleboys—many of them straight but open to queer credit card transactions—each charging higher monthly rates for far thirstier audiences, and offering frequent "collaborations" with other models.

Greg, who has come to comfortably identify as asexual, finds himself more and more a niche product. He's feeling older and smaller and weaker. "I can feel my star fading," he tells me on a Zoom. He hates how his legs look, hates how his hips feel, doesn't feel turned on by himself enough to perform for others, though he takes a workmanlike approach to delivering for his clients. He wishes he could cut his head off and attach it to a bigger body. He wonders how long he'll be able to maintain his size and strength. And he worries a little about how much longer he can count on other men's fantasies to support him.

After fifteen years of online friendship, Greg came last summer to visit me in DC. While he's not really a hugger, I hugged him hello at the airport anyway—and felt the entire concept of "Greg" expand into three dimensions as I squeezed him. He was bigger than I thought he would be. I was bigger than he thought I would be. We both felt small, and we each assured each other we weren't.

We spent a few days strolling around DC (though his hip was killing him) and even got in a couple of workouts at my gym (though my shoulder was killing me). We talked about the other ways our bodies were failing us: I complained about my rotator cuff, my angry knee, and my anxiety attacks. He showed me the constellation of spots that his dermatologist wants dug out with a scalpel. We watched wrestling and old strongman competitions and binged seasons of *Steve Austin's Broken Skull Challenge*. We took naps because we're getting old. He snores. After so many asynchronous years of knowing each other as words in a blinking box or through the consensus of pixels in a picture, it was a relief to be real, to be buddies as bodies.

It's easy to forget that men are real. We do so much to make ourselves the opposite, to privilege fantasy over reality, to make a story out of ourselves. We puff and polish and filter ourselves and wait for clicks to confirm the connections we hope we have. We want to be seen by each other in real life, to be noticed, respected, befriended.

But much like the wrestlers that our young selves saw pretending to destroy each other in the ring to the roar of the crowd, so much of our performance as men is about not allowing ourselves to get hurt.

REAL MEN

T HE HERCULES I love most is a reproduction of an engraving of a marble statue that was itself copied from an ancient bronze sculpture—a copy of a copy of a copy of a copy, like every other Hercules. But Hendrick Goltzius's 1592 engraving of the Farnese Hercules, sometimes known as the "resting Hercules," stands alone.

I've never seen a print of the actual engraving up close—only reprints in the pages of thick tomes on classical sculpture or, most recently, in a high-resolution scan posted by the Metropolitan Museum of Art, where it resides. The latter lets you zoom in on Goltzius's trademark style, an intricate overlapping system of hatchmarks that lend the hero's epic body the illusion of sensual dimensionality.

On this assertive rear view of the massive statue, the ten-and-a-half-foot-tall Hercules leans heavily on his club, weary from his trials—as indicated by the apples of Hesperides, clutched behind his back. Goltzius's lines thicken and taper, curve and crisscross, converge and dissolve like overlapping winds across the rugged landscape of Hercules's colossal body. The exquisite attention paid to every detail by the artist feels like more than an artistic grasp at realism; each line feels like the caress of a lover, an attempt to recall the surfaces of a dream.

From a technical perspective, this Farnese feels like the combination of two artistic inheritances: firstly that of Cornelis Cort, a sixteenth-century Dutch engraver who spent the years before his death in 1578 studying classical forms in Italy and developing the intricate systems of hatchmarks that Goltzius refined into his signature technique, and in Hercules's overstuffed heft, you can also detect the hand of Cornelis Cornelisz van Haarlem, a slightly younger contemporary of Cort, who specialized in beefcake realizations of mythological and biblical heroes.

These two artists, in turn, were inspired by the fleshy splendor of Bartholomeus Spranger, who worked in Prague in the court of the sexually liberated Holy Roman emperor Rudolf II. Spranger's work represents the heights of Mannerism—a post-Renaissance, pre-Baroque pocket of painting that amplifies the naturalism of Michelangelo & Co. into a preternaturally camp-filled virtuality. In Mannerism the symmetry, balance, and order of the Renaissance gives way to an eroticized anarchy, with lots of torsion, tension, flesh, and fecundity. It was less an artistic movement than an outburst.

Goltzius moved from his small German hometown of Brüggen to the Dutch city of Haarlem as a precocious nineteen-year-old engraver. Here, the young artist fell in with the first thrust of Mannerists like Spranger and Karel van Mander, and despite a deformed hand from burns suffered when he was just a year old, he quickly excelled at his craft. By the mid-1580s, Goltzius's style of undulating lines was finding its groove and he was hitting a hot streak. Like many of his fellow Mannerists, his engravings offered viewers what might be their only glimpses of masterworks from across the continent—and engravers worked tirelessly to imbue their copies with verisimilitude. Goltzius's works stand out for their crisp clarity, their enhanced sense of presence, their fleshy generosity.

In 1586, Goltzius fashioned an aggressively callipygian engraving of the Roman decurion Calphurnius, his thick thighs topped with a pronounced booty pop. He's one of a series of muscle-studded "Roman Heroes," including a broad-backed Titus Manlius Torquatus (a Roman politician and general), a rippling Horatius Cocles (a heroic officer in the Roman army), and a ribbon-thonged Marcus Valerius (a military commander and consul).

Hercules makes his first Goltziusian cameo in the artist's 1587 engraving of Spranger's celestially crowded The Wedding of Cupid and Psyche. Herc poses nonchalantly off to the side, draped in the pelt of the Nemean lion, leaning on his favorite club, and supervised by the trumpet-toting Fame, who hovers above him from a perch of muscular clouds.

In 1588, Goltzius teamed with Cornelis Cornelisz van Haarlem to create "The Four Disgracers," a quartet of engravings of doomed, meaty men of ancient myth: a tumbling Tantalus, a falling Phaeton, a flipping Ixion, and an Icarus that's almost entirely undercarriage. Their bodies twisting helplessly, it was as though by freezing them in mid-air Goltzius was offering them safety from their fall, forgiveness for their sins.

Hercules reappears in Goltzius's work as the central hero of his *Great Hercules* of 1589, an original depiction often referred to as the "Knollenman," or "bulbous man." Here, mustachioed and mind-blowingly bulky, a mature Hercules stands surrounded by miniature scenes depicting his many trials. Every available stretch of his flesh is rippled with marbled muscle. His torso could be stuffed with softballs. His legs resemble the trunks of ancient trees. Veins swaddle his forearm and hand, which clutches the torn-off horn of his rival, the river god Achelous. Like some clairvoyant vision of Jay Cutler or Ronnie Coleman, his size is unfathomable, his body unknowable, the glory of his body a factor of its utter impossibility. The historian Beth L. Holman described his musculature as "a densely packed topography of bumps and hillocks" and "not simply overstocked; it is overstated."

Some have interpreted this overinflated body as an embodiment of Dutch might in their rebellion against the Spanish Empire—which intensified between 1588 and 1598—and Herc's figure as a vision of the body politic. "The figure's profusion of relatively small muscles can be compared to the many provinces and towns mustered together in defense of the nascent Republic. The muscles' hyper definition and exaggerated distinctions seem to be an inspired expression of Dutch particularism," suggests Holman.

But the fantasy of the *Great Hercules* also feels intensely personal. Fellow Mannerist van Mander once pointed out that physical size and power had drawn Goltzius's eye since childhood, when he'd paint "camels, elephants and other great things" on his walls. Goltzius was often in poor health, reportedly vomiting blood off and on for years. In the gargantuan Hercules we see a fortress of a body, an impenetrable form, its creator's exact opposite.

By 1590, Goltzius's career was as strong as his health was poor. In an attempt at convalescence, he traveled to Italy for a six-month sojourn, roaming around Rome incognito, keeping even his now-infamous hand disguised. Surrounded by the towering statues of ancient deities and confronted by the gleaming frescoes of celestial heroes in the courtyards and palazzi of Rome, Goltzius had his Sandow moment.

"From this time on he no longer made prints after Spranger's extravaganzas," writes the historian Seymour Slive. "The monstrous muscle-men and over-elongated female nudes with tiny heads . . . were replaced by figures with more normal proportions and movements," inspired by the Grecian proportions preserved from antiquity.

With a new reverence for and fidelity to classical forms, Goltzius sketched a series of divinely inspired (and perfectly proportioned) gods based on Italian Mannerist painter Polidoro da Caravaggio's burly frescoes of Pluto, Neptune, Saturn, Jupiter, and other mythological immortals from the early sixteenth century.

At the Cardinal Alessandro Farnese's Roman palazzo on the banks of the Tiber, Goltzius took in the banquet of mythological bodies collected there: an Atlas, an Artemis, an Aphrodite, and, most impactfully, Hercules in repose, his giant form salvaged from the Baths of Caracalla in 1546, outfitted with new legs in 1560, and centrally situated in a courtyard. Here, Goltzius saw his muscular muse anew, no longer the amorphously ample Herc of his imagination—this one was precisely sculpted, divinely inspired but overwhelmingly human. Goltzius didn't entirely abandon the Mannerist excess of his early training, however; his swaddling lines honor Herc's curvature by amplifying it. There's adoration in its exaggeration.

Perhaps what is most unique about Goltzius's engraving of the Farnese is his inclusion of two spectators peering upward at the edge of the pedestal. Presumed to be Goltzius himself and his nephew, they peer up from over the pedestal's edge, their size an indicator of scale, their gaze an indicator of awe.

Goltzius's male form feels like a Mannerist ancestor to Sandow's neo-classical body goals, to the precisely shaded machismo of Tom of Finland, the CGI superheroes of the Marvel Universe, and the muscle worshipping morph-artists of social media. And his prints spread the fantasy of Herc's body like a flame—one that continues to consume us.

The iron doesn't lie, as Henry Rollins noted, but the Internet does.

Virtual galleries devoted to crudely puffed and pixelated morphs of powerlifters, bodybuilders, and strongmen were once tucked into nichey and largely gay pockets of the Internet. But the recent explosion of publicly available AI tools has enabled millions of idle clickers to instantly transform their bodies into epic proportions and states of superhuman pump.

The week one of these tools was released in early 2023, my Instagram feed was full of uncanny-valley versions of my friends and acquaintances—all of them disconcertingly glossed and flawless, their bodies bulked, buffed, and outfitted with Viking pelts or military regalia or kingly robes and cosplay crowns. Some used the technology to add fifty glistening virtual pounds of muscle to their frames—either to fluff up their profile pictures or to create a personal vision board of sorts for their own bodies. More and more, our avatars are becoming reflections of the identities our bodies keep to themselves.

Social media at large is a procession of deceptively edited and strategically altered photos from advertisers, AI engines, and individual users. Click on any number of Instagram fitness trainers and physique models and you'll find thousands of pics that, once zoomed in on, reveal glaring evidence and sloppy artifacts of digital fuckery.

These conditions have cultivated an entire feeder class of fitness influencers who exist solely to identify the cropped, tweaked, inflated, or otherwise distorted bods among us. These exposés come complete with "receipts"—close-ups of oddly warped backgrounds or implausibly contoured silhouettes. Bodybuilding coach and online influencer John Dorsey, or "goob_U," has attracted hundreds of thousands of followers to his account, which features several videos a week scrutinizing errant pixels and botched Photoshop jobs—the thrill of exposure lending the whole endeavor a vibe of righteousness (swo-cial justice?). And while the technology may be new, as long as there have been beefcakes posing for thirst traps, there have been debunkers devoted to cutting them down to size.

"I could tell you about 'strongmen photography,'" an unknown photographer confessed in 1899 to the *Cincinnati Enquirer*, noting that "professional strong men are as clever at makeup as a society actress." He referred to "one fellow, who visits country fairs and casual shows, goes through tricks of a kind wonderful to the unscientific mind."

"He depends on his photos for advertisement," the anonymous source confided. "In posing he folds his arms tightly, dilates the muscles of his neck, and lines his veins with Prussian blue. His picture gives you Hercules in power of majesty. In private he is a well-developed man without any swagger of sinew or strength."

He coyly adds this blind item, regarding another conspicuously familiar-sounding strongman on the touring circuit: "The veins of a certain professional Hercules protrude like whipcord in the photographic cabinet. He dusts them with powdered ultramarine and treats the high parts of the muscles with Indian red—otherwise his picture would appear quite ordinary."

Alan Calvert of the Milo Barbell Company was a renowned debunker, devoting the entirety of his 1911 book, *The Truth About Weight Lifting*, to debunking deceptive "feats" performed by professional strongmen, revealing the tricks behind dubious stunts such as card tearing, chain snapping, and coin breaking.

Calvert pushed for the creation of a Board of Control to regulate weight lifting competitions, much like the present-day federations that oversee powerlifting and bodybuilding contests, and he pushed against the public stigmas that surrounded weight lifting, such as the superstition that too much lifting would render a man immobile, or "musclebound," and that a man "who is covered with large, knotty muscles" would invariably be "slow and clumsy in his movements."

He also cautioned gawkers to take the bodies of musclemen with a grain of salt. "In regard to the knotted appearance of the strong man's muscles," he writes, "I beg to remind the reader that the man's muscles are knotted only when someone is looking at him, or when he is having his picture taken. Some lifters make a habit of keeping their arms tensed and their shoulders hunched up every minute they are in view of the audience; and when a lifter has his photograph taken his one idea is to make as many muscles prominent as possible. If you are fortunate enough to catch one of these strong men in costume, when he thinks he is not observed, you will find that he is not nearly as heavily muscled as he appears when he is on the stage."

And the contemporaneous fitness guru Earle Liederman devoted an entire chapter of his 1924 book *Muscle Building* to "Posing for Muscular Display," guiding novices through the nuances of posing for photographs. He comments on proper lighting, angling of the body in relation to the position of the lens, and management of each body part to enhance the illusion of increased size. Some of his advice sounds like the internal monologue of a musclehead posting to Instagram: "Do not show the legs," he writes, "for you will look much stronger and heavier in a bust picture than you would in a full-length photo."

But while Liederman advocated for maximizing one's presence in the frame, he was firmly against deception. The body, he believed, was proof of a man's greatness, the photograph merely an attempt to capture it.

"There is no need for anyone to adopt artificial means in order to display the muscles to the best advantage," Liederman writes. "For the one person in all this world whom you do not want to fake, and whom it would never pay you to fool, is yourself."

At any given time, my Instagram feed feels like a scantily clad Turing test of bodies drifting around the bounds of reality. "Photos" rendered by artificial intelligence are becoming harder and harder to discern, and the reality they attempt to reflect is becoming more difficult to delineate.

Recent research suggests that teenage boys and young men are particularly susceptible to these images, and link social media use to an increase in disordered eating behavior, muscle dysmorphia, and steroid use. A pair of recent studies found that a third of teenage boys have tried to actively gain weight, and 22 percent are engaged in some form of muscle-building practice.

The architecture of algorithms driving social media ensures that any expression of interest (a like, a follow, a comment) is exploited into an opportunity for clicks. Platforms like TikTok and Instagram are designed to feed you more and more of what you like (whether you know you like it or not) and the resultant influx of steroidal bodies, jacked-up influencers, and mass-building supplements can foster a distorted outlook that extends far beyond the body.

Increasingly, this virtualization is shaping men's bodies in the real world. The last decade has seen a pronounced spike in men getting cosmetic procedures like filler injections, tummy tucks, liposuction, and hair replacement treatments. Silicone calf and pectoral implants have also increased. In 2020, nearly 2.3 million cosmetic procedures were performed on American men, up from 1.3 million in 2017. This included a 23 percent jump in buttock implants. There's even a (literal) growing number of men opting for painful, expensive leg-lengthening surgeries (in which rods are inserted into severed bones and gradually lengthened), tired of being dismissively looked down upon or written off as "short kings."

Other items in men's palettes of gender affirming care are even more invasive. Synthol, a drug originally developed for topical application to shine up bodybuilders' muscles for posing situations, has recently found its way into men's muscles via injection—a wildly reckless (and medically illicit) practice that instantly engorges and enlarges the muscles, putting users at risk for deadly strokes and complications. Darker corners of the gym Internet host grim galleries of Synthol casualties—men with baggy, bruised, distended arms, their flesh hanging from the bone like punctured tires.

The slower approach to synthetically assisted growth is, of course, steroids. Under the Controlled Substances Act, steroids are considered "Schedule III" substances—meaning they have "a legitimate medical function," but "may lead to moderate or low physical dependence or high psychological dependence." Technically, steroids are illegal to use without a valid prescription and illegal to distribute.

None of this has made them particularly difficult to obtain. Anabolic steroids and other performance enhancing drugs (PEDs) remain easily available through thousands of faceless accounts across social media, their profile pictures typically a stock bodybuilder, their content a grid of little vials and coded contact info.

And while it's impossible to tell whose muscles among the online masses are natural ("natty") and whose are not, the pull of the virtual can double as a push in reality, and it's clear that more young men are experimenting with steroid cycles than ever before. On TikTok, young influencers speak openly about the contents of their "stacks" (the term used for one's regimen of PEDs), and gym bros at large have taken to referring to all steroid use online as HRT (hormone replacement therapy), simply as a way to get it through the gates of permissible discourse.

I've always been steroid agnostic. Personally averse but happy enough to see them safely used by men who feel more drawn to them than repelled. As our society lurches reluctantly but steadily toward an understanding of gender as both existing on a spectrum of experience and also expanding as a social construct into a more material malleability, I find myself having to consciously include masculinity in the mix, recalibrating my view of steroids as something that's not necessarily for me to condone or condemn. It's not lost on me why people hate on steroids—they've been linked to jacked-up aggression and long-term depression, with all kinds of potentially hazardous side effects when abused. They've been long associated with vain, vascular roid ragers, toxed up on their own juice.

But I've also met men for whom the moderated use of steroids allowed them to discover their own mobility on the gender spectrum—albeit deeper into a sense of beckoning masculinity. I also know men, especially men my age, who swear by a sustained boost of testosterone to make them feel more present, more "real." And I certainly know trans men for whom HRT provided essential access to their own internal experience of manhood, their bodies and minds finally fully conversant with one another.

With anti-trans bathroom bills proposed in dozens of states, and already enacted in five, the pressure to conform to traditional gender presentation has become a matter of life and death for many people. (In 2022, according to the Human Rights Campaign, forty-one trans Americans were killed, and the HRC has documented at least 302 violent deaths of transgender and gender nonconforming people since it started tracking in 2013.)

Additionally, hundreds of newly passed and proposed state laws would present increased physical and legal risks to occupying the undefined in-between of nonbinary identity and presentation, or insufficiently "passing" as one's gender as a trans person. The vague language and wide reach of anti-drag laws proposed in states like Florida, Iowa, and Montana put gender nonconforming people at needless risk of fines or even felony prosecution for not adhering closely enough to accepted gender presentation. As the legal scholar Kate Redburn wrote in a June 2023 opinion piece for the *New York Times*: "Gender play through clothing—whether someone is trying out traditionally masculine or feminine styles or selecting gender-neutral options—is more popular than ever. Drag bans strike at this fundamental freedom to express our gender through personal appearance and performance, regardless of our sex assigned at birth." The pressure to uphold legible standards of "realness" when it comes to gender presentation has never been so fraught, nor so fragile.

After all, what does it mean to be "real" as a man? (Or "natty" for that matter?) Why is the value of the real in such constant and curious flux? And since when do we derive our ideal vision of ourselves as men from anything but pure fantasy?

As soon as you walk into the Museo Archeologico Nazionale in Naples, you shrink.

The space seems to grow around you as you navigate its soaring halls. A former cavalry barracks and once home to a grand city university, it now houses substantial permanent holdings of Italian antiquities: sprawling galleries of frescoes, stately marble busts of Roman senators and writers, relics from Pompeii and the Herculaneum, and an assembly of colossi from the Farnese collection, including Hercules himself—*Ercole in riposo*, or "Hercules at rest."

Here, Hercules's body represents the bookends of his twelve trials. He leans on his club, over which is draped the pelt of the prize of his first trial, the Nemean lion. Behind his back, above his ample butt, he clutches the apples of the Hesperides in his hand, the reward of his penultimate trial, nonchalantly obscured from all who approach him.

This is a Hercules who has done his work, performed his labors, atoned for his mistakes. His body is proof of his purchase on mortality, evidence of his bearing the progressively heavier burden of his guilt. Here he is not just full-grown but mature, with nothing left to prove.

"The mind of one familiar with antique models at once turns to the palmy ages of Greek art, and of its Roman copyists," Walt Whitman wrote as Mose in his guide to manly health. "All the grandest characters who appear in it are middle-aged or old men and they rise into colossal proportions."

The streaked marble of his body looks soft to the touch—the bush of his beard, the thick slope of his traps, the broad mounds of his chest and shoulders, the rippling terrain of his torso, the dual plums of his nuts. Goltzius's engraving comes uncannily close to carving his precise curves, but by necessity, its two dimensions only tell you half the story. There's something sublime about circling him in the Naples Museo, negotiating with the space his body takes up, accepting him as real.

At ten-and-a-half-feet tall, Herc silences you, his stony gaze surveys a hall that always seems to hold its breath. Standing at his feet, my husband and I morphed into the two tiny spectators in Goltzius's engraving, gazing up at the exhausted demigod, marveling at the force of his silence, the peace of his presence.

It would be easy to stand before Herc and see an origin point, a beef-cake zero. But just like Goltzius's engraving, he's a copy amplified by desire, a beefed-up dupe.

The Farnese Hercules was modeled after a smaller Grecian bronze by Lysippos, lost to looting Crusaders during the sack of Constantinople in 1205 and melted down into coins by men described in the Annals of the twelfth-century historian Nicetas Choniates as "barbarians" and "haters of the beautiful."

"[Hercules] was thick in the chest and broad in the shoulders, with curly hair," Choniates wrote. "Fat in the buttocks, strong in the arms, he was an incomparable masterpiece fashioned from first to last by the hands of Lysimachos [he likely meant Lysippos] and portrayed in the magnitude which the artist must have attributed to the real Herakles. The statue was so large that it took a cord the size of a man's belt to go round the thumb, and the shin was the size of a man."

But beyond describing the bulk of Hercules's body, Choniates captured the real threat his beauty posed to those who destroyed him: "They who separated manliness from the correspondent virtues and claimed it for themselves did not allow this magnificent Herakles to remain intact, and they were responsible for much more destruction."

Those crusaders failed to contain the multitudes of Hercules's body when they melted it down—if anything, they set his beauty free from its form. The Roman copy inspired a seemingly endless proliferation of his body around the world—the Farnese sprung up in gardens and atop mantles, in plaster, brass, bronze, and polystyrene, as shrine and souvenir. Herc flexes over Florence and Athens, Paris and St. Petersburg, Algeria and Austin.

But in this particular slab of marble, in his hard-earned pose of perpetual repose, he feels alive and present. Standing at his feet feels like reaching the source of a great energy that renders me silent as stone. In the body of the unreal man we can find the promise and the plight of real men: each of us copies without an original, our bodies all carved from the same forgotten dream.

XII

BONES

MY DAD FACETIMED ME the other day to ask if I've ever seen this guy Anatoly.

He's all over TikTok, he says. Or is it Instagram? He's not sure where he saw it. It doesn't matter. The answer was yes, I'd seen him. Anatoly is this unassumingly lanky bearded guy who dresses up in a janitor's jumpsuit and shows up at various gyms to stage a prank that never seems to get old.

Each video finds him pushing his mop bucket up to some unsuspecting heavyweight powerlifter and asking politely if he can step in for a moment and mop up the platform. Once obliged, he picks up the bigger man's 495-pound barbell and casually moves it out of the way with quietly insulting ease, the hidden camera zooming in to capture the cracking face of the reliably emasculated strongman. Technically, Anatoly does indeed mop up the platform.

It's admittedly entertaining stuff, no matter how many reps the routine gets. And while my dad mainly gets a kick out of Anatoly's strength, we both derive a bit of pleasure from his seemingly endless supply of humble pie—and our feeds eagerly serve us more.

The men of the Internet vex my dad to no end. A man of natural and relentless curiosity, he doesn't identify with their weaponized ignorance. A man of easy conversation and effortless grace, he doesn't understand their disposition toward conflict and aggression. A man of deep compassion and silly dad jokes, he can't fathom most men's allergy to empathy and joy. He doesn't understand their obsession with winning, dominance, and control. He knows better.

For the past four years, my father's been entirely devoted to caring for my mother, who in her late sixties started to develop symptoms of Alzheimer's dementia. In less than a decade, my mother went from a vibrant public speaker, social butterfly, natural entertainer, and charismatic fireball to a shadow that only reveals the true shape of its source once or twice a day.

She isn't her body. None of us are. But her body contains and conducts her, lends shape to her spirit, form to her feelings, weight to her words.

When I watch videos of landslides—my feed has become an avalanche of them—they make me think of how things have happened with Mom. A few nervously quaking trees on a cliff drawing attention to themselves. A hard cough of dust from a sudden crack in the ridge. A cluster of tumbling rocks freed from the grip of exposed roots. The sudden slide and collapse of an entire cliff, the grass, the trees, the road—everything engulfed in a rising cloud of dust, everything a roar that devours the past and swallows the present.

My parents live in Maine, and my brothers and I take turns traveling up to help—grocery and pharmacy runs, shoveling snow, filling the freezer with meals, peeling back the pool cover in the spring. Some nights, after a day of staying too busy to feel anything, once Mom is put to bed for the tenth time and it seems like she'll stay there, my father and I will sit at the kitchen table around her empty seat and weep, unsure which direction to aim our mourning. Our bodies quake until they come to rest.

When I hug him good-night, we stay hugging for an extra second—men's way of italicizing silence—and he'll make some mood-saver comment about how big I've gotten, a man of forty-eight still playing at being a growing boy. It's also his way of saying *Look how much I've shrunk, how fragile I've become, how not me I am.*

When my dad was in high school, the other kids all called him Bones. He was a big-grinned slight-framed boy who, by his senior year, was barely scratching 120 pounds. The name left the affectionate bruise of a charley horse.

My dad's only other known nickname came from my grandmother, who dispassionately designated her two sons This and That (my dad was the latter), and he sometimes signed his Christmas and birthday cards to my mother as "Barney," a name that I learned was itself a pseudonym for "Barn Rat"—a moniker that begged me not to pursue further inquiry.

But "Bones," in particular, seemed to stick in his side. The summer after his senior year in Gardner, Massachusetts, he started lifting weights with a couple of buddies in their friend John's garage on Pine Street. It was nothing special—he had a bench, some dumbbells, and a rope-and-pulley system hanging from a girder. My dad spent three months lifting with the guys in the afternoons, between shifts at his job at the town cemetery, planting rows of arborvitae and digging the occasional grave. (The other basis for his nickname.)

Before long, he worked his bench press up to a universally respectable 225 pounds (i.e., two plates on either side) and started requiring alterations to make room in his size 42 jackets, much to the chagrin of his tailor. "Brodeur, you're not doing your body any good," Sammy admonished him.

My dad likes telling me about this whenever I show him one of the shirts I had to get made custom to fit my shoulders or the suit pants tailored to accommodate my butt. Or when one of his FaceTime calls catches me at the gym, asks which exercise I'm doing and thinks fondly back to his max. In my body he sees a memory of his, and in his I see a forecast of mine.

In the time I've known my father, he's had aortic valve replacement, a left lung thoracotomy, type 2 diabetes, endocarditis, viral meningitis, recurrent prostate cancer, several basal cell carcinomas, chronic cellulitis, macular edema, rheumatic fever, Raynaud's syndrome, and, most recently, cold agglutinin disease, a rare blood condition that requires him to keep his body above a certain temperature, like an egg.

His torso is an atlas of scars and little pink divots from scraped melanomas. His blood thinners make him bruise easily, like the bloom of yellow and purple encircling the Dexcom reader stuck to his belly. His eyes have lately been filling with fluid, and his twice-monthly injections to clear them haven't been working and he can no longer drive the car he just bought. On chilly days he holds a two-liter soda bottle filled with hot water to keep the Raynaud's from turning his fingertips tender and purple. His cancer drugs torch him with sudden hot flashes and force his joints and tendons to break out in nasty arguments. Sometimes his feet and ankles swell, sometimes his stomach turns inside out, sometimes searing pains shoot through his body and leave no note as to why.

Other than that, he tells me, he's feeling great.

I know he's not. And he knows I know. But we laugh anyway.

For the past month, he's been back on Orgovyx, a cancer drug so strong that he has to wash his hands after touching the pills. The drug targets the prostate cancer that seems to have made a particulate reappearance in his PSA numbers last month—a measurement of prostate-specific antigens in the blood. For a long time after his first bout and treatment, his testosterone levels were "undetectable," but a trace amount in his last blood test raised concern.

It was 2004 when his doctor referred him to the Dana-Farber Cancer Institute. He was terrified, sitting with my mother in a drab examination room awaiting the oncologists. A team of women with clipboards arrived with a list of questions. How is your urination? Are you able to perform? How would you rate your erection?

At this last one my dad told them that while he used to be able to hang a towel on it, now he was lucky if it held the facecloth. The whole room fell apart laughing. They told him that the cancer feeds on testosterone, that the hormone had to go from his body, and that the best treatment would involve drugs that would essentially chemically castrate him.

"There are two ways of doing it," he said, to set up his joke. "I'd prefer the chemical one."

Twenty years later he still likes to make bad jokes about his "transition" ("Am I they now?") which I shoo away with soft reprimands. And he barely thinks about it, except when the commercial breaks blast him with ads for Nugenix and Super-T, bemoaning the scourge of diminishing manhood. But I know he must feel unmoored from his former sense of What Makes a Man.

My dad's dad was a fireman whom none of us ever met. He died fighting a house fire before my parents even started dating. And while my dad wasn't on the local force himself, he had some firefighter in his blood. When a wildfire once broke out on a small island in the middle of the town lake, he paddled out in his canoe with a tank of water to douse it.

He was big into camping and ice fishing. He listened to Cream and Moby Grape and Quicksilver Messenger Service and liked nights out dancing to ska bands at the Buttercup, where one night he met the prettiest girl he'd ever seen. My mom negged him for being drunk.

My family is proof that you must always try again. By the time I showed up in 1976, he and my mother already had two toddlers and were never not working—my dad at his job as a foreman at a turbine plant (until an accident left him deaf in one ear), my mother at the Old Mill, the pharmacy, the bank. Whenever they were off work together, they were building their home—my dad hauling sheets of plywood by himself up a wobbly ladder, tearing down walls with a crowbar and dragging in lumber and drywall, pushing teetering wheelbarrows of mulch and soil, grabbing a corner of old carpet and peeling it back like turf from the earth. Each of my brothers has inherited what we call his "work face"—eyes squinted, teeth bared, a single drop of sweat dangling from the tip of the nose, the breath of an angry bull. I pull it every time I deadlift.

For my entire childhood, work was his identity and our lives at home his legacy. After the accident at the turbine plant, he put himself through night school, started working as a financial planner, then as a trainer of financial planners, filling out fresh new suits and filling conference halls of men in fresh new suits. He treated our home like a castle, tending its gardens and never quite finishing its finishes. He wore the regalia of dadhood proudly, his increasingly ample belly a trophy of hard-earned pleasure and long-delayed leisure.

Four decades later, my dad groans when he stands, feels the walls when he walks, regards the burden of every movement with a mix of grief and gratitude. Sometimes I see pain run up the faults of his face like the first cracks in a landslide.

And yet I can't help but see his body as Herculean—a living archive of his trials, a record of survival, proof of purchase.

Deep down I know that one of the reasons I lift is a futile attempt to ironclad my body, to swaddle myself in armor, to gird my bones with muscle and meat. But as I get older, the more my muscles feel like decorations that I leave up all year.

My dad isn't his body. None of us are. And in the ways that don't involve the body, the ways that matter as men, he's way bigger than me, way stronger than me. I think about how he carried me until he couldn't. The inheritance of cells he gave me. The way his body contains the story of mine, the way he's the source of my multitudes.

What form will I take at the end of my labors? Will it be the stony pose of a passed-down fantasy? Or will I be a real man? One who bears the burden of his body and the weight of his world with kindness, compassion, empathy, and courage? One who knows that strength is not the pursuit of power—it's the path to lightness.

ACKNOWLEDGMENTS

M Y DEEPEST THANKS go to my editor, Catherine Tung (and everyone at Beacon Press giving this book a place on the shelf), and my agent, Will Lippincott. You're both paragons of patience and extremely good at what you do. This book couldn't have happened without either of you and I'm eternally grateful.

Before writing a word of this book, I had long conversations with dozens of men for whom size has played an outsized role in their identity. While this book centers on my story, I owe any understanding I've acquired of how men relate to their bodies from these men and their much-appreciated candor. So thank you, Bob, David, Mike M., Shaun, Sean, Steve, Mike H., Balde, Nard, Brandon, Rob, James, Matt, J.P., Matthew, Nate, Gregory, Colin, Dale, Mike, Steve B., Marcos, Chris, Gabe, Jeph, Kahan, Steve S., Dominic, Matt, and Scott, among others, for your generosity and time.

I'd like to thank David L. Chapman, whose guidance early in the conception of this book and whose own extensive and illuminating histories of Eugen Sandow, physical culture, and the role of muscles and masculinity in mass media were essential to my own understanding and research.

Huge thanks also go to Jan Todd, who, along with her late husband, Terry, founded the H. J. Lutcher Stark Center at the University of Texas at Austin, the world's largest archive devoted to physical culture, sport, resistance training, and alternative medicine, and whose extensive research and writing on the history of weight training were invaluable to this project.

I owe an additional debt of gratitude to writers including Randy Roach, Eric Chaline, Daniel Kunitz, Kenneth R. Dutton, and Bob Whelan; and thanks as well to the many random muscle blogs that helped guide various wormholes, including *Sandow & the Golden Age of Iron Men: The Online*

Physical Culture Museum (https://www.sandowplus.co.uk), *The Tight Tan Slacks of Dezso Ban* (http://ditillo2.blogspot.com), *Quest for Beauty* (https://hadrian6.tumblr.com/archive), and *80s Muscle* (https://80smuscle.tumblr.com).

Thanks to librarians at Harvard University, the Whitney Museum of Art, and the Montreal Museum of Fine Arts for vital assistance in research.

Perpetual and boundless thanks and appreciation go to my family—especially my three brothers, Emmy, Jim, Denise, and everyone on #TeamRosie. It was only because of you that I was able get through the past three years in one piece.

Thanks also to my Nautical Thanksgiving crew and support system of friends, with honorable mentions to Lena and Darcy, Avery and Gary, Davey and Brie, Brian and Matt—all of whom gave space and encouragement for this book to be written.

And not a page of *Swole* would have been possible without the love and support of my husband, Evan, who pushed and pulled me through the most difficult parts of the process and made every burden bearable. I love you more than anybody.

WORKS CITED

INTRODUCTION—MIKEY

bell hooks, *The Will to Change: Men, Masculinity and Love* (New York: Washington Square Press, 2004).

Brett R. Gordon, Cillian P. McDowell, Mats Hallgren, Jacob D. Meyer, Mark Lyons, and Matthew P. Herring, "Association of Efficacy of Resistance Exercise Training with Depressive Symptoms: Meta-Analysis and Meta-Regression Analysis of Randomized Clinical Trials," *JAMA Psychiatry*, Department of Physical Education and Sport Sciences, University of Limerick, Ireland, June 1, 2018, https://pubmed.ncbi.nlm.nih.gov/29800984.

"Male Depression: Understanding the Issues," Mayo Clinic, https://www.mayoclinic.org/diseases-conditions/depression/in-depth/male-depression/art-20046216.

1—ADAM

"MOTU—Creation of He-Man Action Figure," *80TOYSHOP*, July 28, 2012, http://80toyshop.wordpress.com/2012/07/28/motu-creation-of-he-man-action-figure.

Martin Goodman, "Dr. Toon: When Reagan Met Optimus Prime," Animation World Network, October 12, 2010, http://www.awn.com/animationworld/dr-toon-when-reagan-met-optimus-prime.

Michael Isikoff, "FCC Weakens Policy on TV for Children," *Washington Post*, December 23, 1983, https://www.washingtonpost.com/archive/business/1983/12/23/fcc-weakens-policy-on-tv-for-children/f1404264-0c27-42ba-862a-ded4c9a7e435.

Glenn Collins, "Controversy About Toys, TV Violence," *New York Times*, December 12, 1985, http://www.nytimes.com/1985/12/12/garden/controversy-about-toys-tv-violence.html.

Peter J. Boyer, "Toy-Based TV: Effects on Children Debated," *New York Times*, February 3, 1986, http://www.nytimes.com/1986/02/03/arts/toy-based-tv-effects-on-children-debated.html.

Associated Press, "Court Orders F.C.C. Review of Policy on Children's TV," *New York Times*, June 27, 1987, http://www.nytimes.com/1987/06/27/arts/court-orders-fcc-review-of-policy-on-children-s-tv.html.

"The He-Man Market," *New York Times*, June 25, 1988, http://www.nytimes.com/1988/06/25/opinion/the-he-man-market.html.

Peter J. Boyer, "CBS Plans 'Noids' Cartoon Series," *New York Times*, January 25, 1988, https://www.nytimes.com/1988/01/25/movies/cbs-plans-noids -cartoon-series.html.

Edmund L. Andrews, "Toy-Based TV Shows Win Ruling," *New York Times*, November 9, 1990, http://www.nytimes.com/1990/11/09/business/toy -based-tv-shows-win-ruling.html.

"The Birth of He-Man," *The Sneeze*, April 18, 2006, www.thesneeze.com/mt -archives/000500.php.

Brian Cronin, "Movie Legends: Was He-Man Originally a Toy Tie-In for the Conan Film?," CBR.com, February 25, 2018, https://www.cbr.com/he -man-conan-toy-tie-in.

Lee Leslie, "The Surprisingly Awesome Comics History of 'Masters of the Universe,'" Comics Alliance, April 16, 2013, www.comicsalliance.com /masters-of-the-universe-comics-history.

John DeVore, "He-Man Is My Gender Icon," *Humungus*, August 9, 2020, https://medium.com/humungus/he-man-is-my-gender-icon-b95b27d00675.

Jordan Zakarin, "Why One Expert Says He-Man Is the 'Gayest Show Ever,'" *Syfy Wire*, September 17, 2020, https://web.archive.org/web/2021030 3025556/https://www.syfy.com/syfywire/why-one-expert-says-he-man -is-the-gayest-show-ever-fandom-files-14.

Alexander Huls, "Who's Afraid of a Gay He-Man?," *Men's Health*, September 21, 2020, https://www.menshealth.com/entertainment/a33446186/gay -he-man.

Michael O'Rielly, "It's Time to Reexamine the FCC's KidVid Requirements," *FCC Blog*, January 26, 2018, https://www.fcc.gov/news-events/blog/2018 /01/26/its-time-reexamine-fccs-kid-vid-requirements.

I—FORM

Andrew Stewart, *One Hundred Greek Sculptors, Their Careers and Extant Works*, Gregory R. Crane, ed., Perseus Digital Library, Tufts University, http:// www.perseus.tufts.edu/hopper.

Andrew Stewart, "The Canon of Polykleitos: A Question of Evidence," *Journal of Hellenic Studies* 98 (1978): 122–31.

Hugh McCague, "Pythagoreans and Sculptors: The Canon of Polykleitos," *Rosicrucian Digest* 87, no. 1 (2009), https://www.perkiomen.org/uploaded /faculty/jthobaben/art_history/ap_homework/canon_polykleitos.pdf.

Kenneth R. Dutton, *The Perfectible Body: The Western Ideal of Male Physical Development* (New York: Continuum, 1995).

II—PETER

"Peter Cullen Explains How He Created the Voice for Optimus Prime," TFCon, September 3, 2018, www.youtube.com/watch?v=zryfjSaxXLo.

Mike Ryan, "'You're Like a Nerd': Larry King & Peter Cullen, Voice of Optimus Prime, Interviewed at Comic-Con," *HuffPost*, July 16, 2012, https:// www.huffpost.com/entry/youre-like-a-nerd-larry-king-optimus-prime _n_1676914.

Joel Searls, "How the Voice of Optimus Prime Was Inspired by a Marine," *We Are the Mighty*, March 19, 2023, https://www.wearethemighty.com /popular/optimus-prime-voiced-by-marine.

Darren Bonthuys, "Batman 1989 Thirty Years Later—How the Batsuit Was Designed to Be Iconic, Intense and Mythical," *Critical Hit*, June 5, 2019, https://www.criticalhit.net/entertainment/batman-1989-thirty-years -later-how-the-batsuit-was-designed-to-be-iconic-intense-and -mythical.

II—ON MANLY HEALTH

Alex Abad-Santos, "Why It's So Hard to Find Dumbbells in the US," *Vox*, August 24, 2020, https://www.vox.com/the-goods/21396116/dumbbell -set-shortage-nordictrack-bowflex.

Alex Shultz, "Inside the Great Kettlebell Shortage of 2020," *GQ*, April 7, 2020, https://www.gq.com/story/inside-the-great-kettlebell-shortage.

Stephen G. Miller, *Arete: Greek Sports from Ancient Sources, Expanded Edition* (Berkeley: University of California Press, 1991).

Eric Chaline, *The Temple of Perfection: A History of the Gym* (London: Reaktion Books, 2015).

Friedrich Ludwig Jahn, Charles Beck (trans.), *A Treatise on Gymnasticks* (Northampton, MA: Simeon Butler, 1828).

Thomas Wentworth Higginson, "Saints, and Their Bodies," *The Atlantic Monthly*, March 1858.

Thomas Hughes, *Tom Brown at Oxford* (Cambridge and London: British Library, 1861).

Daniel Kunitz, *Lift: Fitness Culture, from Naked Greeks and Acrobats to Jazzercise and Ninja Warriors* (New York: Harper Wave, 2016).

David L. Chapman, *Sandow the Magnificent: Eugen Sandow and the Beginnings of Bodybuilding* (Urbana: University of Illinois Press, 2006).

Donald Walker, *British Manly Exercises: In Which Rowing and Sailing Are Now First Described; and Riding and Driving Are for the First Time Given in a Work of This Kind* (London: T. Hurst, 1834).

Walt Whitman, *Manly Health & Training: With Off-Hand Hints Toward Their Conditions*, 1858 (Carlisle, MA: Applewood Books, 2017).

Ed Boland Jr., "FYI," *New York Times*, February 24, 2002, https://www.nytimes .com/2002/02/24/nyregion/fyi-760579.html.

Edward T. O'Donnell, "154 Years Ago: The Mose, America's 1st Superhero Is Born," *Irish Echo*, February 16, 2011, https://group.irishecho.com/2011 /02/154-years-ago-the-mose-americas-1st-superhero-is-born-2.

"Frank S. Chanfrau Dead; Struck Down by Apoplexy Without Warning . . ." *New York Times*, October 3, 1884, https://www.nytimes.com/1884/10/03 /archives/frank-s-chanfrau-dead-struck-down-by-apoplexy-without -warning-his.html.

"Frank Chanfrau Dead," *New York Clipper*, October 11, 1884.

Jan Todd, "From Milo to Milo: A History of Barbells, Dumbbells and Indian Clubs," *Iron Game History* 3, no. 6 (April 1995).

M. Jimmie Killingsworth, "Whitman's Anonymous Self-Reviews of the 1855 *Leaves*," *Walt Whitman: An Encyclopedia*, ed. J.R. LeMaster and Donald D. Kummings (New York: Garland Publishing, 1998).

III—LOU

"The First Black Bodybuilder to Be the Incredible Hulk," Nick's Strength and Power, www.youtube.com/watch?v=xKMXT88Z9rs.

Greg Merritt, "Manny Perry, '70s Bodybuilder and Hollywood Stuntman," *Flex*, May 2006, https://www.ironmagazineforums.com/threads/manny -perry-70s-bodybuilder-and-hollywood-stuntman.111149.

bell hooks, *The Will to Change: Men, Masculinity and Love* (New York: Washington Square Press, 2004).

Allan Cole, "Lou Ferrigno and the Harley Hulkout," *My Hollywood Misadventures*, November 4, 2011, allangcole.blogspot.com/2011/11/lou-ferrigno -and-harley-hulkout.html.

Lisa Capretto, "How Lou Ferrigno Went from Bullied, Skinny Kid to 'Incredible Hulk,'" *HuffPost*, January 29, 2014, www.huffpost.com/entry/lou -ferrigno-bullied-bodybuilding-hulk_n_4676191.

Bill Dobbins, "Lou Ferrigno: From the Hulk to Hercules," *Muscle & Fitness*, September 1982.

Jay, Carr, "'Hercules' Labors in Vain," *Boston Globe*, August 27, 1983, https:// ghostarchive.org/archive/sohPM.

Chris Walters, "Only Muscle Stunts Can Help 'Hercules,'" *Austin-American Statesman*, August 27, 1983, https://ghostarchive.org/archive/hGuLd.

Steve Watkins, "Not Even the Strength of Steel Can Save, Hercules'," *Tallahassee Democrat*, August 28, 1983, https://ghostarchive.org/archive /NxzUA.

Henry Edgar, "Sets, Costumes, Effects Are Good, but Boring 'Hercules' Has No Heart," *Daily Press*, August 28, 1983, https://ghostarchive.org/archive /JNrrv.

Dave Karger, "'The Hulk' Tramples Its Box Office Competition," *Entertainment Weekly*, June 20, 2003, https://ew.com/article/2003/06/20/hulk -tramples-its-box-office-competition.

III—WILD AT HEART

Steffi Cao, "Liver King Might Be the Biggest Bro Influencer We Have Ever Seen," *BuzzFeed News*, March 2, 2022, www.buzzfeednews.com/article /stefficao/liver-king-tik-tok-influencer.

Madeleine Aggeler, "In the Court of the Liver King," *GQ*, May 5, 2022, https://www.gq.com/story/in-the-court-of-the-liver-king-brian-johnson -ancestral-supplements.

Alice Hearing, "YouTube 'Primal Living' Guru Liver King, Who Built a $100M Fitness Empire, Admits He's Actually on Steroids," *Fortune*, December 6, 2022, https://fortune.com/well/2022/12/06/liver-king-leaked -steroids-email-apology-video.

Walt Whitman, *Manly Health & Training: With Off-Hand Hints Toward Their Conditions*, 1858 (Carlisle, MA: Applewood Books, 2017).

Eugen Sandow with G. Mercer Adam, *Sandow on Physical Training: A Study in the Perfect Type of the Human Form* (London: Gale & Polden, 1894).

George Hackenschmidt, *The Way to Live in Health and Physical Fitness*, 1908 (n.p.: Physical Culture Books, 2011).

Robert Bly, *Iron John: A Book About Men*, 1990 (Boston: Da Capo Press, 2004).

Sam Keen, *Fire in the Belly: On Being a Man* (New York: Bantam Books, 1991).

bell hooks, *The Will to Change: Men, Masculinity and Love* (New York: Washington Square Press, 2004).

Phil McCombs, "Men's Movement Stalks the Wild Side," *Washington Post*, February 3, 1991.

Neil Howe, "You're Not the Man Your Father Was," *Forbes*, October 2, 2017, www.forbes.com/sites/neilhowe/2017/10/02/youre-not-the-man-your -father-was/?sh=a28fa668b7fd.

Thomas G. Travison, Andre B. Araujo, Amy B. O'Donnell, Varant Kupelian, and John B. McKinlay, "A Population-Level Decline in Serum Testosterone Levels in American Men," New England Research Institutes, www .pubmed.ncbi.nlm.nih.gov/17062768, published in *Journal of Clinical Endocrinological Metabolism*, January 2007.

R. Vigen et al., "Association of Testosterone Therapy with Mortality, Myocardial Infarction, and Stroke in Men with Low Testosterone Levels," *JAMA*, November 6, 2013.

FDA Drug Safety Communication, "FDA Evaluating Risk of Stroke, Heart Attack and Death with FDA-Approved Testosterone Products," January 31, 2014, https://wayback.archive-it.org/7993/20161022203724/http:// www.fda.gov/Drugs/DrugSafety/ucm383904.htm.

Norse Fitness, Facebook post, September 14, 2019, https://www.facebook. com/norsefitness/posts/modern-culture-stands-for-mediocritymodern -culture-seeks-out-comfort-instead-of-/2532203846844592/.

IV—FRIEDRICH

Andy Grundberg, "The Allure of Mapplethorpe's Photographs," *New York Times*, July 31, 1988, https://www.nytimes.com/1988/07/31/arts/photography -view-the-allure-of-mapplethorpe-s-photographs.html.

Eugen Sandow, *Strength and How to Obtain It* (London: Gale & Polden, 1897).

David L. Chapman, *Sandow the Magnificent: Eugen Sandow and the Beginnings of Bodybuilding* (Urbana: University of Illinois Press, 2006).

Robert Mapplethorpe, *Black Book* (New York: St. Martin's Press, 1986).

Eugen Sandow with G. Mercer Adam, *Sandow on Physical Training: A Study in the Perfect Type of the Human Form* (London: Gale & Polden, 1894).

"WPA Teacher Wins Sculpture Award; Work of Michael Lantz of New Rochelle Is Chosen for Apex Building at Capital," *New York Times*, January 27, 1938, https://www.nytimes.com/1938/01/27/archives/wpa-teacher-wins -sculpture-award-work-of-michael-lantz-of-new.html.

Martin Austermule, "'We're The Ones Who Saved Congress': Meet Three D.C. Police Officers Who Fought For The U.S. Capitol," *Deist*, January 15, 2021, https://dcist.com/story/21/01/15/were-the-ones-who-saved -congress-meet-three-d-c-police-officers-who-fought-for-the-u-s-capitol.

IV—FLEX

Eugen Sandow with G. Mercer Adam, *Sandow on Physical Training: A Study in the Perfect Type of the Human Form* (London: Gale & Polden, 1894).

David L. Chapman, *Sandow the Magnificent: Eugen Sandow and the Beginnings of Bodybuilding* (Urbana: University of Illinois Press, 2006).

John F. Kasson, *Houdini, Tarzan and the Perfect Man: The White Male Body and the Challenge of Modernity* (New York: Farrar, Straus & Giroux, 2001).

"Thought He Was Like Sandow," *The Sun*, New York, September 6, 1894.

V—ARNOLD

Rita Beaming, "Bush Leads 'Great American Workout,'" Associated Press, May 1, 1991, https://apnews.com/article/65d8fd231441906b236daef7552f3ba2.

"Pumping Firewood with the President," UPI, November 29, 1983, https://www.upi.com/Archives/1983/11/29/Pumping-firewood-with-the-president/5756438930000.

Jazzercise, "More Than 50 Years After Its Beginning, Jazzercise Remains as Popular as Ever," news release, December 18, 2020, https://www.jazzercise.com/Media-center/Press-Releases/Press-Release-Wrap/More-than-50-years-after-its-beginning,-Jazzercise-remains-as-popular-as-ever.

D. J. R. Bruckner, "Film: Schwarzenegger, 'Commando,'" *New York Times*, October 4, 1985, https://www.nytimes.com/1985/10/04/movies/film-schwarzengger-commando.html.

Bernard Weinraub, "On the Set With—Arnold Schwarzenegger; Big Guy. Big Star. Big Deal, Baby," *New York Times*, March 4, 1993, https://www.nytimes.com/1993/03/04/garden/on-the-set-with-arnold-schwarzenegger-big-guy-big-star-big-deal-baby.html.

Ken Chowder, "Muscle Beach," *Smithsonian Magazine*, November 1, 1998, https://www.smithsonianmag.com/travel/muscle-beach-62784377.

V—TO FAILURE

Jan Todd, "The Strength Builders: A History of Barbells, Dumbbells and Indian Clubs," *International Journal of the History of Sport* 20, no. 1 (March 2003).

Alan Calvert, *The Truth About Weight Lifting*, 1911 (n.p.: Physical Culture Books, 2011).

John D. Fair, *Muscletown USA: Bob Hoffman and the Manly Culture of York Barbell* (University Park: Pennsylvania State University Press, 1999).

VI—ANGELO

Robert H. Boyle, "The Report That Shocked the President," *Sports Illustrated*, August 15, 1955, https://vault.si.com/vault/1955/08/15/the-report-that-shocked-the-president.

Denis Bertacchi, "Lou Ferrigno Shares Bullying Advice and the Hardest Part of Being the Hulk with Kids at West County's D1 Gym," *St. Louis Magazine*, April 5, 2019, https://www.stlmag.com/family/lou-ferrigno-west-county-d1-bullying.

Andrew Fenton, "Dwayne Johnson Recalls Being Bullied as a Kid and Arrested for Theft," News Corp Australia, June 30, 2016, https://www.news.com.au/entertainment/movies/new-movies/dwayne-johnson-recalls-being-bullied-as-a-kid-and-arrested-for-theft/news-story/bc2c2adc55e77670da5b30eaa612cfoe.

Kevin Slane, "John Cena Reveals Why He Was Bullied as a Kid Growing Up in Massachusetts," Boston.com, October 29, 2019, https://www.boston.com/culture/entertainment/2019/10/29/john-cena-bullied-as-a-kid.

Barsha Roy, "Sylvester Stallone's Rocky Past: Actor Shoveled Lion Dung and Teachers Voted Him 'Mostly Likely to End Up on Electric Chair," Meaww.com, July 4, 2023, https://meaww.com/sylvester-stallones-rocky-past-actor-shoveled-lion-dung-and-teachers-voted-him-mostly-likely-to-end-up-on-electric-chair.

Robby Robinson, *The Black Prince: My Life in Bodybuilding: Muscle vs. Hustle*, self-published, 2001.

George Barker Windship, "Autobiographical Sketches of a Strength-Seeker," *The Atlantic Monthly*, January 1862, https://www.theatlantic.com/magazine/archive/1862/01/autobiographical-sketches-of-a-strength-seeker/627985.

Jan Todd, "Strength Is Health: George Barker Windship and the First American Weight Training Boom," *Iron Game History*, September 1993.

"Charles Atlas, the Body-Builder and Weightlifter, Is Dead at 79," *New York Times*, December 24, 1972, https://www.nytimes.com/1972/12/24/archives/charles-atlas-the-bodybuilder-and-weightlifter-is-dead-at-79.html.

Robert Ernst, *Weakness Is a Crime: The Life of Bernarr Macfadden* (Syracuse, NY: Syracuse University Press, 1991).

Maria Newman, "Hey, Skinny! Charles Atlas Lives!; The Man Is Dead, but the Name Has Kept Its Muscle," *New York Times*, May 31, 2001, https://www.nytimes.com/2001/05/31/nyregion/hey-skinny-charles-atlas-lives-the-man-is-dead-but-the-name-has-kept-its-muscle.html.

P.L. "The Insult That Made a Man Out of 'Mac,'" *American Heritage*, October/November 1978, https://www.americanheritage.com/insult-made-man-out-mac.

"(Body)Building an Empire," *New York Times*, November 28, 1981, https://www.nytimes.com/1981/11/28/business/body-building-an-empire.html.

Dieter Wolke, "Big Men Feeling Small: Childhood Bullying Experience, Muscle Dysmorphia and Other Mental Health Problems in Bodybuilders," Department of Psychology and Health Sciences Research Institute, University of Warwick Medical School, Coventry, April 24, 2007, www.sciencedirect.com/science/article/abs/pii/S1469029207001033.

Jason Shurey and Jan Todd, "Joe Weider, All-American Athlete, and the Promotion of Strength Training for Sport: 1940–1969," *Iron Game History* 12, no. 1 (August 2012), https://starkcenter.org/igh/igh-v12/igh-v12-n1/igh1201p04.pdf.

Robert D. McFadden, "Joe Weider, Creator of Bodybuilding Empire, Dies at 93," *New York Times*, March 23, 2013, https://www.nytimes.com/2013/03/25/sports/joe-weider-founder-of-a-bodybuilding-empire-dies-at-93.html.

Joe Weider and Ben Weider with Mike Steere, *Brothers of Iron: How the Weider Brothers Created the Fitness Movement and Built a Business Empire* (Champaign, IL: SportsPublishing, 2006).

David Ferrell, "Body Building : Joe Weider's Iron Grip on an Empire," *Los Angeles Times*, March 2, 1989, https://www.latimes.com/archives/la-xpm -1989-03-02-mn-254-story.html.

Andrew Tate, "Accidentally Pimpin' Hoes," Rumble.com. https://rumble.com /v35ha40-accidentally-pimping-hoes.html.

VI—THE ALPHAS

L. David Mech, *The Wolf: The Ecology and Behavior of an Endangered Species* (1970) (Minneapolis: University of Minnesota Press, 1981).

L. David Mech, "Wolf News and Information," Mech's homepage, https:// davemech.org/wolf-news-and-information.

Jordan Peterson, *12 Rules for Life: An Antidote to Chaos* (Toronto: Random House Canada, 2018).

Timothy Bella, "Vaccine Scientist Says Anti-Vaxxers 'Stalked' Him After Joe Rogan's Challenge," *Washington Post*, June 19, 2023, https://www .washingtonpost.com/nation/2023/06/19/joe-rogan-hotez-rfk-vaccine -debate.

Al Tompkins, "Joe Rogan Apologizes for Vaccine Misinformation and Promises to 'Do Better,'" Poynter, February 1, 2022, https://www.poynter.org /reporting-editing/2022/joe-rogan-apologizes-for-vaccine-misinformation -and-promises-to-do-better.

Staff, "Joe Rogan Apologizes for 'Regretful,' 'Shameful' Use of Racial Slur After Clips Circulate," *USA Today*, February 6, 2022, https://www.usatoday .com/story/entertainment/celebrities/2022/02/06/podcaster-joe-rogan -apologizes-using-racial-slur-spotify-controversy/6683805001.

J. Kim Murphy, "Joe Rogan Faces New Criticism for Promoting 'Antisemitic Tropes About Jews and Money' on Podcast," *Variety*, February 7, 2023, https://variety.com/2023/digital/news/joe-rogan-antisemitic-controversy -jewish-1235516253.

Alex Paterson, "Spotify's Joe Rogan and Guest Jordan Peterson Suggest Trans People Are a Sign of 'Civilizations Collapsing,'" Media Matters, January 26, 2022, https://www.mediamatters.org/joe-rogan-experience/spotifys -joe-rogan-and-guest-jordan-peterson-suggest-trans-people-are-sign.

"Joe Rogan: Podcast Host, 'The Joe Rogan Experience,'" GLAAD Accountability Project, April 21, 2023, https://glaad.org/gap/joe-rogan.

VII—HENRY

"Altered Beast: The Complete History," SGR, October 27, 2019, https://www .youtube.com/watch?v=KD57JOqG5Ro.

Henry Rollins, *The Portable Henry Rollins* (New York: Villard, 1997).

Marlo Stern, "Henry Rollins Opens Up About Toxic Masculinity and Abuse: 'I Hate Men,'" *Daily Beast*, June 14, 2020, https://www.thedailybeast .com/henry-rollins-opens-up-about-toxic-masculinity-and-abuse-i -hate-men.

Alan Pendergrast, "The Angriest Man in Los Angeles: Rock Poet Henry Rollins Doesn't Drink, Smoke or Do Drugs—He Just Burns," *Los Angeles Times*, June 14, 1987, https://www.latimes.com/archives/la-xpm-1987-06 -14-tm-7341-story.html.

VII—THE DRAG OF BIG

Shawna Mizelle, "Republicans Across the Country Push Legislation to Restrict Drag Show Performances," CNN, February 5, 2023, www.cnn.com/2023 /02/05/politics/drag-show-legislation/index.html.

Stephen Elliott, "GOP Lawmakers Aim to Criminalize Drag Shows Where Children Could Be Present," *Stateline*, December 14, 2022, www.pewtrusts .org/en/research-and-analysis/blogs/stateline/2022/12/14/gop-lawmakers -aim-to-criminalize-drag-shows-where-children-could-be-present.

James Factora, "Anti-Drag Legislation Isn't Just About Drag," *Them*, February 13, 2023, www.them.us/story/anti-drag-legislation-trans-community-drag -queens.

Ellie Silverman, "Montgomery Police to Patrol Drag Story Hours After Proud Boys Protest," *Washington Post*, February 21, 2023, https://www.washington post.com/dc-md-va/2023/02/21/maryland-drag-queen-story-hour-proud -boys.

Edith Hamilton, *Mythology* (New York: Little, Brown, 1942).

Stephen O'Donnell, "Three Paintings of Maurice Deriaz, by Gustave Courtois," *Gods and Foolish Grandeur*, April 19, 2014, http://godsandfoolishgrandeur .blogspot.com/2014/04/three-paintings-of-maurice-deriaz-by.html.

VIII—TOUKO

"HIV and AIDS Timeline," Centers for Disease Control and Prevention, https://npin.cdc.gov/pages/hiv-and-aids-timeline.

"The AIDS Epidemic, 1991–1993," *New York Times*, https://archive.nytimes .com/www.nytimes.com/library/national/science/aids/timeline91–93.html ?scp=8&sq=1991&st=cse.

Philip J. Hilts, "F.D.A. Backs a New Drug to Fight AIDS," *New York Times*, December 9, 1995, https://www.nytimes.com/1995/12/08/us/fda-backs -a-new-drug-to-fight-aids.html.

VIII—BEAUTY AND THE BEEF

Katharine Lowry, "The Show of Muscles at the Whitney Was Vitiated by Academic Flabbiness," *Sports Illustrated*, June 7, 1976, https://vault.si.com /vault/1976/06/07/the-show-of-muscles-at-the-whitney-was-vitiated-by -academic-flabbiness.

Ian Frazier, "Muscles at the Whitney," *New Yorker*, March 14, 1976, https:// www.newyorker.com/magazine/1976/03/22/muscles-at-the-whitney.

Vicki Goldberg, "Is It an Art, a Sport or Sheer Exhibitionism?," *New York Times*, November 30, 1975, https://www.nytimes.com/1975/11/30/archives /b-o-is-it-an-art-a-sport-or-sheer-exhibitionism.html.

Walt Whitman, *Manly Health & Training: With Off-Hand Hints Toward Their Conditions*, 1858 (Carlisle, MA: Applewood Books, 2017).

Eugen Sandow with G. Mercer Adam, *Sandow on Physical Training: A Study in the Perfect Type of the Human Form* (London: Gale & Polden, 1894).

David K. Johnson, *Buying Gay: How Physique Entrepreneurs Sparked a Movement* (New York: Columbia University Press, 2019).

Stephen Birmingham, "For Love of Muscle," *Sports Illustrated*, August 3, 1959, https://vault.si.com/vault/1959/08/03/42792#&gid=cio258bf26000d278a&pid=42792—065—image.

"Bob Mizer's Story," Bob Mizer Foundation, https://www.bobmizer.org/bobmizer.

Bob Mizer, *The Complete Reprint of Physique Pictorial, 1951–1990* (London: Taschen, 1997).

Burkhard Riemschneider, ed., *Tom of Finland: The Art of Pleasure* (London: Taschen, 2004).

Micha Ramakers, *Dirty Pictures: Tom of Finland, Masculinity and Homosexuality* (New York: St. Martin's Press, 2000).

IX—BIG LITTLE

Daniel Goleman, "When Ugliness Is Only in Patient's Eye, Body Image Can Reflect Mental Disorder," *New York Times*, October 2, 1991, https://www.nytimes.com/1991/10/02/health/when-ugliness-is-only-in-patient-s-eye-body-image-can-reflect-mental-disorder.html.

"Body Dysmorphic Disorder," Mayo Clinic, https://www.mayoclinic.org/diseases-conditions/body-dysmorphic-disorder/symptoms-causes/syc-20353938.

"Anabolic Steroids and Other Appearance and Performance Enhancing Drugs (APEDs)," National Institute on Drug Abuse, May 2023, https://nida.nih.gov/research-topics/anabolic-steroids.

"Steroid Fast Facts," National Drug Intelligence Center, archived January 1, 2006, https://www.justice.gov/archive/ndic/pubs5/5448/index.htm.

Bonnie Berkowitz and William Neff, "What Bodybuilders Do to Their Bodies—and Brains," *Washington Post*, December 8, 2022, https://www.washingtonpost.com/investigations/interactive/2022/bodybuilding-health-risks/?itid=bodybuilders-series-box.

IX—THE PUMP

Arnold Schwarzenegger with Bill Dobbins, *The New Encyclopedia of Modern Bodybuilding* (New York: Simon & Schuster, 1985).

Arnold Schwarzenegger with Douglas Kent Hall, *Arnold: The Education of a Bodybuilder* (New York: Simon & Schuster, 1977).

"Interview with Mr. Olympia Frank Zane," *Muscle & Strength*, September 2010, https://www.muscleandstrength.com/articles/interview-with-mr-olympia-frank-zane.html.

X—MEMBERSHIP

Daniel A. Cox, "Men's Social Circles Are Shrinking," American Survey Center, June 29, 2021, https://www.americansurveycenter.org/why-mens-social-circles-are-shrinking.

"Demographic Data Project: Gender and Individual Homelessness," National Alliance to End Homelessness, 2018, https://endhomelessness.org/demographic-data-project-gender-and-individual-homelessness.

John Gramlich, "Black Imprisonment Rate in the U.S. Has Fallen by a Third Since 2006," Pew Research Center, May 6, 2020, https://www.pewresearch.org/short-reads/2020/05/06/share-of-black-white-hispanic-americans-in-prison-2018-vs-2006.

"Suicide Data and Statistics," Centers for Disease Control and Prevention, https://www.cdc.gov/suicide/suicide-data-statistics.html.

"Men and Mental Health," National Institute of Mental Health, https://www.nimh.nih.gov/health/topics/men-and-mental-health.

"Men and Mental Health," Mental Health America, https://www.mhanational.org/infographic-mental-health-men.

"Men: A Different Depression," American Psychological Association, https://www.apa.org/topics/men-boys/depression.

"Men's Mental Health," Anxiety and Depression Association of America, https://adaa.org/find-help/by-demographics/mens-mental-health.

"Men's Rights Activist (MRA)," Anti-Defamation League Glossary of Extremism, https://extremismterms.adl.org/glossary/mens-rights-activist-mra.

Brendan Bures, "Guys Are Paying $10,000 to Become Real Men at Warrior Camps," *Vice*, January 24, 2022, https://www.vice.com/en/article/4awnqm/what-are-man-warrior-camps.

Adam Nagourney, Michael Cieply, Alan Feuer, and Ian Lovett, "Before Brief, Deadly Spree, Trouble Since Age 8," *New York Times*, June 1, 2014, https://www.nytimes.com/2014/06/02/us/elliot-rodger-killings-in-california-followed-years-of-withdrawal.html.

Megan Garvey, "Transcript of the Disturbing Video 'Elliot Rodger's Retribution,'" *Los Angeles Times*, May 24, 2014, https://www.latimes.com/local/lanow/la-me-ln-transcript-ucsb-shootings-video-20140524-story.html.

Laura Bates, "Men Going Their Own Way: The Rise of a Toxic Male Separatist Movement," *Guardian*, August 26, 2020, https://www.theguardian.com/lifeandstyle/2020/aug/26/men-going-their-own-way-the-toxic-male-separatist-movement-that-is-now-mainstream.

"MGTOW Means Men Going Their Own Way," Mgtow.com archive, https://web.archive.org/web/20130806115314/http://www.mgtow.com, accessed September 20, 2023.

XI—REAL MEN

Earle Liederman, *Muscle Building*, 1924 (n.p.: Physical Culture Books, 2011).

Earle Liederman, *Secrets of Strength*, 1925 (n.p.: Triarius Publishing, 2013).

Ian McMahan, "Body Dysmorphia in Boys and Men Can Fuel Muscle Obsession, Doctors Say," *Washington Post*, April 14, 2023.

Jan Todd, "The History of Cardinal Farnese's 'Weary Hercules,'" *Iron Game History* 9, no. 1 (August 2005), https://starkcenter.org/igh_article/igh0901d.

Roger Pearse, "Melting Down the Statues in Constantinople in 1204," Roger-Pearse.com, December 14, 2013, https://www.roger-pearse.com/weblog/2013/12/14/melting-down-the-statues-in-constantinople-in-1204.

Seymour Slive, *Dutch Painting, 1600–1800* (New Haven, CT: Yale University Press, 1998).

Beth L. Holman, "Goltzius' 'Great Hercules': Mythology, Art and Politics," *Netherlands Yearbook for History of Art* 42/43 (1991–92), https://www.jstor.org/stable/24705375.

Allison Tierney, "Why More Men Are Getting Calf and Pec Implants," *Vice*, August 9, 2018, https://www.vice.com/en/article/wjk74y/why-more-men-are-getting-calf-and-pec-implants.